# Entrepreneurial Financial Literacy During Crisis Conditions

Fatemeh Dekamini
*Mahan Business School, Iran & Islamic Azad University, Iran*

Abbas Dastanpour Hossein Abadi
*Ehraz Argamauditory Institution, Iran*

Amin Entezari
*Allameh Tabataba'i University, Iran*

Ramona Birau
*Constantin Brâncuși University of Targu Jiu, Romania*

Rezvan Pourmansouri
*Islamic Azad University, Iran*

IGI Global
Scientific Publishing
Publishing Tomorrow's Research Today

Vice President of Editorial　　　　　　Melissa Wagner
Managing Editor of Acquisitions　　　　Mikaela Felty
Managing Editor of Book Development　Jocelynn Hessler
Production Manager　　　　　　　　 Mike Brehm
Cover Design　　　　　　　　　　　　Phillip Shickler

Published in the United States of America by
　　IGI Global Scientific Publishing
　　701 East Chocolate Avenue
　　Hershey, PA, 17033, USA
　　Tel: 717-533-8845
　　Fax:  717-533-8661
　　E-mail: cust@igi-global.com
　　Website: https://www.igi-global.com

Copyright © 2025 by IGI Global Scientific Publishing. All rights reserved. No part of this publication may be reproduced, stored or distributed in any form or by any means, electronic or mechanical, including photocopying, without written permission from the publisher.
Product or company names used in this set are for identification purposes only. Inclusion of the names of the products or companies does not indicate a claim of ownership by IGI Global Scientific Publishing of the trademark or registered trademark.

　　　　　　　　　Library of Congress Cataloging-in-Publication Data


CIP PENDING

ISBN13: 9798369394151
Isbn13Softcover: 9798369394168
EISBN13: 9798369394175



British Cataloguing in Publication Data
A Cataloguing in Publication record for this book is available from the British Library.

All work contributed to this book is new, previously-unpublished material.
The views expressed in this book are those of the authors, but not necessarily of the publisher.
This book contains information sourced from authentic and highly regarded references, with reasonable efforts made to ensure the reliability of the data and information presented. The authors, editors, and publisher believe the information in this book to be accurate and true as of the date of publication. Every effort has been made to trace and credit the copyright holders of all materials included. However, the authors, editors, and publisher cannot assume responsibility for the validity of all materials or the consequences of their use. Should any copyright material be found unacknowledged, please inform the publisher so that corrections may be made in future reprints.

# Table of Contents

**Preface** ................................................................................................ v

**Chapter 1**
Introduction to Entrepreneurial Financial Literacy ............................... 1

**Chapter 2**
History of Financial Management ....................................................... 11

**Chapter 3**
An Overview of the Specialized Topics of Financial Management and the Duties of Financial Managers ............................................................. 21

**Chapter 4**
Basic Concepts in Financial Management of Companies ................... 35

**Chapter 5**
Financial Concepts for Non-Financial Managers ............................... 83

**Chapter 6**
Financial Markets and Its Tips .......................................................... 115

**Chapter 7**
Financial Intelligence ........................................................................ 141

**Chapter 8**
Financial Management During the Crisis ......................................... 159

**Chapter 9**
Business Intelligence for Financial and Non-Financial Managers .... 169

**Chapter 10**
Effective and Key Financial Management Solutions for Entrepreneurs and Business Owners ............................................................................. 195

**Chapter 11**
Entrepreneurship and Financial Management .................................. 231

**Chapter 12**
Conclusion ................................................................................................................ 259

**Compilation of References** ............................................................................. 283

**About the Authors**............................................................................................ 289

**Index**..................................................................................................................... 291

# Preface

The book entitled "Financial literacy and investment of entrepreneurs in crisis conditions" represents an original approach on topics of great current interest. The structure of this book is original and provides an innovative perspective. The book includes certain contents, such as: "Introduction", "History of financial management", "An overview of the specialized topics of financial management and the duties of financial managers", "Basic concepts in financial management of companies", "Financial concepts for non-financial managers", "Financial markets and its tips", "Financial Intelligence", "Financial management during the crisis", "Business intelligence for financial and non-financial managers", "Effective and key financial management solutions for entrepreneurs and business owners", "Entrepreneurship and financial management" and "Conclusion".

As a conceptual approach, organizational entrepreneurship can be defined as the process of innovation and taking advantage of opportunities with a lot of effort and perseverance along with accepting financial, psychological, and social risks. We mentioned the fact that financial literacy is necessary and useful for the progress of young entrepreneurs. Moreover, considering the knowledge structures of entrepreneurship, using orientation theory there are certain influential factors such as: organizational learning, entrepreneurial leadership, entrepreneurial culture, entrepreneurial thinking, entrepreneurial strategy, entrepreneurial orientation, entrepreneurial spirit and risk taking.

The major aim and motivation of the book entitled "Financial literacy and investment of entrepreneurs in crisis conditions" is focused on achieving our objective of creating a complex research-based knowledge based on relevant literature, and original contributions establish on the critical analysis of the current state of knowledge compared to the latest results and empirical and theoretical achievements quoted in the mainstream research papers or books. This original and exhaustive research book can be perceived as a landmark for researchers and professionals in the financial field.

The target audience of this book will be composed of University Professors, Academics, Researchers, Students, Advanced-Level Students and PhD Students, Policy Makers, Government Officials, Professionals, Entrepreneurs and Shareholders, Business Analytics and Financial Consultants, working in the financial field.

The book entitled "Financial literacy and investment of entrepreneurs in crisis conditions" provides significant contributions to the existing literature. In addition, it is important to mention that this book has a very original structure which differs greatly from other books that have a generally academic course content based on definitions, concepts, categories, classifications etc.

**Fatemeh Dekamini**
*Mahan Business School, Iran & Islamic Azad University, Iran*

**Abbas Dastanpour Hossein Abadi**
*Ehraz Argamauditory Institution, Iran*

**Amin Entezari**
*Allameh Tabataba'i University, Iran*

**Ramona Birau**
*Constantin Brâncuși University of Targu Jiu, Romania*

**Rezvan Pourmansouri**
*Islamic Azad University, Iran*

# Chapter 1
# Introduction to Entrepreneurial Financial Literacy

## ABSTRACT

*Entrepreneurial knowledge is the ability to recognize or create opportunities and take action to achieve goals based on innovative knowledge. Knowledge entrepreneurship differs from traditional economic entrepreneurship in that it focuses on realizing opportunities to improve knowledge production and efficiency rather than maximizing financial profit. Entrepreneurship and knowledge management have an inseparable link that together form entrepreneurial knowledge. Entrepreneurship is analyzed from a psychological point of view and based on personality traits. It is also examined from the perspective of management and based on organizational structures. From an economic point of view, an entrepreneur is a self-employed person who has the power of good economic forecasting, has a tendency to take risks, and in this way makes profit or loss, and thus contributes to the balance and stability of the market economy.*

## INTRODUCTION

Entrepreneurial knowledge is the ability to recognize or create opportunities and take action to achieve goals based on innovative knowledge. Knowledge entrepreneurship differs from traditional economic entrepreneurship in that it focuses on realizing opportunities to improve knowledge production and efficiency rather than maximizing financial profit.

Entrepreneurship and knowledge management have an inseparable link that together form entrepreneurial knowledge. Entrepreneurship is analyzed from a psychological point of view and based on personality traits. It is also examined from the perspective of management and based on organizational structures. From an economic point of view, an entrepreneur is a self-employed person who has the power of good economic forecasting, has a tendency to take risks, and in this way makes profit or loss, and thus contributes to the balance and stability of the market economy.

Organizational entrepreneurship is the process of innovation and taking advantage of opportunities with a lot of effort and perseverance along with accepting financial, psychological, and social risks. Entrepreneurial management brings financial gain, seeking success, personal satisfaction, and seeking independence. Knowledge of entrepreneurship plays a fundamental role in this, which is necessary for both entrepreneurs and economic development at the micro and macroeconomic levels. In this section, the definition and importance of entrepreneurial knowledge are discussed.

## Definition of Entrepreneurial Knowledge

Entrepreneurial knowledge encompasses a wide range of concepts, skills, and mindsets that are essential for business owners to navigate the complexities of starting and running a successful enterprise. This multifaceted knowledge draws from various interdisciplinary fields, integrating both technical expertise and practical skills that can be taught and enhanced over time. It involves not just understanding the mechanics of business operations but also cultivating an entrepreneurial attitude that encourages continuous improvement and adaptability in a rapidly changing economic landscape.

The term "entrepreneurial knowledge" was first introduced by the American economist Richard Cantillon in the early 18th century. He described economic actors who engage in ventures involving expenses while anticipating uncertain and potentially risky returns in the future. According to Cantillon, an entrepreneur is fundamentally a risk-taker who purchases goods at a known price and sells them at an unpredictable price. This definition highlights the entrepreneur's role as a coordinator and integrator of production factors, emphasizing the necessity for individuals to effectively combine resources—such as labor, capital, and materials—to produce goods, offer services, or engage in trade. Furthermore, the renowned economist Joseph Schumpeter expanded on the concept of entrepreneurship in his influential work "The Theory of Economic Development." He made a critical distinction between innovation and invention, asserting that innovation involves taking risks to develop and commercialize new products or services. Schumpeter posited that innovation serves as the driving force behind wealth creation and the stimulation of demand in the economy. Thus, he characterized entrepreneurs as managers or owners who leverage inventions by establishing commercial production units, ultimately facilitating economic growth and transformation. This perspective underscores the significance of entrepreneurial knowledge in fostering an environment conducive to innovation and economic advancement.

## The Importance of Entrepreneurial Knowledge

Knowledge is a factor by which entrepreneurs can differentiate themselves from competitors. It is with this knowledge that one can organize the business environment well and achieve goals. Entrepreneurs who have more knowledge are more confident in their effectiveness. These people can learn and pay attention to market changes faster.

The role of knowledge entrepreneurs in economics is still vital for strengthening and economic prosperity in any society. Therefore, it is very important that entrepreneurs are aware of the importance of improving their knowledge and the reasons for its need. Acquiring knowledge is a special process for entrepreneurs. They usually learn the best things. It can be said that there is no limit to entrepreneurial knowledge. By combining new tools, technologies, resources and opportunities, entrepreneurs can continuously create new added value.

The three main reasons for the importance of entrepreneurship are the creation of wealth, the development of technology and the creation of productive employment. According to belief, in today's societies, it is necessary to have an entrepreneurial revolution. Entrepreneurship is a combination of many factors. These factors shape the characteristics of entrepreneurs and employees. Fostering entrepreneurship includes two main aspects: First, the impact of economic, political, social, and cultural factors should be considered. These factors may affect the choices of entrepreneurial people. Second, the sources of support for organizational entrepreneurship should be examined. It is very important to support entrepreneurs. Use the entrepreneurial knowledge questionnaire to measure this category (Zarefard, 2018).

## Dimensions of Entrepreneurial Knowledge

Various research has been done on the knowledge structures of entrepreneurship. Based on the orientation theory, a set of factors can be proposed that can directly affect the formation of entrepreneurial knowledge. Some of these factors are:

- Organizational learning

- Entrepreneurial leadership
- Entrepreneurial culture
- Entrepreneurial thinking
- Entrepreneurial strategy
- Entrepreneurial orientation
- Entrepreneurial spirit
- Risk taking

An entrepreneur is someone who has knowledge and information in the field of special innovation. This innovation can be in providing a new product, providing a new service, designing a new process, innovating in customer satisfaction, etc. Entrepreneurs see change as a defining factor, they change values and transform their nature. They use their risk-taking power to realize this idea. They make the right decision and therefore anyone who makes the right decision is considered as an entrepreneur.

According to Schumpeter, the entrepreneur is the driving force and engine of economic development. He considers the characteristic of an entrepreneur to be innovation. Also, "Jeffrey Timmons" believes that an entrepreneur is a person who creates a valuable insight from nothing. A process that can use creativity to create something new with new value by using time, resources, risk and employing partners is called entrepreneurship. Entrepreneurship is not only individual and can also be organizational. Even large companies, both public and private, can engage in entrepreneurship. Today, there is even talk of an entrepreneurial government.

Now knowledge has become one of the main topics among economists and politicians. All economies are based on knowledge and cannot be expected otherwise. Economic knowledge is the dominant economic force in today's world and is developed and strengthened at the micro level by entrepreneurs.

Entrepreneurship is a purposeful activity that includes a series of coherent decisions by an individual or a group of individuals to create, develop or maintain an economic unit. Entrepreneurship is considered as accepting risk, pursuing opportunities, satisfying needs through innovation, and establishing a business. According to "Peter Drucker", entrepreneurship is a behavior and in fact it is the application of management concepts and techniques, product standardization, and the establishment of work based on education.

There are several definitions of entrepreneur and entrepreneurship. Based on the definition of Webster's academic culture, an entrepreneur is someone who undertakes to organize, manage, and assume the risks of an economic activity. Also, based on the definition of Cambridge culture, an entrepreneur is someone who tries to make a profit by starting his own company or acting alone in the world of economy, especially those who must accept risks. In the Encyclopaedia Britannica, an entrepreneur is a person who organizes and manages a business or economic institution and accepts the risks arising from it.

## FINANCIAL LITERACY IS NECESSARY FOR THE SUCCESS OF YOUNG ENTREPRENEURS

Have you ever wondered what financial literacy is? Why is it important for entrepreneurs? Do you have financial skills? If you want to be a successful entrepreneur, these are questions that must be answered with a "yes". Because entrepreneurship along with financial skills leads to success. In this book, we try to show that financial literacy is one of the most important success factors for entrepreneurs.

We are surrounded by people who do different jobs for a living or provide different services to the society to earn a living. Why do you think entrepreneurs run similar or different businesses? I don't mean what they offer, but basically why the way they offer is different?

One of the most important reasons for their distinction is actually their difference in financial knowledge. Yes, you can argue that entrepreneurs can be very different. That's true, but what really sets them apart is whether or not they have financial skills.

Financial literacy refers to the availability of acumen or knowledge about business finances. Entrepreneurs' financial skill sets allow them to make decisions based on available financial information. In fact, financial literacy provides a solid foundation for their business decisions (Zulfiqar, 2017).

### Why is Financial Literacy Important for the Success of Entrepreneurs?

In 2019, CB Insights conducted a survey of the top 20 reasons startups fail. 29% of the respondents stated that lack of money was the main reason for their failure. Another 18% had pricing and cost problems. The sum of these two categories shows that 47% of people whose business failed actually failed in evaluating the financial aspects of their startup. Be aware that as an entrepreneur, with a lack of financial skills, not only is your business at risk, but the livelihoods of the people who work in your business are also at risk.

The only goal of any startup is to gain a good market share and stay profitable with steady growth. Therefore, a financially skilled entrepreneur is likely to make a wise decision based on financial principles, which makes him more likely to succeed than other people.

You might say, there are millions of entrepreneurs running their businesses without these kinds of skills. The answer is clear; There are always exceptions. Furthermore, we need to analyze that if the same people used financial literacy tools in their business, wouldn't they achieve more success in a shorter time? (Ali Nejad,2017).

*"Never spend your money before you have it."*

We have seen a lot of people around us who do not pay attention to their financial management in their daily life, and this issue eventually causes serious problems for them. There are so many people around us who can't pay their credit card due to financial principles or can't save enough from their income to live a part of their life more easily later. There are so many people around us who can't afford their education or health care bills. These are all good examples of bad financial management. In other words, people are not financially literate to do their existing financial affairs in a better way to achieve good and different results.

## Benefits of Having Financial Literacy for Entrepreneurs?

An entrepreneur who runs a business should be aware of its health like anything else that has an expiration date. Just as someone who doesn't know how to read the expiration date on a drug is sure to get into trouble, so is financial literacy for business (Dekamini et al,2023). If an entrepreneur does not know about the financial conditions of his business, sooner or later he will face serious problems in his work. In the following, we have tried to mention the benefits of financial skills for the success of entrepreneurs:

1. **Financial Literacy Provides the Possibility of Proper Budgeting**

Business forecasting is an important thing that should be addressed in time. No part of the business can be done without proper budgeting. An entrepreneur who is financially literate will take care of his budget throughout the year so that he can achieve his predetermined goal with reasonable expenses, whether this goal is to earn more profit or income or manage expenses.

Imagine, as a supplier or product provider, not having the tools you need before the start of the season. what will happen? The opportunity is completely lost. On the other hand, if at the beginning of the year, you had prepared a suitable budget plan according to your previous year's performance, for example, it will be easy for you to provide inventory levels in accordance with the budget.

Budgeting allows you to take control of your business and not let things go to waste. It has been seen that many entrepreneurs, without realizing it, have not been able to properly consider their expenses, which have led to losses, or properly evaluate their claims or debts.

We should consider what we really want instead of our wishes.

2. **Financial Literacy Allows Credit Management**

Most business empires or even countries in the world operate on debt. Debt itself is not a cause for concern, what matters is how you manage it. Without having financial literacy, entrepreneurs cannot do this important work well. You should manage your debts for the same purposes for which you incurred them. In the following, you explain the types of debt:

- **Working Capital Liabilities:** Loans that a business receives to manage the working capital of the business or to fill the gap between its receivables and payables.
- **Capital Loans:** These loans are used to increase your business capital in the form of adding machinery, etc.
- **Car Loan:** These loans are mainly used to provide motor vehicles for your business employees or sometimes for business purposes as well.
- **Credit Cards:** A credit card is an expense that you spend now and then pay off the loan later. It is very common among people; however, it is still a loan that requires financial management.
- **Mortgage Loans:** These loans are usually requested to acquire a building for personal use or sometimes for business purposes.

If an entrepreneur wants to be successful in his business, he must use these debts for the specific purposes for which they were approved. Because each loan was received for a specific need and should have its own added value for the business. but, an entrepreneur who does not have enough financial literacy, when he receives a loan, instead of spending it, he may ruin it all by doing some international trips, spending nights in hotels, sunbathing on beaches, and going bankrupt(Andreou,2017).

*"A person either controls his finances, or his finances discipline him"*

3. **Financial Literacy Makes it Possible to Make Decisions Based on Analysis**

An entrepreneur who is proficient in financial literacy can read income statements, balance sheets, cash flows, and financial ratios correctly and will be more successful in properly analyzing business conditions. In other words, the right decision will be based on proper knowledge of business and on the basis of proper foundations to improve business situations.

*"You cannot progress without making decisions."*

### 4. Financial Literacy Helps Business Growth

If you don't run the business using financial tools, no one should expect to achieve long-term success. You can have small wins, but in the long run, small wins will be difficult to maintain. Startups often face many problems such as liquidity after development and professionalization, and eventually fail and cease to exist. However, startups that have professional financial and accounting systems, due to the considered financial management of their business, have the ability to face any adversities, and as a result, they are more likely to survive.

### 5. Financial Literacy Gives You Control

I personally am a strong advocate of financial literacy, it is true that you can still control your business to some extent without financial knowledge, but even if you do it well, are you doing the right thing? Certainly not!

Financial literacy allows you to monitor your business by reviewing the financial statements your business is on. This gives you enough time to plan and take action before it's too late to find solutions. Don't forget that whenever you are good at finances, it will be difficult for employees to damage your business internally.

*"You must control your money or the lack of it will control you forever."*

## How to Be Financially Literate?

There are no limits in today's world. So if a person needs improvement, there will be several options available to him:

- **Books:** If you want to improve your financial literacy, you should spend hours reading books such as "Financial Literacy Starter Package", and "Rich Dad Increases Your Financial Intelligence".
- **Training Courses:** There are various institutions that offer financial literacy courses. In order to improve your financial knowledge and skills, you should enroll in free or paid financial literacy courses. To improve your financial skills and literacy level, you can participate in Warli School's financial literacy training workshops for children and teenagers.
    **Financial Management Tools:** There are numerous financial management tools available over the internet to improve understanding and increase business financial literacy that you can use to learn well. Few of them have been prepared as handbooks and practical books.
    1- My Financial Toolbox
    2- Financial Accounting: Tools for Business Decision Making

      3- Facilitating Financial Health: Tools for Financial Planners, Coaches
      4- The Financial Controller and CFO's Toolkit
      5- The Essential Financial Toolkit
      6- The New Accounts Payable Toolkit

- Financial newspapers and newsletters: To improve your financial skills and increase your economic knowledge and financial literacy, regularly read financial newspapers or newsletters. Regular reading will often show you something relevant to your business.

# REFERENCES

Andreou, P. C., Karasamani, I., Louca, C., & Ehrlich, D. (2017). The impact of managerial ability on crisis-period corporate investment. *Journal of Business Research*, 79, 107–122. DOI: 10.1016/j.jbusres.2017.05.022

- Zulfiqar, S., Asmi, F., Sarwar, B., &Aziz.S. (2017). Measuring Entrepreneurial Readiness among Youth in Pakistan through Theory of Planned Behavior (TPB) Based Approach. Business and Economic Research, 7(1), 149–167. - https://www.investopedia.com/terms/f/financial-market.asp

Zarefard, M., & Beri, S. E. C. (2018). Entrepreneurs' Managerial Competencies and Innovative Start-Up Intentions in University Students: Focus on Mediating Factors. *International Journal of Entrepreneurship*, 2(2), 2–22.

Dekamini, Fatemeh, Javanmard, Habibollah, & Ehsanifar, Mohammad. (2023). Identifying the factors of the financial crisis and presenting a model in the hotel industry in the critical conditions of COVID-19 (5 and 4-star hotels in Iran). *The Quarterly Journal of Transformative Human Resources*, 2(6).

Nejad, Ali, & Mehdi, Tarfi, Setareh. (2017). The Impact of Management Ability on Financing Policy. *Accounting Knowledge Quarterly*, 8(2), 180–159.

# Chapter 2
# History of Financial Management

**ABSTRACT**

*By reviewing the changes and developments of financial management during the last hundred years, it can be concluded that this field of management emerged as an independent scientific field in the early years of the 20th century. This is despite the fact that before that time and during the 1890s and 1900s, financial management was considered a part of applied economics. During this period, with the merger of large American companies, which was influenced by the development of the product market after the construction of the national railway, half of the industrial production was under the control of 78 companies. These mergers required huge capitals and in addition, capital structure management became one of the important tasks of managers. It should be noted that in this period of time, the process of compiling financial statements and analyzing them was at the beginning of the growth and development period, and presenting financial analyzes to investors was not common. (https://hbr.org/1996/11/the-questions-every-entrepreneur-must-answer)*

## INTRODUCTION

The evolution of financial management over the past century highlights its transformation into a distinct and essential scientific discipline. While initially considered a subset of applied economics during the late 19th and early 20th centuries, financial management emerged as an independent field in response to economic complexities and the growing needs of businesses. The expansion of large American corporations during the industrial boom and the need for managing significant capital and structuring financial resources underscored its importance. This section explores the historical development of financial management, tracing its progression from its rudimentary beginnings to the sophisticated, technology-

DOI: 10.4018/979-8-3693-9415-1.ch002

driven practices of today. Early efforts in financial management focused on basic tasks such as financial statement preparation and managing corporate mergers. Over time, as industries grew and economic challenges such as the Great Depression and World Wars reshaped global markets, financial management adapted to include more structured approaches to liquidity, investment, and capital management. The 20th century witnessed substantial advancements in financial strategies, including cash budgeting, risk management, and the optimal allocation of financial resources. The field further expanded in recent decades, driven by technological innovations, globalization, deregulation, and fluctuating economic conditions. Financial management now integrates complex methodologies, such as econometric modeling, operational research, and data analytics, reflecting its pivotal role in modern business operations. This chapter delves into the milestones of financial management, from its origins to its current status as a cornerstone of organizational strategy and decision-making. By examining its historical trajectory, readers will gain insights into the dynamic nature of financial management and its enduring relevance in addressing contemporary economic challenges.

## THE EVOLUTION OF FINANCIAL MANAGEMENT: FROM APPLIED ECONOMICS TO A DYNAMIC SCIENTIFIC DISCIPLINE

By reviewing the changes and developments of financial management during the last hundred years, it can be concluded that this field of management emerged as an independent scientific field in the early years of the 20th century. This is despite the fact that before that time and during the 1890s and 1900s, financial management was considered a part of applied economics. During this period, with the merger of large American companies, which was influenced by the development of the product market after the construction of the national railway, half of the industrial production was under the control of 78 companies. These mergers required huge capital and in addition, capital structure management became one of the important tasks of managers. It should be noted that in this period, the process of compiling financial statements and analyzing them was at the beginning of the growth and development period, and presenting financial analyses to investors was not common[1].

In the 1920s, major industries such as steel, automobile manufacturing, and chemical industries began to grow and develop. Due to the increase in profit margins and the decrease in the inventory of companies due to the decrease in prices in 1920 and 1921, the issue of financial structures became more important. Price changes made companies and industries aware of the importance of liquidity control and capital structure.

Next, the recession or economic crisis of 1929, which was unique in its duration and severity, brought a wave of bankruptcy and capital restructuring. Liquidity was severely reduced and large companies were faced with back-breaking fixed costs. These issues caused traditional financial management to face the luck of companies once again. This process was affected by the beginning of the Second World War in the 1940s, and the industries started to invest in the defense industry's demand through the attraction of resources and government financial support, which brought financial management with new complications. The first years of the 1950s witnessed the growth and prosperity of the American economic system, parallel to which some cash budget forecasting methods were presented. Financial management initiatives and innovations, with the reduction of corporate profitability during the 1960s and the contractionary policies of the American government, leaned towards the financial evaluation of capital plans and the optimal allocation of financial resources, which was more focused on investment decisions in corporate financial management (Lusardi,2019).

During the last forty years, there have been many changes and developments in financial management, which are mostly focused on the increase of global competition, technological advances, the removal and cancellation of some previous laws and regulations, and exchange rate fluctuations. In general, it can be said that with the emergence of new industries and the actions of old industries in the way of achieving the changes caused by new technologies and adapting to them, the subject of financial management has also faced numerous innovations. The increasing use of computer science and new mathematical models, operational research, and econometrics, is one of the financial management innovations that has been strengthened by the intensification of the competitive environment in recent years and continues to evolve. According to what has been said so far, the evolution of financial management has three important features as follows:

1. Financial management is a relatively new field and one of the branches of management science.
2. Financial management as currently used is based on decision-making and uses the tools and methods of data analysis, computer, economics, and financial accounting.
3. The continuous movement and increasing speed of economic developments promises that financial management will not only assume a more important role; Rather, the speed of progress of this scientific field will increase again; To be able to open the way for managers of companies that are always facing new issues and challenges in the field of finance and capital provision.

# FINANCIAL MANAGEMENT: MEANING, OBJECTIVES, AND FUNCTIONS

Providing financial needs and related matters is one of the first and most important requirements that different businesses face in today's competitive world. In a way, it can be said that all organizational activities are somehow dependent on financial affairs, and if the organization faces a problem in terms of financial affairs, the entire life of the organization is endangered. In this article, an attempt has been made to introduce and explain some of the most important processes related to this field at the company level by briefly reviewing the concepts and definitions related to financial management[2].

## Financial Management: Definitions and Concepts

If we want to express a scientific and academic definition of financial management, we can say: "Financial management means planning, organizing, directing, and controlling financial activities, such as funding and using company funds. In addition, applying the principles of general management to the financial resources of the company is one of the other things that are done in financial management (Pourmansouri et al, 2022).

Financial management can be seen as the application of economic principles and concepts for decision-making and problem-solving; In simple words, financial management is applied economics, which should be done by applying the principles and concepts of micro and macroeconomics and other topics related to economics in the management of business finances. In general, the concept of "financial management" can be divided into three major and at the same time-related areas:

1. **Business Financial Management:** This field, which is called "Corporate Finance" or "Business Finance", focuses on the financial processes of business enterprises, which will ultimately lead to the adoption of financial decisions in different business units. One of the main duties of a financial manager is to maintain and control the company's liquidity, manage matters related to borrowing from the bank and issuing bonds and shares.
2. **Investment:** This area deals mostly with the pricing of securities and the behavior of financial markets. For example, an investment manager's job might include valuing stocks, selecting securities for a pension fund, or evaluating the performance of a company's investment portfolio.
3. **Financial Institutions:** This field is somewhat larger than the previous ones and is mostly related to financial companies such as banks.

It should be noted that regardless of the field of financial management and the small and large differences between them, the general processes are similar in all cases and the same knowledge is needed for its proper management. The following are the most important features of financial management:

- Analytical knowledge based on economic principles
- Uses financial data and accounting information as input for decision-making
- Its main goal is how to optimally use financial assets and increase investment productivity
- Is constantly changing
- It has a global perspective

## Scope and Key Elements of Financial Management

In the financial management of a business, various decisions are made about how to use financial resources, whether the company's financial assets or external financial resources, cash flow control, and investment strategies. Based on this, the most important components of financial management of a business can be summarized in the following cases:

A) **Investment Decisions:** Investing in fixed assets and allocating funds to different assets, under the title of capital budget, is one of the most important things that must be done in financial management. Investing in current assets is also a part of investment decisions known as working capital decisions[3].
  b) **Financial Decisions:** This case is related to increasing the budget from different sources, which is done according to indicators such as the type of source, financing period, financing cost, and return on investment.
  c) **Deciding on Profit Distribution:** The financial manager must make a decision on the distribution of net profit. In general, net profit is divided into two parts: "dividend of profit for shareholders" and "ordinary profit". In the decisions related to the determination of shareholders' profit, the amount of profit and how it is distributed is determined. In conventional profit, the amount of net profit is finalized, which is completely dependent on the development plans and structural changes of the organization, (Pourmansouri et al, 2022).

## Objectives of Financial Management

The objectives of financial management are fundamental to the effective operation of any organization and are centered around the provision, allocation, and control of financial resources. These objectives can be summarized as follows:

1. **Ensuring Regular and Appropriate Supply of Financial Resources:** One of the primary goals of financial management is to guarantee that the organization has a consistent and adequate supply of financial resources. This involves careful planning and forecasting to ensure that funds are available when needed for operational activities, investments, and other financial obligations.
2. **Acquiring Sufficient Profit for Shareholders:** Financial management aims to maximize the profitability of the organization, which is crucial for meeting shareholders' expectations. This includes focusing on the company's earning capacity, maintaining a favorable share price in the market, and aligning corporate strategies with the interests of shareholders. By doing so, financial management seeks to create value and provide satisfactory returns to investors.
3. **Optimal Use of Financial Resources:** After securing and allocating the necessary budget, it is vital to monitor the utilization of financial resources effectively. This involves ensuring that the funds are spent efficiently and that the allocated budget achieves its intended purpose. Financial managers are tasked with implementing control measures to evaluate performance and optimize resource allocation for enhanced operational efficiency.
4. **Ensuring Safety in Investment**: Financial management also focuses on safeguarding investments by ensuring that capital is allocated to ventures with appropriate return rates. This objective involves assessing the risk associated with different investment opportunities and making informed decisions that prioritize capital preservation while seeking growth.
5. **Planning a Correct Capital Structure:** Establishing a sound capital structure is another essential objective of financial management. This entails creating a balanced mix of debt and equity financing to support the organization's operations while minimizing the cost of capital. A well-planned capital structure helps maintain financial stability and ensures that the organization can meet its long-term obligations while also pursuing growth opportunities.

By achieving these objectives, financial management plays a critical role in enhancing the overall financial health of an organization, enabling it to navigate challenges and capitalize on opportunities in a competitive business environment.

## Financial Management Functions

A financial manager should be able to make various decisions regarding the financial affairs of the company. Obviously, due to the influence of some of these decisions on different aspects of the business, the final decision is made in coordination with the senior management in order to avoid conflict and align with the company's macro strategies. In these cases, the information and estimates required for decision-making will be prepared by the financial management and provided to the senior managers of the organization. In the following, some of the most important duties of the financial manager of the company are introduced:

1. **Estimating Capital Needs:** A financial manager must have an accurate and comprehensive estimate of the company's capital needs. It depends on the expected costs, profits, future development plans and related policies. Estimates should be selected sufficiently to increase the earning capacity of the company.
2. **Determining the Composition of the Capital:** After the necessary capital estimate is made, a decision must be made for the capital structure. This includes short-term and long-term stock value analysis. Determining the structure and composition of the company's capital also depends on the proportion of the company's capital and additional funds that must be provided from outside the company.
3. **Choosing Funding Sources:** A company has several options in front of it to receive additional funding, the choice of each of which depends on the relative advantages and disadvantages of each source and funding period. Some of the most important budget sources are:
    - Issuance of stocks and bonds
    - Loans taken from banks and financial institutions
    - Public deposits in the form of bonds
4. **Investment:** The financial manager should make a decision to allocate funds to profitable companies in order to create a minimum level of investment security. In this case, the investment return will also increase in proportion to the investment security.
5. **Profit Determination:** Net profit decisions should be taken by the financial manager. This can be done in two ways:
    - *Dividend Declaration:* which includes the recognition of dividend rates and other benefits, such as bonuses.
    - *Retained Profit:* a part of the company's profit that must be decided on how to allocate it. Usually, the allocation of retained earnings will depend on the company's development, innovation, and diversification plans.

6. **Cash Management:** The financial manager must make decisions related to the management and control of the company's cash flow. Cash is required for various purposes such as payment of wages and salaries, payment of electricity and water bills, payment to creditors, current liabilities, maintaining sufficient stock, purchase of raw materials, etc. and for this reason there should be minimum cash flow in the business.
7. **Financial Control:** The financial manager must not only plan, prepare and use funds, but also focus on financial control. This issue can be done using many techniques such as ratio analysis, financial forecasting, cost, and profit control, etc.

## CONCLUSION: THE ROLE OF TECHNOLOGY IN FINANCIAL MANAGEMENT; THE EMERGENCE OF FINTECHS

One of the characteristics of today's life is the penetration of technology in all dimensions and aspects of human life, which has caused many changes and transformations in various industries and businesses. The intensification of competition and the substantial change of the competitive environment of the last century have prompted companies and economic enterprises to use new technologies to increase efficiency and productivity. Reviewing the experiences of successful companies of recent years, such as Google, Apple and Microsoft, shows the importance of technology as one of the most important elements of sustainable competitive advantage in today's world.

Financial management has always been affected by the increasing role of technology; The use of various types of financial software and the introduction of computer calculations and mathematical programming are examples of the introduction of technology into financial management, which began in the last years of the last century (Fallahet al,2024). However, this trend has accelerated dramatically over the past decade. Today, the financial technology "Financial Technology" which is called "FinTech" in short, has been welcomed by startup companies active in this field. From an economic point of view, financial technology is a type of industry that consists of a group of companies with the aim of improving the performance of financial services with the help of new technologies. In simpler terms, financial technology is synonymous with "innovation in financial services" (Banga, 2019).

Since many experts and analysts believe that the future of the banking industry as well as the financial management of large companies depends on the growth of such startups, the desire to invest in FinTechs has increased. According to published statistics, global investment in financial technology increased almost 12 times between 2008 and 2014 and increased from 930 million dollars to more than 12 billion dollars. The interesting point is that this amount has increased by 4 billion dollars compared to 2013.

It seems that the combination of entrepreneurs and technologists with investors and traditional financial managers of the previous generation is going to change the future of financial services. The new generation of start-ups is being formed to penetrate the heart of the financial and banking industry, and it is predicted that in the next few years, financial management will face many changes and developments, at least in large companies and banks.

According to experts and experts in the field of technology and financial services, seven important technologies that have the ability to make changes in financial services and that financial and banking companies can use are:

- **Cloud Computing:** This technology allows new computer structures to work more creatively, and for this reason, it can create more and more convenient security and access for financial and banking institutions.
- **Blockchain Technology "Block Chain":** This technology, which is a chain of databases for maintaining and storing a huge amount of information, has a good potential for timely access to various information, reducing costs and increasing transparency in companies and financial institutions. Currently, about a thousand fintech startups are working in this field.
  - **Big data and Detailed Analysis:** these technologies will be very useful when accessing intuitive information and analyzing them is not possible. Artificial intelligence systems will play a big role in the future development of this technology in the banking and financial services industry.
- **Personalization:** Each customer interaction can be considered as a very important piece of information that identifies subtle and small differences between each person's financial needs.
- **Advanced Financial Transaction Processing Systems:** These systems can help differentiate the services provided by fintech institutions and startups.
- **New Patterns in Personal Processing:** Apple Watch and virtual reality glasses are two examples of these new patterns that allow customers to create new patterns of behavior and create ways for customers to interact more actively with companies and manage their financial resources. do
- **Super-Converged Systems:** through these systems, it is possible to integrate storage, inventory processing, and equipment networks, thus providing the possibility of providing better and more coherent services in the field of financial management (Ai,2018).

# REFERENCES

Banga, J. (2019). The green bond market: A potential source of climate finance for developing countries. *Journal of Sustainable Finance & Investment*, 9(1), 17–32. DOI: 10.1080/20430795.2018.1498617

Fallah, M. F., Pourmansouri, R., & Ahmadpour, B. (2024). Presenting a new deep learning-based method with the incorporation of error effects to predict certain cryptocurrencies.[-. *International Review of Financial Analysis*, 103466, 103466. Advance online publication. https://climbtheladder.com/sales-planning-manager/. DOI: 10.1016/j.irfa.2024.103466

Lusardi, A. (2019). Financial literacy and the need for financial education: Evidence and implications. *Swiss Journal of Economics and Statistics*, 155(1), 1. DOI: 10.1186/s41937-019-0027-5

Ai, H., Croce, M., & Li, K. (2018). News shocks and the production-based term structure of equity returns. *Review of Financial Studies*, 31(7), 2323–2467.

Pourmansouri, R., Mehdiabadi, A., Shahabi, V., Spulbar, C., & Birau, R. (2022). An investigation of the link between major shareholders' behavior and corporate governance performance before and after the COVID-19 pandemic: A case study of the companies listed on the Iranian stock market. *Journal of Risk and Financial Management*, 15(5), 208. DOI: 10.3390/jrfm15050208

# ENDNOTES

[1] https://www.netsuite.com/portal/resource/articles/financial-management/financial-management.shtml

[2] https://www.lsbf.org.uk/blog/news/importance-of-financial-management/117410

[3] https://managementstudyguide.com/financial-planning.htm

# Chapter 3
# An Overview of the Specialized Topics of Financial Management and the Duties of Financial Managers

## ABSTRACT

*Organizations usually deal with dynamic and variable environments, and their managers are required to carefully and sensitively monitor the organization's financial flows while paying attention to production, support and control activities, because financial management or management of cash flow and financial obligations are among the most important organizational issues. For this reason, experienced managers usually emphasize the continuity of the flow of financial reports and information. Financial management is the administration of cash flow and supervision of the accurate recording of financial affairs and the process of fulfilling the organization's obligations and control of reports and financial information in order to analyze economic activities and plan to improve the organization's financial performance.*

## INTRODUCTION

In today's rapidly changing economic landscape, financial management stands as a critical function for the survival and growth of organizations. The complexity of global markets, economic fluctuations, and technological advancements demand a strategic approach to managing financial resources. Financial managers play a pivotal role in ensuring the effective allocation of resources, maintaining liquidity,

DOI: 10.4018/979-8-3693-9415-1.ch003

and optimizing profitability, thereby directly influencing the organization's success. This section explores the specialized topics in financial management, including public finance, international finance, and the operations of monetary and financial institutions. These areas highlight the diversity of financial management practices, encompassing government resource allocation, cross-border financial transactions, and the critical roles of financial intermediaries. Understanding these topics provides a holistic view of the financial mechanisms that drive both organizations and economies. Additionally, the chapter examines the key responsibilities of financial managers. From liquidity control and cash flow forecasting to enhancing profitability and safeguarding organizational assets, their duties underscore the strategic importance of financial oversight in navigating challenges and capitalizing on opportunities. Through this analysis, readers will gain insights into the multifaceted nature of financial management and its profound impact on organizational stability and growth. The section also emphasizes the significance of financial literacy for managers across all departments, fostering informed decision-making and collaborative efforts toward achieving organizational objectives. This chapter serves as a guide for understanding the intricate relationship between financial expertise and business success in a competitive global environment.

## THE CRITICAL ROLE OF FINANCIAL MANAGEMENT IN ORGANIZATIONAL SUCCESS: A DYNAMIC APPROACH TO ECONOMIC STABILITY

Organizations often operate in dynamic and ever-changing environments, requiring their managers to closely monitor financial flows while managing production, support, and control activities. This close supervision is essential because financial management, including the handling of cash flow and financial obligations, stands among the most critical aspects of organizational success. For this reason, seasoned managers place significant emphasis on the continuity and accuracy of financial reports and information, which serve as the foundation for informed decision-making.

Financial management is the administration of cash flow and supervision of the accurate recording of financial affairs and the process of fulfilling the organization's obligations and control of reports and financial information in order to analyze economic activities and plan to improve the organization's financial performance.

In fact, financial managers are interested in the application of economic and financial theories and accounting within the framework of their professional attitudes. Financial flows are one of the most important factors affecting the mobility and life of an organization; For this reason, the task departments in charge of controlling and managing these flows have a critical position in the organization (Babiak,2023).

# Specialized Topics of Financial Management

## Public Finances

Public finances encompass the processes by which governments manage their financial resources, focusing on the collection, allocation, and oversight of these resources. These financial resources are primarily collected through taxation, borrowing, government fees, and, in some cases, profits from state-owned enterprises. The ultimate goal of public finance is to support the functioning of the state and its institutions while promoting social welfare, economic growth, and stability.

At its core, public finance is concerned with how governments fund their operations and distribute resources to meet various objectives. These objectives may include providing public goods and services, such as education, healthcare, infrastructure, and national defense, or supporting social safety nets like unemployment benefits and pensions. Public finance also plays a crucial role in achieving economic stability through countercyclical fiscal policies, where governments may adjust spending or taxation levels to stabilize the economy during periods of recession or inflation.

Effective public finance management requires careful planning, budgeting, and financial analysis. Governments must consider the long-term sustainability of their financial policies, ensuring they do not accumulate excessive debt or implement measures that could harm the economy. For instance, a government may face the challenge of balancing the need to fund essential services with maintaining a manageable level of public debt.

Public finances are also linked to issues of fairness and equity. Policymakers must decide how to distribute the tax burden among citizens and how to allocate resources to maximize social benefits. This often involves difficult trade-offs, as governments must prioritize spending across competing areas, such as healthcare, education, and infrastructure, while addressing pressing challenges like poverty, inequality, and climate change.

In recent years, public finance has expanded to include a greater focus on transparency and accountability, driven by the increasing demand for governments to be more open about how they use public funds. Public financial management reforms aim to improve efficiency, reduce corruption, and ensure that governments remain fiscally responsible while achieving their social and economic goals. Public debt management, fiscal responsibility laws, and independent auditing institutions are some of the key mechanisms used to enhance accountability in public finance systems. Public finance is a multifaceted field that involves the collection, allocation, and oversight of financial resources by governments. It requires a delicate balance between raising adequate revenues, ensuring efficient and fair distribution of resources, and promoting economic growth and stability while maintaining transparency and accountability. The ultimate aim is to use these resources to benefit society as a whole and ensure long-term fiscal sustainability.

## International Finance

International finance is a comprehensive field that delves into the intricate dynamics of financial transactions occurring between individuals, businesses, and governments across national borders. This discipline encompasses a wide array of activities, from analyzing international investments to understanding the flow of capital and the implications of exchange rate fluctuations. One of the core components of international finance is the examination of the balance of payments, which serves as a critical indicator of a country's financial health in its dealings with the rest of the world. The balance of payments is essentially a systematic record of all economic transactions between residents of a country and the rest of the world over a specific period. It is divided into two main accounts: the current account and the capital account. The current account reflects the trade balance, including exports and imports of goods and services, as well as income earned from abroad and payments made to foreign entities. Conversely, the capital account captures financial transactions, such as foreign direct investments, portfolio investments, and other capital flows. A thorough analysis of these accounts enables financial managers and policymakers to assess the quality of a government's balance of payments and identify any potential imbalances that could lead to economic instability.

In the context of multinational corporations, international finance plays a crucial role in facilitating their operations across different countries. These corporations often engage in complex financial transactions that involve multiple currencies, diverse regulatory environments, and varying economic conditions. Financial managers within these firms are tasked with navigating these complexities to optimize capital allocation, manage currency risk, and ensure compliance with local regulations. They must also consider the potential impact of political and economic factors on their international operations, as geopolitical tensions or economic sanctions can significantly affect profitability and operational viability.

Furthermore, international finance encompasses the study of foreign exchange markets, where currencies are traded, and the dynamics of exchange rates are determined. Fluctuations in exchange rates can have profound effects on the profitability of international transactions, making effective currency risk management a key focus for financial professionals. This often involves employing hedging strategies, such as using forward contracts or options, to mitigate the adverse effects of exchange rate volatility on cash flows and profit margins, (Pourmansouri et al,2024).

Another vital aspect of international finance is the evaluation of global investment opportunities. Investors increasingly seek to diversify their portfolios by exploring opportunities in emerging markets and other countries. However, such investments carry inherent risks, including political instability, economic fluctuations, and differences in regulatory frameworks. As a result, financial managers must conduct thorough risk assessments and perform due diligence to make informed investment decisions that align with their organizations' strategic objectives. In summary, international finance is a multifaceted discipline that encompasses the examination of financial transactions between individuals, businesses, and governments on a global scale. By assessing the balance of payments and managing the risks associated with international trade and investment, financial managers play a pivotal role in fostering stable financial relationships between countries. Through a comprehensive understanding of currency dynamics, global market trends, and the regulatory environment, they are better equipped to navigate the complexities of international finance and contribute to the sustainable growth of their organizations in an increasingly interconnected world.

## AFFAIRS OF MONETARY AND FINANCIAL INSTITUTIONS

The examination of monetary and financial institutions encompasses a thorough analysis of the economic structures underlying financial and credit institutions, such as banks, credit unions, and investment firms. These entities are integral to the economy as they are responsible for collecting deposits from savers and investing those funds in a variety of ventures, including personal loans, mortgages, business financing, and public projects.

Financial institutions serve as intermediaries between savers and borrowers, facilitating the flow of capital within the economy. By attracting deposits from individuals and businesses, these institutions create a pool of available funds that can be allocated toward productive investments. This process not only generates returns for savers in the form of interest payments but also fosters economic growth by providing necessary capital for enterprises to expand, innovate, and create jobs.

Moreover, the economic structure of these institutions is characterized by a complex network of regulations, risk management practices, and financial instruments designed to ensure their stability and efficiency. Regulatory frameworks, established by government entities and central banks, play a critical role in overseeing these institutions, promoting transparency, and safeguarding the interests of depositors and investors. Compliance with these regulations helps mitigate risks associated with lending and investment activities, thereby enhancing the resilience of the financial system.

The proper functioning of financial and credit institutions is vital for maintaining economic stability. When these institutions operate efficiently, they contribute to a stable financial environment that encourages consumer confidence and stimulates investment. In contrast, failures or mismanagement within these institutions can lead to financial crises, resulting in severe economic repercussions, including increased unemployment, reduced consumer spending, and lower overall economic growth. The affairs of monetary and financial institutions are a cornerstone of the modern economy. By effectively collecting savers' money and channeling it into productive investments, these institutions play a pivotal role in supporting business development, fostering innovation, and promoting economic stability. A comprehensive understanding of their economic structures and functions is essential for policymakers, financial analysts, and industry professionals as they navigate the complexities of the financial landscape.

This area examines the economic structures of financial and credit institutions, such as banks and investment firms, which play pivotal roles in collecting deposits from savers and channeling those funds into productive investments. The proper functioning of these institutions is essential for maintaining economic stability and supporting business development.

## Duties of Financial Managers

Financial managers play a crucial role in the organization by overseeing its financial health and ensuring that resources are effectively managed. They are responsible for not only safeguarding the organization's financial stability but also working in tandem with other departments to align financial strategies with the overall business goals. Some of the core duties of financial managers are outlined below, including liquidity control, credit monitoring, and resource development.

1. **Liquidity Control and Credit Circulation Monitoring**

Liquidity management is the backbone of any organization's financial stability. Financial managers are tasked with monitoring the flow of cash and credits, ensuring that the company can meet its obligations promptly. This involves managing funds received from various sources such as bank facilities, product sales, or financial instruments like stocks and bonds. Effective liquidity management ensures that the organization maintains its reputation and avoids the risk of defaulting on payments, which can severely damage its credibility.

A) **Forecasting the Cash Flow of the Organization**

Accurate cash flow forecasting is one of the most important tasks of financial managers. By predicting when cash inflows will occur and matching them with the company's obligations, managers can ensure that all debts, such as loan repayments, supplier payments, and wages, are met in a timely manner. This requires close coordination with sales, procurement, and operational departments to accurately project income from sales or services and plan for future cash outlays. Failure to fulfill obligations on time not only tarnishes the company's reputation but may also lead to penalties, higher borrowing costs, or strained relationships with creditors and suppliers. Therefore, financial managers strive to predict the amount and timing of incoming funds to balance obligations effectively.

B)  **Development of Financial Resources**

Another key duty is identifying and securing additional sources of financing. Diversifying funding sources is critical for the organization's long-term stability. Financial managers are constantly evaluating different financial sources—such as loans, equity financing, and bond issues—to determine the best fit for the company's needs. Not all financial sources are equal. Some offer better terms, lower costs, or more flexible repayment schedules. Managers must evaluate these options by considering factors such as the interest rates, fees, timeframes, and risks associated with each option. They need to carefully weigh these characteristics to secure the most favorable funding while ensuring that the company is not overburdened with debt or exposed to unnecessary financial risk.

C)  **Control of Cash and Credits**

In many organizations, different bank accounts are used for various purposes, such as payroll, operations, and capital investments. Without proper oversight, this can lead to inefficiencies where cash is underutilized in some accounts, while others face shortages. Financial managers are responsible for optimizing the organization's overall cash balance by transferring funds between accounts to minimize borrowing and ensure liquidity is available where needed.By closely monitoring cash balances, financial managers can make sure that the organization makes the best use of available resources, reducing the need for costly short-term borrowing. This also enables the company to take advantage of investment opportunities or deal with unexpected expenses without compromising financial stability.

2.  **Increasing Profitability**

Financial managers play a pivotal role in enhancing profitability and improving the overall efficiency of organizations. By preparing, analyzing, and adjusting financial reports and data, they enable informed decision-making, particularly in areas concerning profit-generating activities. Their responsibilities go beyond mere financial oversight; they include providing insights and strategies for optimizing profitable activities, cost management, pricing decisions, and profit forecasting. Below are the key areas through which financial managers contribute to earning profit.

A) **Cost Control**

In large organizations, managing operational and administrative costs is critical to profitability. Financial managers often rely on industrial accounting and cost accounting methods to gain a clear understanding of how resources are allocated. The modern integration of technology, particularly the use of computer-based systems, allows for the detailed tracking and reporting of expenses across various departments. These detailed expense reports provide financial managers with critical data, enabling them to analyze cost patterns and identify inefficiencies. Once the costs are thoroughly reviewed, financial managers propose actionable strategies aimed at cost reduction. This might involve renegotiating supplier contracts, optimizing resource use, or identifying unnecessary expenditures that can be eliminated. Their ultimate goal is to ensure that operational costs are kept under control without sacrificing the quality of goods or services, thus safeguarding the organization's profitability. For example, in manufacturing companies, this could involve analyzing production costs and seeking ways to reduce material waste or improving labor efficiency through better scheduling and resource management.

B) **Pricing**

Pricing strategy is one of the most significant levers a financial manager can pull to influence profitability. Financial managers must continuously monitor market conditions and the organization's position within the market to establish appropriate pricing policies. This involves performing a thorough cost-benefit analysis, taking into account several key factors:

- **Market Share:** Financial managers need to understand how their organization's pricing strategy affects its competitive position within the market.
- **Competitor Analysis:** Monitoring competitors' pricing strategies and adjusting accordingly helps in maintaining competitiveness without compromising profitability.

- **Production and Marketing Costs:** Prices must reflect not only the costs of production but also the associated costs of bringing products or services to market.
- **Organizational Values:** Financial managers must ensure that pricing aligns with the brand's values and reputation. For instance, premium products may demand higher prices that reflect quality, while a cost-leader strategy may focus on affordability.

In developing a pricing strategy, financial managers consider both short-term and long-term profit goals. They must balance the need for immediate revenue with sustaining profitability over time. Dynamic pricing models, which adjust prices based on market conditions or customer demand, are often employed to maximize profitability. By fine-tuning pricing strategies, financial managers ensure that the organization remains competitive while capturing the maximum potential revenue from its offerings.

C) **Predicting the Amount of Profit**

Forecasting future profits is a crucial task for financial managers. Accurate profit predictions enable organizations to plan investments, allocate resources effectively, and set realistic financial targets. To do so, financial managers consider several important factors:

- **Current Costs and Possible Changes:** Understanding existing operational costs and predicting future cost fluctuations, such as changes in raw material prices or labor costs, is essential in making accurate profit forecasts.
- **Sales and Service Capabilities:** Financial managers analyze the organization's capacity to sell products or provide services at projected volumes, based on historical performance and market demand forecasts.
- **Future Organizational Plans:** Long-term plans, such as entering new markets, launching new products, or expanding operational capacity, influence profit forecasts. Financial managers take these future initiatives into account when estimating profits.

The estimated profit data is typically recorded in a profit estimation worksheet, which helps assess whether the projected profits can cover the organization's initial operating costs. This type of analysis helps managers determine the feasibility of new ventures or investments, providing a risk assessment that compares potential returns against the risks involved. Organizations require these assessments to avoid losses and ensure that any new undertaking is profitable. Additionally, these predictions are made with error margins, accounting for uncertainties and potential market changes. For example, unexpected economic downturns or shifts in consumer demand could impact the organization's ability to achieve forecasted profits. A well-constructed profit forecast includes these factors and applies error probabilities to ensure that decision-makers have a clear understanding of potential risks (Boratyńska,2016).

3. **Taking Care of Property and Assets**

The assets of any organization play a critical role in its operational success and long-term sustainability. These assets encompass a wide range of items, including buildings, vehicles, machinery, equipment, inventory, cash, credits, and any other resources that are essential to the organization's functioning. Proper care, maintenance, and protection of these assets are vital responsibilities for financial managers.

Financial managers must ensure that these assets are safeguarded from damage, theft, or depreciation, while also monitoring their utilization to optimize efficiency. This includes keeping accurate records, scheduling regular maintenance, and evaluating whether certain assets are still serving their purpose or need to be upgraded or replaced. Furthermore, determining the current value of the organization's assets, through regular assessments and appraisals, is a crucial aspect of financial management. This helps in understanding the financial health of the company and making informed decisions about future investments or divestments. In addition to protection and valuation, managing the organization's assets also involves strategically allocating resources to ensure that each asset contributes to the overall productivity and profitability of the company. This requires a careful balance between investing in new assets and maintaining existing ones. Financial managers are tasked with ensuring that the organization's capital is utilized effectively, reducing waste, and increasing returns on assets, which ultimately contributes to the financial stability and growth of the organization.

## Familiarity with Financial Management

Financial management is the backbone of any successful organization, encompassing the careful planning, control, and utilization of the company's financial resources. At its core, financial management involves ensuring that the organization's resources are used most efficiently and effectively to achieve its goals. The primary objective is to control and optimize resource usage while preventing waste. This ensures that every dollar spent is contributing to the organization's strategic objectives.

Another critical aspect of financial management is increasing the organization's capital. Growing capital is vital not only for ensuring success in the short term but also for providing a cushion during challenging economic times. By efficiently managing the organization's resources and capital, financial managers help to ensure that the company remains competitive and has the necessary financial reserves to face any future challenges. Capital growth also facilitates investment in new opportunities, which in turn fuels innovation and expansion. Budget allocation is another key responsibility. Financial managers must determine how to distribute the budget across various departments and projects, making decisions based on current priorities, organizational needs, and long-term strategic goals. This requires financial managers to have a deep understanding of the organization's operational requirements and market conditions to make decisions that maximize value.

Ultimately, the overarching goal of financial management is to drive the organization toward high profitability and to enhance shareholder wealth. Profitability not only measures the success of an organization but also directly impacts shareholder confidence and the overall market value of the company. A robust financial management strategy ensures that the organization can generate consistent profits even during economic downturns by effectively navigating uncertainties and maintaining operational efficiency.

In today's volatile economic environment, organizations often face unexpected challenges, such as market fluctuations, regulatory changes, or shifts in consumer behavior. Strong financial management helps companies weather these storms by providing the framework needed to maintain liquidity, reduce financial risk, and sustain profitability. A well-executed financial management plan is essential for any organization looking to achieve long-term success and stability. Experts in the field often describe financial management as the proper application of economic principles in a business setting. When applied effectively, it ensures that the company can achieve maximum profitability in the best economic conditions. Furthermore, sound financial management strategies can significantly increase the company's stock value, which benefits shareholders and investors. This makes financial management not only crucial for the organization's internal operations but also for its external reputation and financial standing. (Campbell, 2018).

## The Role of Managers in Financial Literacy

Financial management is a critical skill that extends beyond the confines of finance departments. Every manager, whether overseeing human resources, operations, marketing, or any other department, must possess a basic understanding of financial principles to contribute effectively to their organization's success. Financial literacy enables managers to make more informed decisions, allowing them to align their departmental actions with the broader financial goals of the organization. This ensures that managers are not just focused on their immediate responsibilities but are also contributing to the long-term profitability and sustainability of the organization.

One of the key advantages of financial literacy for managers is the ability to allocate resources more effectively. When managers understand how to manage their departmental budgets, they are better equipped to make decisions that optimize spending and avoid waste. For example, a marketing manager with financial knowledge will be able to assess the return on investment (ROI) of various campaigns and allocate resources toward initiatives that yield the highest value. Similarly, an operations manager can analyze the costs associated with production processes and implement cost-saving measures without compromising quality. This strategic allocation of resources ensures that each department functions efficiently and contributes to the overall financial health of the organization.

Another critical aspect of financial literacy for managers is the ability to assess the financial implications of their decisions. Managers are often responsible for implementing projects, making investments, or introducing new processes that have significant financial ramifications. Without a solid understanding of financial principles, they may inadvertently make decisions that strain the organization's resources or fail to deliver a positive financial outcome. For instance, a human resources manager who understands financial management can evaluate the costs and benefits of hiring new employees, offering benefits, or implementing training programs. They can ensure that their decisions not only enhance employee performance and development but also align with the organization's budgetary constraints and profitability goals.

Moreover, financial literacy empowers managers to contribute to the organization's profitability by identifying opportunities for growth and cost reduction. Managers who are financially literate can analyze financial reports, key performance indicators (KPIs), and other metrics to identify trends that may indicate opportunities for expansion or areas where the organization can reduce costs. For example, a manager in the supply chain department may identify inefficiencies in the procurement process, leading to significant cost savings that can be reinvested into other areas of the business. Similarly, a sales manager with financial acumen can design strategies that not only drive revenue but also enhance profitability by focusing on high-margin products or customer segments.

In addition to operational decision-making, financial literacy equips managers to engage more effectively in strategic planning and forecasting. By understanding financial principles, managers can contribute valuable insights during the budgeting process, helping to create realistic financial plans that reflect both the opportunities and challenges facing the organization. This can lead to better financial outcomes, as managers can identify potential risks or bottlenecks and proactively suggest solutions that minimize financial disruptions. Furthermore, during times of financial uncertainty or economic downturns, financially literate managers are better positioned to navigate challenges, as they can quickly adjust strategies to maintain financial stability and avoid long-term damage. Finally, promoting financial literacy across all management levels fosters a more cohesive and financially sound organization. When every manager, regardless of their department, understands the financial implications of their decisions, they can work together more effectively toward common financial goals. This leads to improved communication, collaboration, and coordination between departments, as all managers share a common understanding of the organization's financial priorities. It also creates a culture of accountability, where managers are more mindful of their spending and resource allocation, knowing that their decisions directly impact the organization's financial performance.

## CONCLUSION

In conclusion, financial management is at the heart of any organization's success, and every manager, irrespective of their specific role, must be equipped with financial knowledge. From safeguarding assets and ensuring efficient resource allocation to increasing capital and maximizing profitability, financial literacy enables managers to support the organization's strategic goals and contribute to its overall success. By embedding financial literacy into all levels of management, organizations can create a more financially resilient, efficient, and profitable business.

# REFERENCES

Babiak, M. (2023). Generalized disappointment aversion and the variance term structure. *SSRN*, 1–48. DOI: 10.2139/ssrn.4197174

Boratyńska, K. (2016). FsQCA in corporate bankruptcy research. An innovative approach in food industry. *Journal of Business Research*, 69(11), 5529–5533. DOI: 10.1016/j.jbusres.2016.04.166

- Campbell, J. (2018). Financial decisions and markets: A course of asset pricing. Princeton University Press.de Groot, O., Richter, A., & Throckmorton, N. (2018). Uncertainty shocks in a model of effective demand: Comment. Econometrica, 86(4), 1513–1526. - https://managementstudyguide.com/financial-planning.htm

Pourmansouri, R., Fallahshams, M. F., & Afshani, R. G. G. (2024). Designing a Financial Stress Index Based on the GHARCH-DCC Approach and Machine Learning Models. *Journal of the Knowledge Economy*, ●●●, 1–30. DOI: 10.1007/s13132-024-02075-9

# Chapter 4
# Basic Concepts in Financial Management of Companies

## ABSTRACT

*Before we examine the topic of financial management of companies, we must deal with the basic concepts in economics and explain the place of financial knowledge in economics and specify the difference between finance and accounting science and express a clear demarcation of them. After a proper understanding of the concepts and basic principles of financial management of companies, we will continue to discuss specialized topics in financial management of companies. Financial knowledge is examined in the framework of economics. The financial sector that is not part of finance or public finance and is not related to the government, and the issues related to the private sector and non-governmental enterprises, is classified in the field of "micro economy". If we want to speak more precisely, non-governmental finance is included in the framework of the "theory of the firm". Therefore, the financial position is in the field of economy; We are talking about the economy, and of course that part of the economy that is called financial economics.*

## INTRODUCTION

Financial management, as a cornerstone of corporate success and sustainability, focuses on analyzing and making financial decisions to allocate resources effectively and enhance organizational value for stakeholders. Understanding the fundamental concepts of financial management, including financial and real assets, financial instruments, balance sheets, and the roles of financial managers, is essential for delving into more advanced topics in this field. This chapter begins by examining the role of

DOI: 10.4018/979-8-3693-9415-1.ch004

financial knowledge within economics to clarify the relationship between financial markets and economic activities. It then distinguishes between financial and real assets, highlighting the differences between tangible properties and financial claims on these assets. Additionally, the chapter introduces financial instruments, financial institutions, and financial markets as the foundational infrastructure for corporate financial management. A critical section of this chapter focuses on analyzing the financial balance sheets of both financial and non-financial companies. By emphasizing the recording of assets and liabilities, it explores the hierarchy of stakeholders' claims and methods for evaluating a company's financial position. Key topics such as financing, risk management, and the roles of financial managers and portfolio managers in both financial and non-financial companies are also discussed. This chapter is designed to provide a comprehensive understanding of the fundamental principles and concepts of financial management, creating a strong foundation for exploring more advanced topics in the field. A thorough grasp of these concepts will empower managers and professionals to make informed decisions and steer their organizations toward growth and sustainability.

## FOUNDATIONS OF FINANCIAL MANAGEMENT: UNDERSTANDING ITS ECONOMIC ROOTS AND DISTINCTION FROM ACCOUNTING

Before we examine the topic of financial management of companies, we must deal with the basic concepts in economics explain the place of financial knowledge in economics specify the difference between finance and accounting science and express a clear demarcation of them. After a proper understanding of the concepts and basic principles of financial management of companies, we will continue to discuss specialized topics in financial management of companies.

### Where is the Place of Financial Knowledge in Economics?

Financial knowledge plays a crucial role in the broader framework of economics, influencing both theoretical and practical aspects of economic theory and application. Understanding the intersection between finance and economics helps clarify how financial markets operate, the behavior of economic agents, and the allocation of resources within an economy. This connection can be explored through several key concepts and frameworks.

While finance and economics are closely related disciplines, they have distinct focuses. Economics broadly examines how societies allocate scarce resources among competing uses, exploring factors such as supply and demand, production, consumption, and distribution. In contrast, finance specifically addresses the management of money and investments, the mechanisms of financial markets, and the behavior of financial instruments. Within economics, the financial sector can be viewed from different angles:

1. **Macroeconomics:** This branch of economics focuses on the overall performance and behavior of an economy, including national income, inflation, unemployment, and government policies. Financial knowledge is essential in macroeconomic analysis, as it informs understanding of monetary policy, interest rates, and the implications of financial crises.
2. **Microeconomics:** This branch deals with individual economic agents, such as households and firms, and their decision-making processes. Financial knowledge becomes particularly relevant here, especially concerning how firms manage their finances, make investment decisions, and respond to market conditions.

When considering financial knowledge within the microeconomic framework, it is important to note that non-governmental finance—relating to private sector enterprises—falls under the category of the "theory of the firm." This theory examines how firms operate, make decisions regarding production and pricing, and interact with markets. Financial knowledge in this context includes understanding:

- **Capital Structure:** Firms must decide on the optimal mix of debt and equity financing to fund their operations and growth. Financial knowledge enables firms to analyze their options and manage financial risks effectively.
- **Investment Decisions:** Firms often face choices regarding where to allocate their financial resources. Knowledge of financial markets, risk assessment, and potential returns is critical for making informed investment decisions that maximize shareholder value.
- **Cost-Benefit Analysis:** Businesses frequently engage in cost-benefit analyses to determine the financial viability of projects or investments. A solid understanding of financial principles helps firms evaluate potential risks and returns associated with their choices.
- **Financial Performance Metrics:** Understanding key financial metrics, such as return on investment (ROI), profit margins, and cash flow analysis, is vital for firms to assess their operational effectiveness and make strategic adjustments.

Within the realm of economics, the subfield known as financial economics specifically focuses on the relationship between financial variables and economic activity. Financial economics examines topics such as:

- **Market Behavior:** Understanding how financial markets function, including price formation, market efficiency, and the impact of information on asset prices.
- **Risk Management:** Evaluating how individuals and firms manage financial risks, including the use of derivatives, insurance, and diversification strategies.
- **Investment Theory:** Exploring how investors make decisions based on risk and return trade-offs, asset pricing models, and behavioral finance.
- **Impact of Financial Policy:** Analyzing how financial regulations, monetary policy, and fiscal policy influence economic conditions, growth, and stability.

The interdependence between finance and economics highlights the importance of financial knowledge in understanding economic phenomena. For example, the performance of financial markets can significantly affect overall economic growth. Conversely, changes in economic conditions can impact financial stability and the functioning of financial institutions (Pourmansouri et al, 2023). Moreover, the study of economics provides insights into broader economic trends and policies that can influence financial decision-making. Financial professionals rely on economic principles to inform their strategies and adapt to changing market conditions. In conclusion, financial knowledge occupies a pivotal place within the field of economics, particularly in the realms of microeconomics and financial economics. By examining how financial principles intersect with economic theories, individuals and organizations can better understand the dynamics of financial markets, make informed decisions, and navigate the complexities of resource allocation. This integration of financial knowledge into economic frameworks ultimately enhances our understanding of both disciplines and their relevance to the functioning of modern economies.

## What is the Definition of Financial Economics?

Financial economics is a specialized subfield within economics that focuses on the dynamics of financial markets, the behavior of financial instruments, and the impact of financial decisions on economic outcomes. It seeks to understand how individuals, institutions, and governments allocate resources over time, considering the risk and uncertainty inherent in financial transactions. This field integrates theoretical frameworks and quantitative models to analyze various aspects of finance, including asset pricing, capital structure, corporate finance, and investment strategies.

The prominence of financial economics in contemporary economic discourse can be attributed to its significant influence on both academic research and practical applications in financial markets. Notably, it occupies a considerable space within the broader field of economics, primarily due to the substantial investments made in research and development within this area. In fact, following the field of medicine, financial economics is one of the most heavily researched domains, highlighting its critical importance in understanding modern economies. The substantial financial resources of various financial institutions also facilitate extensive research in this field, enabling scholars and practitioners to explore complex financial phenomena. While discussing financial economics, it is essential to recognize its foundational relationship with microeconomics. Finance is often viewed through the lens of microeconomic principles, emphasizing individual and firm behavior regarding financial decisions. However, in many discussions within our country, there tends to be an overlap and sometimes confusion between the domains of finance and accounting. This is understandable, especially given the historical context in which financial education in Iran began. Approximately four decades ago, when finance courses were first introduced, a clear demarcation was established between finance and accounting. At that time, the narrative often emphasized that "finance" and "accounting" were distinct and unrelated fields.

However, upon closer examination, it becomes evident that while finance and accounting are indeed separate disciplines, they are interrelated and share a symbiotic relationship. Finance is concerned with the allocation of resources and the management of financial assets and liabilities, while accounting focuses on the systematic recording, reporting, and analysis of financial transactions. The interplay between these fields is crucial for effective financial decision-making. Financial analysts often rely on accounting data to inform their investment strategies, while accountants must understand financial principles to accurately report and analyze financial statements. Therefore, rather than viewing finance and accounting as mutually exclusive domains, it is more productive to appreciate them as complementary fields that together enhance our understanding of economic behavior and financial markets.

In summary, financial economics not only delves into the mechanisms of financial markets and the implications of financial decisions but also underscores the intricate relationship between finance and accounting, emphasizing the importance of both disciplines in fostering a holistic understanding of the economic landscape.

## What is the Definition of Accounting Science?

Accounting science is a systematic discipline that focuses on the collection, processing, and presentation of financial data, transforming it into meaningful information for decision-making. Within the broader framework of information science, accounting plays a pivotal role by specializing in financial data, which is expressed in the domestic currency of a given country. This financial data is critical for economic enterprises, as it forms the foundation for understanding an organization's financial health and performance. To delineate what constitutes financial data, it is essential to recognize that while various types of information are significant to an organization—such as the skills and number of employees or engineering designs—these do not fall under the umbrella of financial information. For instance, assessing workforce efficiency involves numerical data that, although important, is not inherently financial. In contrast, financial data specifically pertains to figures that represent monetary values, such as revenues, expenses, assets, and liabilities, quantified in the local currency, such as riyals.

The primary objective of accounting is to transform raw financial data into a structured format that enhances usability for decision-makers. This transformation process involves several steps, including the collection of financial transactions, classification into appropriate categories, and summarization in the form of financial statements. These statements, such as balance sheets and income statements, present a clear picture of an organization's financial status and performance over a specific period. For managers, raw accounting figures alone provide insufficient insight for informed decision-making. It is only when this data is organized and classified into specific formats that meaningful analyses can occur. For example, understanding the relationship between incurred costs and generated revenues requires contextual interpretation, which is facilitated through detailed financial reporting. This process of transforming raw data into actionable insights serves various stakeholders, including investors, managers, and government authorities.

In essence, accounting science encompasses the methods and techniques for converting raw financial data into valuable information that aids in strategic planning and operational decision-making. It is an indispensable tool for organizations seeking to navigate their financial landscape effectively, ensuring that stakeholders have access to relevant, accurate, and timely information necessary for assessing performance and making informed choices. By bridging the gap between raw data and decision-making, accounting science plays a crucial role in the overall functioning and sustainability of economic enterprises.

## What is the Meaning and Concept of Audit?

The concept of an audit is multifaceted and plays a crucial role in enhancing the integrity and transparency of a company's financial reporting. At its core, an audit system serves as a mechanism that assists a company's accounting department in preparing accurate financial data. Auditors work closely with accountants, facilitating the transformation of raw financial data into meaningful and useful information that stakeholders can rely on for decision-making.

One of the primary responsibilities of auditors is to ensure compliance with a company's internal controls. This emphasis on internal controls is vital as it helps safeguard assets, ensures the accuracy of financial reporting, and promotes operational efficiency. Auditors are tasked not only with identifying and reporting any instances of wrongdoing or non-compliance that they encounter during their work but also with fostering an environment of improvement (Pourmansouri et al,2024). Their main objective is to assist accountants in enhancing the quality of financial information, ensuring that it meets the required standards for reliability and relevance. Both accountants and auditors base their work on established accounting principles and theories that are typically taught in universities. They operate within a framework of accounting standards, which serve as guidelines for how financial transactions should be recorded and reported. These standards, developed over years of professional practice, provide a summary of best practices within the field rather than legal mandates. For instance, accounting standards dictate how accounts should be organized to ensure comparability, how depreciation should be recorded, how profit should be identified, and when income should be recognized. Accountants adjust their financial statements by these national or international standards, ensuring consistency and compliance.

Accountants play a pivotal role in collecting financial data and organizing it into formats that are usable by various stakeholders, including managers. Among the key users of this financial information is the financial manager, who relies heavily on the data presented in financial reports to make informed decisions. However, it is essential to distinguish between the fields of finance and accounting. While financial managers utilize accounting information extensively, finance encompasses broader concepts that are defined within the academic discipline of economics.

Accounting focuses primarily on the collection, processing, and reporting of financial information, making it understandable and accessible to a wide range of audiences, including the public, managers, and investors. This distinction highlights the complementary yet distinct roles that accounting and finance play within an organization, emphasizing the importance of both in driving informed decision-making and fostering financial accountability. Through effective auditing, organizations can enhance the reliability of their financial information, ultimately contributing to better governance and more robust economic performance.

# What are the Differences Between Financial Accounting and Management Accounting?

Financial accounting and management accounting are two distinct branches of accounting that serve different purposes, audiences, and regulatory requirements. Here are the key differences between the two:

1. **Purpose of Reporting:**
   - *Financial Accounting:* The primary purpose of financial accounting is to provide a clear and accurate representation of an organization's financial performance and position to external stakeholders, including investors, creditors, regulatory agencies, and the public. It focuses on the overall financial health of the organization over a specified period.
   - *Management Accounting:* In contrast, management accounting is designed to assist internal management in decision-making processes. It provides detailed financial and non-financial information that helps managers plan, control, and evaluate organizational operations.
2. **Audience:**
   - *Financial Accounting:* The reports generated from financial accounting are intended for external parties, such as shareholders, regulators, and potential investors, who need insights into the organization's financial stability and profitability.
   - *Management Accounting:* Management accounting reports are tailored for internal users, primarily the organization's management team. These reports are used for strategic planning, performance evaluation, and operational decision-making.
3. **Regulatory Requirements:**
   - *Financial Accounting:* Financial accounting adheres to established accounting standards and frameworks, such as Generally Accepted Accounting Principles (GAAP) or International Financial Reporting Standards (IFRS). Compliance with these standards ensures consistency and comparability across organizations.
   - *Management Accounting:* Management accounting is not bound by external regulations or standards. It is more flexible and can be customized to meet the specific needs of the organization and its management team.
4. **Types of Reports:**
   - *Financial Accounting:* The reports generated in financial accounting include the balance sheet, income statement, cash flow statement, and statement of changes in equity. These reports provide a summary of financial activities over a defined period.

- *Management Accounting:* Management accounting produces various reports, such as budget forecasts, variance analyses, cost analyses, and performance reports. These reports focus on detailed operational metrics and are often produced more frequently than financial accounting reports.

5. **Time Orientation:**
   - *Financial Accounting:* Financial accounting is retrospective, focusing on historical data and providing insights into past performance. It typically covers a specific reporting period, such as quarterly or annually.
   - *Management Accounting:* Management accounting is more forward-looking, emphasizing planning and forecasting. It helps management project future financial scenarios and makes informed decisions based on anticipated performance.

6. **Detail and Scope:**
   - *Financial Accounting:* Financial accounting provides a broad overview of the organization's financial status, often at a summarized level. It does not delve deeply into individual operational aspects.
   - *Management Accounting:* Management accounting goes into greater detail, analyzing specific areas of the business. It can include segment reporting, departmental budgets, and performance metrics, allowing for granular analysis of operations.

7. **Decision-Making Focus:**
   - *Financial Accounting:* The decision-making information provided by financial accounting is primarily related to external stakeholders, helping them assess the organization's financial viability and investment potential.
   - *Management Accounting:* Management accounting directly supports internal decision-making by providing actionable insights, enabling managers to optimize resources, improve efficiency, and align operations with strategic objectives.

While both financial accounting and management accounting are essential for an organization's success, they serve different purposes and audiences, adhere to different regulatory frameworks, and focus on distinct aspects of financial information. Financial accounting provides an overarching view for external stakeholders, while management accounting offers detailed insights for internal management, facilitating informed decision-making and effective operational control.

## What is the Definition of Financial Accounting?

Financial accounting is a crucial branch of accounting that focuses on systematically recording, summarizing, and presenting a company's financial transactions over a specific period. Its primary purpose is to create financial statements—such as the balance sheet, income statement, and cash flow statement—that provide a comprehensive overview of a company's financial performance and position. These financial statements are designed for external stakeholders, including investors, creditors, regulators, tax authorities, and the general public, who rely on this information to make informed decisions regarding their involvement with the company.

At the heart of financial accounting is the principle of transparency. By adhering to generally accepted accounting principles (GAAP) or International Financial Reporting Standards (IFRS), companies ensure that their financial statements are accurate, consistent, and comparable across different periods and industries. This consistency enables stakeholders to assess a company's financial health and performance reliably. Investors, for example, use financial statements to evaluate a company's profitability and growth potential, while creditors examine them to determine the company's ability to meet its debt obligations.

In addition to providing insights into financial performance, financial accounting serves as a key tool for regulatory compliance. Many countries require publicly traded companies to regularly publish audited financial statements, ensuring that businesses operate within the legal and regulatory frameworks. This legal obligation promotes transparency, reduces the risk of fraud, and enhances public trust in the integrity of the financial markets. Moreover, financial accounting often extends beyond traditional financial metrics, encompassing areas like environmental and social reporting as part of a company's broader corporate responsibility initiatives. One significant aspect of modern financial accounting is its increasing emphasis on non-financial disclosures, particularly those related to Environmental, Social, and Governance (ESG) factors. With growing concerns over sustainability and corporate accountability, financial accountants are now tasked with providing information on a company's environmental performance. This may include data on carbon emissions, waste management, water usage, and other sustainability metrics. Such reporting is important not only for compliance with regulations but also for meeting the expectations of socially conscious investors and customers. Companies that transparently report on their ESG efforts can enhance their reputation and attract stakeholders who prioritize responsible business practices.

Furthermore, financial accounting also involves the communication of various types of risks that a company might face. These risks include market risk, which refers to potential losses due to changes in market conditions; credit risk, which pertains to the possibility of default by borrowers; and operational risk, which arises from failures in internal processes or external events. Accurate risk reporting is essential because it allows external stakeholders to gauge the potential threats to a company's future financial performance. For example, investors may reconsider their investment if a company is exposed to high levels of credit or market risk, while regulators may require additional safeguards if significant operational risks are identified. While the primary role of financial accounting is external reporting, it also plays a vital role in internal decision-making. Managers and executives rely on financial accounting information to monitor the company's financial health, assess its profitability, and make strategic decisions regarding investments, cost management, and future growth. Financial statements offer key insights into operational efficiency, helping managers identify areas for improvement and make data-driven decisions to optimize performance. However, what distinguishes financial accounting from managerial accounting is its outward focus; the primary audience for financial accounting reports is external stakeholders, as opposed to the internal users targeted by managerial accounting.

Financial accounting is a discipline that involves the preparation and presentation of a company's financial data to external stakeholders. It serves as a foundation for transparent communication, regulatory compliance, and stakeholder decision-making. By adhering to established accounting standards and incorporating both financial and non-financial information, financial accounting provides a holistic view of an organization's financial position and risk profile. It plays a pivotal role in fostering trust, ensuring accountability, and supporting the broader goal of corporate sustainability and governance.

## What is the Definition of Management Accounting?

Management accounting, on the contrary, primarily reports inside the organization and for managers to make decisions. Of course, the tax officer can request management accounting reports to check the accounts, or the shareholders' meeting will have access to these reports if they wish; But management accounting is primarily aimed at reporting to the organization. Cost accounting, whose old name was industrial accounting, is somewhere between these two disciplines and is part of financial accounting as far as it calculates the cost price; As it examines performance and future planning, standard costs, and finding discrepancies and budgets, it is classified under management accounting. Basic accounting equality Let's talk a few sentences about basic accounting equality. This may help the audience who are not familiar with accounting or financial concepts, or who work in technical and engineering fields.

Assets = Liabilities + Capital

This equation is only relevant in accounting, and we will see that it does not have much use in economics.

## What is the Definition of Property?

Anything that has economic value. In the past, these assets were mostly physical, and in the digital age, many assets are intangible and spiritual. So, the program you wrote, the copyright on your book, or your company's brand (trademark) are all intangible assets and have value in their own right. Consider wherever you are now as your business location. Everything around you are an asset: furniture, computers, desks, machines, equipment, land, buildings, etc.

$70 + 30 = 100$

Assume that the value of everything around you is equal to 100 of your company's assets. The equation says, 100 of you is equal to 30 units of debt and 70 units of capital. We know what property is; It is something that has transactional value, is tradable, and has intrinsic value. Now we need to know what debt or capital means (Chiaramontea et al,2017).

## What is the Definition of Debt or Capital?

Debt and capital are not separate from assets. Assets belong to those whose title in the company is owner, shareholder, or shareholder. Or belongs to those whose title is creditor. 70 units of the assets belong to those who have the title of owner or capital owner, and 30 units belong to those who hold the title of creditor or creditor of the company. Therefore, debt is not something separate from assets; Capital is nothing but assets, but debt and capital are rights governing assets. That is, out of those 100 assets, 70% belong to those who have the legal title of owner or shareholder, and 30% belong to those who have the legal title of creditor or creditor, for example, they are the holders of company bonds.

## Who are the Shareholders and Debt Holders?

The owner of shares and the owner of debt (for example, the owner of partnership bonds) have different possibilities and priorities from a legal point of view. This is the division of accountants and at the same time, it is a kind of legal division. If the owners of those 100 monetary units (assets) are 10 people, and one is the owner and the other 9 are creditors, the rights of those 9 people have a different definition than ownership. In a stock exchange company that has two groups of investors with a ratio of 70 to 30, the company's shareholders may be several thousand people; Creditors may be 20 institutions, two banks, the government, and thousands of creditors who are holders of partnership bonds or sukuk bonds of the company.

From the point of view of the economist, these natural or legal persons are all investors, with the difference that the name of one is the owner of the shares and the name of the other is the creditor, the holder of the sukuk lease or the holder of the company's partnership bonds. It is clear that major shareholders stay in the company longer, but small shareholders may leave the company tomorrow while holding the company's bonds for two years. So, who stays longer with the company is not a criterion to separate the owner of the capital from the owner of the debt. The criterion for distinguishing the capital owner from the debt owner is the priority of receiving profits.

This priority belongs to the holder of sukuk bonds, bonds, and partnership bonds, or any other debt holder, who receives the interest first, and if there is anything left, it is given to the stockholder or the owner of the company. The owner of the company does not have priority in this case. Interest is paid first, and then the rest of the company's profit goes to the owner. When we want to collect the company or the company is bankrupt and we want to close it, this priority is still with the creditor; Then if there is anything left, the owner of the capital receives, and hence the owner of the capital is called the recipient of the remainder. From the economist's point of view, these two groups are all capital investors; But from the point of view of the company itself, from the point of view of the accountant and the lawyer, this separation is necessary (Hasler,2019).

## What is the Difference Between Accounting and Financial Management in Companies?

Finance works on market values and accounting on historical figures, one area that separates them is the definition of capital in accounting and economics. Capital accounting considers the company's shareholders and distinguishes the quality of shareholders' claims on assets from those of lenders. However, the economist believes that anyone who has a claim to the assets in the balance sheet and brings resources to the company is considered an investor and is no different from others.

For the economist, the word equity has the general meaning of bringing financial resources, and the quality of the claim that the owner of resources has, the type of contract he has as a money bringer, whether it is an ownership contract or a claim contract, is not important. The economist has nothing to do with the contract; He says that all these are owners of capital in its general sense.

Financial approaches, meanwhile, have both views on the matter: sometimes they look at the matter from the shareholder's point of view and ask how much return this stock or debt bond have? Sometimes he looks at all those who have brought money and asks, what is the return on the whole investment? When we calculate the return on the company's investments, that is, the return for all those who brought money; That is, we consider the return on all assets, we look at the problem like an economist. But when we pay attention to the return on equity, we look at the problem like an accountant. In terms of investment, the accounting perspective is different from the financial one. In accounting, the title "investment" refers to assets that are considered assets according to accounting standards, while in economics, the focus is more on productive assets that generate cash flows in the future.

Buying productive goods is not for their immediate consumption but for their use in the production of goods or services in the future. Therefore, in the economic definition, investment means using funds to start or develop businesses. Finance considers investment to include both groups and considers the purchase and maintenance of financial assets as investments. Sometimes he looks at investments like an accountant. According to the point of view of the accountant and economist, financial knowledge can be defined as knowledge that makes extensive use of accounting data, takes advantage of economic knowledge, to perform one of its most important tasks, which is to calculate the current value of assets.

## What are the Duties of the Accountant in Front of the Financial Manager?

The duties of the accountant in relation to the financial manager encompass a wide range of critical responsibilities that are essential for ensuring the organization's financial health, operational efficiency, and strategic success. At the core of an accountant's role is the meticulous task of ensuring accurate financial reporting. This involves the careful recording of all financial transactions in compliance with established accounting standards and principles. Accountants must differentiate between various types of costs—such as direct and indirect costs—as well as ensure that overhead costs are properly allocated across different departments and projects. This detailed classification is crucial, as it enables the financial manager to understand the true cost structure of the organization, allowing for informed decision-making regarding pricing strategies, budgeting, and resource allocation.

In addition to financial reporting, accountants are responsible for preparing timely and accurate tax reports. This duty is paramount, as compliance with tax regulations is essential for avoiding legal complications and potential penalties from government authorities. By managing tax obligations diligently, accountants not only protect the organization from financial risks but also help maintain its reputation in the marketplace. Their expertise in navigating complex tax laws can lead to optimized tax positions, ultimately contributing to the company's bottom line. Moreover, accountants play a vital role in cost management by analyzing and monitoring overhead allocations, which can significantly impact the organization's profitability. By providing insights into cost behaviors and trends, accountants empower financial managers to make strategic decisions that enhance efficiency and reduce unnecessary expenditures. For instance, understanding where costs can be trimmed or controlled allows financial managers to allocate resources more effectively, thus maximizing returns on investments.

Accountants also oversee inventory management, ensuring that the organization maintains an accurate and efficient inventory system. Proper inventory management is crucial for safeguarding the company's assets and ensuring that sufficient stock levels are maintained to meet customer demands. By keeping track of inventory turnover rates and associated costs, accountants provide financial managers with essential information that influences purchasing decisions and production planning, ultimately leading to better cash flow management. IN the realm of personnel management, accountants are responsible for calculating and maintaining accurate payroll data. This involves not only determining salaries and wages but also ensuring compliance with labor laws and regulations regarding employee benefits and deductions. Timely and accurate payroll processing is critical for maintaining employee morale and trust, as delays or errors can lead to dissatisfaction and turnover. By ensuring that employees are compensated correctly and on time, accountants contribute to a positive workplace culture, which in turn supports overall organizational performance. Furthermore, accountants are tasked with processing raw financial data into actionable information. This data serves as the foundation for financial managers to make strategic decisions regarding investments, capital budgeting, and liquidity management. By providing reliable and comprehensive financial reports, accountants enable financial managers to assess the company's financial health accurately, identify trends, and forecast future performance.

While accountants focus on these detailed financial operations and compliance aspects, financial managers take a broader view of the organization's financial strategy. They are primarily concerned with maximizing shareholder value by making strategic investment decisions, managing capital structures, and optimizing the company's cost of capital. Financial managers must navigate the complexities of the financial markets, assess risks, and determine the best funding sources to ensure the organization's long-term sustainability and growth. They analyze various investment opportunities, evaluate potential returns against associated risks, and make critical decisions that can involve significant amounts of capital. The interplay between accountants and financial managers is vital for the successful functioning of any organization. Accountants lay the groundwork by ensuring accurate financial records, compliance, and detailed analyses of financial data, while financial managers leverage this information to make strategic decisions that drive the company's growth and profitability. This division of responsibilities highlights the unique contributions each role brings to the organization, underscoring the importance of collaboration between these two functions to achieve overall financial stability and success.

## What are the Duties of the General Accountant in the Organization?

The work of the general accountant (controller) is completely different from that of the financial deputy and the chief financial officer. Financial data processing is the main mental occupation of the general accountant, while the financial expert looks for cheap money for the company using the information of the accounting system, he wants to make sure that the financial resources are used correctly in the company. The financial mission is the effective use of funds within the company. If it is the work of the production manager of labor and raw materials, the work of the personnel manager of labor and training methods to improve the quality of work, and the work of the production manager of raw materials; It is the hand of the financial manager of the funds that he wants to use in the company profitably. The mission of the financial manager is to raise the value of the company. Financial managers like managers with other duties in the company. Stock companies seek to maximize the stock value (Li,2023).

## THE EXACT DEFINITION OF VALUE MAXIMIZATION AND FISHER'S SEPARATION PRINCIPLE

Value maximization is a fundamental concept in finance that refers to the objective of a company to maximize the wealth of its shareholders. This idea suggests that all business decisions—whether related to production, financing, or investment—should be geared toward increasing the company's market value, thereby benefiting its shareholders. In essence, it's the driving force behind corporate decision-making, aiming to enhance the company's long-term value. A key principle associated with value maximization is Fisher's separation principle, proposed by economist Irving Fisher. According to this principle, a company's investment decisions are independent of the personal preferences of its shareholders regarding consumption. This means that as long as the company focuses on value maximization, the specific preferences of individual shareholders—whether they prefer immediate dividends or future capital gains—do not influence the optimal investment strategy of the company. In simpler terms, the principle separates the firm's decisions about its operations and investments from the personal preferences of its owners. As long as the firm maximizes its value, shareholders can individually adjust their consumption patterns, borrowing or lending on their own if needed.

However, the environment in which a company operates has a significant impact on its ability to achieve value maximization. A company's external environment consists of factors that it cannot control, such as government regulations, competition, the availability and pricing of goods and services, and customer behavior. These external conditions impose constraints on the company, influencing its operational decisions and its ability to maximize value. For instance, changes in government policies, fluctuating market prices, or aggressive competition may affect a company's profitability and ability to generate shareholder returns. To cope with these external forces, companies engage in various projects to drive production and service delivery. These projects require significant resources, including financial resources from shareholders and lenders, as well as human resources, technology, and equipment. Shareholders, who provide equity, assume higher risks and thus expect higher returns, while lenders, who provide debt financing, take on less risk and expect lower but more secure returns.

Historically, companies have evolved from simple structures, such as sole proprietorships, to more complex entities, such as private and public corporations. In a sole proprietorship, the owner typically manages all aspects of the business, from operations to marketing and finance. Since the owner makes all the decisions, there is minimal internal conflict, and the company's finances are tightly controlled. However, these businesses often have limited access to financial resources, relying mainly on the owner's personal wealth and avoiding significant debt. In such businesses, value maximization is a more straightforward process because the owner is both the decision-maker and the primary beneficiary of the profits. For example, the owner of a small confectionery shop will oversee everything—managing the production, purchasing ingredients, selling products, and handling customer relations. The owner's sole focus is on maximizing personal profits, ensuring that all operational decisions, from pricing to procurement, align with the goal of increasing the business's value. As businesses expand and adopt more complex structures, such as corporations with multiple shareholders, the decision-making process becomes more complicated. Different stakeholders, including shareholders and managers, may have conflicting interests. Shareholders want to maximize their returns, while managers may focus on other goals, such as personal compensation or job security. This divergence of interests can create what is known as an agency problem, where managers do not always act in the best interest of shareholders. Fisher's separation principle, however, provides a theoretical solution to this issue by emphasizing that the company should focus solely on value maximization, leaving shareholders to manage their individual consumption preferences. The concept of value maximization and Fisher's separation principle are central to corporate finance, guiding companies in making decisions that increase shareholder wealth. While the external environment poses challenges, companies must carefully balance their resource allocation and project management to achieve this goal. The evolution from sole proprietorships to complex corporate structures highlights the growing importance of aligning management strategies with shareholder interests in the pursuit of long-term value maximization.

## What are the Conflicting Interests of the Manager and Owner of the Companies?

As an owner, he has limited financial resources; As a sole proprietor, of course, he cannot borrow a thousand billion dollars. For this, he has to move in the form of a company. In a joint-stock company, the responsibility of the owner and manager is separated, and we immediately find ourselves in a dilemma where the interests of the manager or agent are separate from the interests of the owner (principle) and a conflict is created. At the same time, the investment opportunity increases. Responsibilities are separated and conflicts increase. In a public company, the distance between the manager and the owner increases. The company faces more investment opportunities. Active and passive investors enter the ownership of the company. The financial resources of the company increase, and professional people are hired in the financial field.

Conflicts naturally intensify in public companies. Not only financial economics theorists deal with these contradictions, but scholars in the fields of social sciences and psychology are also interested in investigating these contradictions. The shareholders of each public company pursue different goals.

A pension fund is a second shareholder that prefers long-term investment in large projects and does not require dividends. The third investor is a businessman himself; he predicts that prices will rise, and it is better for the company not to sell its assets and wait for the future. In this public company that the manager pursues the goal of maximizing investors' wealth, what should he do with these different preferences of investors and how should he respond to them. I The manager of this public company is faced with different investment preferences. An investor wants to get to cash flow sooner and enjoy constant cash flow. The second wants to have no immediate cash flow, and the third prefers that the company sell part of its assets and distribute profits, and the other part is invested. This is where we see that there may be a conflict between investor wealth maximization and investor preferences.

The financial manager is uncertain about which path to follow in the investors' preferences, which is helped by Fisher's principle of differentiation. This principle seeks to separate managers' investment decisions from shareholders' preferences. It says that investors can borrow and borrow at the interest rate in the market to estimate their time preferences. Thus, the optimal point of investment will be where the final return rate of investment opportunities is equal to the market interest rate, and where the time preferences of consumption (current and future consumption) maximize the investor's utility. So, if the investor has the necessary dividends to consume, or doesn't have and has future consumption, the debt market allows these time preferences to be pursued there. Because of investors' preferences, investment opportunities and the goal of maximizing the investor's wealth should not be forgotten. There is a place called the market, and those preferences are settled there (Christensen,2016).

## What are the Strategies for Maximizing Shareholders' Profits?

Maximizing shareholders' profits is a core responsibility of financial managers and is achieved through a series of well-defined strategies designed to enhance shareholder wealth. These strategies aim to optimize the value of investments and ensure that the company's projects deliver high returns, regardless of the personal preferences of individual shareholders. The overarching goal is to grow the overall value of the firm, allowing shareholders to adjust their financial decisions based on their unique consumption needs and liquidity requirements.

One key strategy for maximizing shareholder value is "investing in high-return projects". Financial managers prioritize investment opportunities that promise to generate positive cash flows and increase the company's market value. These projects are selected based on rigorous financial analysis, which often includes evaluating the risk and return of each potential investment. When financial managers focus on such value-enhancing projects, shareholders benefit through increased stock prices or higher dividends, depending on the company's dividend policy. For shareholders, one of the most important aspects of profit maximization is the "flexibility provided by liquidity options". Shareholders have different preferences when it comes to consumption and investment timing. Some may prefer immediate returns, while others might be focused on long-term growth. A strategy that allows shareholders to trade their shares or adjust their financial positions is essential. For example, a shareholder in need of cash can sell a portion of their shares at a favorable market price if the company's value has increased. This flexibility is critical because it enables shareholders to access liquidity without affecting the company's overall investment strategy or growth potential.

The "role of dividends" in profit maximization is another strategic component. Financial managers must decide whether to distribute cash profits to shareholders through dividends or reinvest those profits back into the company. In cases where a company has profitable reinvestment opportunities, managers may choose to retain earnings, which can further drive the company's growth and increase its stock price.

However, when appropriate, dividends can provide shareholders with immediate cash returns, which they can either spend or reinvest based on their individual financial goals.

One of the most critical elements in profit maximization is the "alignment with Fisher's Separation Principle", which emphasizes that investment decisions should remain independent of shareholders' consumption preferences. According to this principle, the financial manager's task is to focus solely on selecting projects that maximize the company's value. If shareholders require cash for immediate consumption, they can access financial markets to meet those needs by selling shares or borrowing, while the company continues its focus on value-enhancing investments. This principle aligns with the "Modigliani-Miller theorem", which posits that the capital structure—whether financed by equity or debt—does not affect the firm's value or investment decisions, further reinforcing that shareholders' liquidity preferences should not interfere with the company's broader financial strategy. Moreover, financial managers can adopt strategies that cater to shareholders with varying risk appetites. For instance, "diversifying the company's investment portfolio" can ensure stable returns while managing risks effectively. This diversification allows the company to pursue both high-risk, high-reward projects, and more conservative investments, thus appealing to shareholders who may have different risk tolerance levels. Additionally, maintaining "a balance between debt and equity financing" helps optimize the firm's capital structure, ensuring that the company can leverage opportunities without taking on excessive risk, which could potentially dilute shareholder value.

Lastly, the "efficient use of market mechanisms" plays a vital role in maximizing shareholder profits. In a liquid stock market, shareholders can adjust their portfolios by buying or selling shares according to their financial needs. This adaptability provides shareholders the ability to control their wealth and consumption, even if the company decides to reinvest profits rather than distribute them. Financial managers facilitate this by ensuring that the company remains attractive to investors, maintaining strong performance metrics, and fostering positive investor sentiment. For example, "transparent financial reporting" and regular updates on the company's performance build trust and encourage shareholder confidence, ultimately supporting higher stock valuations. The strategies for maximizing shareholders' profits revolve around making value-driven investment decisions, providing liquidity and flexibility through stock markets, and balancing the use of dividends and reinvestments. By adhering to these principles, financial managers can create an environment where both the company and its shareholders thrive. As shareholders adjust their personal investment strategies, financial managers continue to focus on long-term growth and profitability, ensuring a harmonious alignment of interests and optimal financial outcomes for all parties involved.

## What is the Importance of Cash Flow in Financial Management of Companies?

The importance of cash flow in the financial management of companies cannot be overstated, as it serves as a critical component in both financing and investment decisions. At its core, effective financial management revolves around answering two fundamental questions: "Where do we get money from?" and "What projects should we invest in?" These inquiries are essential for ensuring the sustainability and growth of a business.

Cash flow provides a clear picture of a company's liquidity position, enabling managers to understand how much cash is available for operations, investments, and other financial commitments. The distinction between inflows and outflows is crucial; cash inflows include revenues from sales and any financing activities, while outflows encompass expenses, investments, and loan repayments. A positive cash flow indicates that a company can cover its operational costs and invest in growth opportunities, whereas negative cash flow can signal financial distress.

In the context of investment decisions, the net present value (NPV) criterion plays a pivotal role in assessing the viability of projects. NPV is calculated by subtracting the present value of cash outflows from the present value of cash inflows. This calculation is essential for determining whether an investment will yield a positive return. If the NPV is positive, it suggests that the project is expected to generate more cash than it costs, making it an attractive option for investment. This process helps companies prioritize projects that maximize shareholder wealth. Moreover, cash flow analysis aids in evaluating the performance of financial managers. A key indicator of managerial effectiveness is whether the market value of the company exceeds its book value. If the market capitalization is greater than the book value, it suggests that the company has successfully created added value through its investments and operational decisions. Thus, a focus on cash flow not only guides investment strategies but also serves as a benchmark for assessing the overall health of the organization.

Cash flow is a vital element in the financial management of companies, influencing both financing and investment decisions. By understanding and managing cash flow effectively, businesses can ensure liquidity, evaluate potential projects accurately through NPV calculations, and gauge managerial performance in terms of value creation. This comprehensive approach allows companies to make informed decisions that enhance their long-term sustainability and profitability.

## What is Added Economic Value?

Added economic value (AEV) refers to the value generated by a company beyond the costs of its capital. It is an important measure of performance that assesses whether a company's operating profit after tax exceeds its after-tax cost of capital. When operating profit surpasses this threshold, it indicates that the company is creating additional value for its shareholders, signifying effective management performance and operational efficiency. A critical distinction exists between profit and cash flow in the context of added economic value. While profit can be reported on financial statements, it is often subject to manipulation through various accounting methods, which can distort the actual financial health of a business. For instance, a company may show substantial profits—such as reporting 10,000 units from an investment of just 100 units—yet if these profits do not translate into cash inflow (i.e., if customers do not pay for sales), the company may face severe liquidity issues, ultimately impacting its stock price negatively.

Cash flow is the lifeblood of any organization; it represents the actual movement of money into and out of the company. Unlike profit, which can be inflated through accounting practices like asset revaluation or recognition of revenue before payment is received, cash flow reflects real economic activity and the company's ability to sustain operations and meet obligations. For shareholders, cash flow is a more reliable indicator of financial health because it demonstrates the company's capacity to generate returns, pay dividends, and reinvest in growth opportunities. Moreover, relying solely on profit figures to gauge a company's value can be misleading. For example, if a company reports high profits through accounting maneuvers—such as selling long-term debt or revaluing assets—it raises the question of what real value has been created for shareholders. In this scenario, the profits reported do not contribute to the company's long-term viability or shareholder wealth if they are not accompanied by corresponding cash flows.

Ultimately, added economic value emphasizes the importance of focusing on cash flow rather than just profit figures. A company may showcase impressive profits but still face bankruptcy if it lacks sufficient cash flow to cover its liabilities. Therefore, for a comprehensive evaluation of a company's financial performance and to assess whether it is genuinely adding value for shareholders, attention should be directed towards cash flow, which provides a realistic picture of the company's operational success and sustainability in the long run.

# ACCURATE DEFINITION OF FINANCIAL ASSET VERSUS REAL ASSET

A car is a real asset; Real property does not necessarily have to be tangible and physical. Your copyright is a real asset that has intrinsic value. But a financial asset has no value in itself, it is a claim on real assets. You have a share; This paper itself has no value in itself, it is a digital number in the stock exchange depository company's computer. It is not like a car to get a service from it. This share represents the right that participate. That company has an activity that leads to cash flow, and that cash flow is something real inside the company. The value of real assets is derived from physical properties, such as buildings, land, and machinery. The value of financial assets is derived from claims on future earnings, such as stocks and bonds. When a bank makes a loan, the loan agreement is an asset of the bank, but that asset has no intrinsic value. Its value is the cash flow that will result from the loan in the future. Therefore, financial assets are represented by real assets.

Our interest in financial assets is that they represent real assets and have cash flows. In the general formula that we talked about earlier, that is, assets are equal to liabilities plus capital (capital+debt=assets), we talked about two sides of the coin, that is, we said that assets are one thing and liabilities, and capital are not separate things. Capital and debt are the governing rights of those assets. Now let's look at the problem from different people's points of view to better understand the concept of financial assets. Assets are equal to liabilities plus capital. Now, if we have 100 units of real assets, for example, we are a car manufacturer, and the equation of assets is equal to 30+70. Investment 30 is related to those who have bonds or sukuk in their hands; These bonds or sukuk are considered financial assets for their holders. In addition, 70 units of the company's value is related to those who hold shares, and they also own financial assets.

This financial asset is a reflection of the value of the car manufacturing plant. If we simplify the formula now, from an economic point of view, real assets are equal to financial assets; That is, the value of real assets is equal to the rights governing those assets. Those who own the company have financial assets. Financial asset = real asset. Financial assets represent ownership of real assets. Stocks, a good insurance plan, a retirement plan, and a savings account are among these financial assets. These have no value in themselves, and their value is related to the cash flow from the real asset. From this point of view, financial assets are the same as debt and capital in non-financial companies from the point of view of accountants. Of course, financial companies have financial assets on both sides of the balance sheet.

The term financial instruments refers to a legal obligation that one party gives to another party (or parties to each other) to transfer value (money) at a future time under certain conditions. We can take the terms financial instruments, financial bonds, and securities as synonyms; When we talk about financial instruments, we mean a set of securities that are formed in the form of debt and capital.

## What is the Definition of Financial Instruments, Financial Institutions, and Financial Markets?

Types of business units are divided into financial and non-financial companies: financial companies such as banks, and non-financial companies such as car dealers or manufacturers or hospitals. All of these can be considered non-financial enterprises. A trading company, a heavy industry company, and a furniture manufacturing company are all non-financial corporations. Pension funds, mutual funds, banks, credit institutions, exchanges, and brokerages are all financial institutions. They sell financial goods, and non-financial units of non-financial kind.

The first group are shops that sell stocks, bonds, sukuk bonds, and insurance policies, and the second group are shops that sell houses, education, medicine, hairdressing, cars, and heavy machinery. Financial firms are entities that provide services related to financial assets or sell those assets. When we say financial institutions or financial companies, we mean financial companies. Usually, the word institution is mostly used for financial companies. When we say financial institutions, we mean banks, insurance, and financing (Cohn,2022).

## What is the Exact Definition of Financial Markets?

Financial markets are structured platforms where financial instruments, securities, and other related assets are traded. They operate within the broader context of money and capital markets, facilitating the exchange of funds between various participants, including individuals, institutions, and governments. In financial markets, financial companies, such as banks, investment firms, and insurance companies, engage in the buying and selling of financial goods. This differentiates them from non-financial markets, where companies providing services or goods unrelated to finance operate. For instance, a sports club offering fitness services, a hospital providing healthcare, or a supermarket selling consumer products all function within non-financial markets.

At their core, financial markets serve as essential mechanisms for price discovery, liquidity, and capital allocation. They enable participants to raise funds for investment through the issuance of securities, such as stocks and bonds and allow investors to buy and sell these instruments based on their expectations of future performance. For example, the stock market is a critical component of financial markets, where shares of publicly traded companies are bought and sold. Investors participate in the stock market to seek capital appreciation, dividend income, or a combination of both, while companies use it to raise capital for expansion, research, and development.

In addition to stock markets, financial markets encompass various other segments, including bond markets, foreign exchange markets, and derivatives markets. Each segment plays a vital role in the global economy by providing avenues for investment, risk management, and hedging strategies. For instance, the bond market enables governments and corporations to borrow funds at fixed interest rates, while the foreign exchange market facilitates the trading of currencies, allowing businesses to conduct international transactions and manage exchange rate risks. As we delve deeper into financial knowledge, it becomes evident that the vast array of financial concepts and topics taught across faculties of finance, management, and economics can be categorized into four primary areas. These areas encompass:

1. **Corporate Finance:** This area focuses on the financial management of corporations, including capital structure decisions, investment appraisal, and dividend policy. It examines how companies raise capital and allocate resources to maximize shareholder value.
2. **Investments:** This field covers the study of various investment vehicles, portfolio management, and asset allocation strategies. It explores how investors can effectively analyze and select securities to achieve desired financial goals.
3. **Financial Institutions and Markets:** This area examines the role of financial institutions, such as banks, insurance companies, and investment firms, in the functioning of financial markets. It also explores the regulatory framework governing these institutions and their impact on economic stability.
4. **International Finance:** This area addresses financial transactions and investment decisions in a global context. It involves the analysis of foreign exchange rates, international capital flows, and the impact of global economic events on financial markets.

Financial markets are dynamic environments that facilitate the trading of financial instruments, playing a crucial role in capital allocation and economic development. By understanding the various components and areas of financial knowledge, participants can better navigate these markets and make informed financial decisions.

## What are the Main Topics in Financial Management of Companies?

In the financial management of companies, several core topics can be systematically categorized into four distinct groups: "corporate finance, investment management, financial markets, and institutions," and "financial engineering and risk management". At the center of this framework lies corporate finance, which focuses on the critical aspects of managing a company's capital structure, investment decisions, and financial strategies aimed at maximizing shareholder value. This encompasses a variety of subtopics, including capital budgeting—where financial managers evaluate potential investments to determine their viability—and working capital management, which ensures the company maintains sufficient liquidity for its operational needs.

Surrounding corporate finance, investment management plays a pivotal role in guiding how a company allocates its financial resources across various assets to achieve optimal returns. This area includes portfolio management, where the emphasis is on constructing and balancing investment portfolios to mitigate risk while maximizing returns, alongside asset valuation and the development of investment strategies tailored to specific financial goals.

Financial markets and institutions form another peripheral component, providing the necessary infrastructure for the movement of capital within the economy. This includes understanding the workings of different markets, such as primary and secondary markets, and the impact of interest rates on borrowing and lending activities. Knowledge of the regulatory environment governing these markets is also essential for ensuring compliance and stability. Finally, financial engineering and risk management serve as a foundational support system that underpins the other three areas. This field focuses on the design and implementation of innovative financial products and strategies to manage various types of risks, including market, credit, and operational risks. By utilizing sophisticated quantitative techniques and derivatives, financial engineering helps companies navigate uncertainties and make informed financial decisions. These four topics represent the essential framework of financial management in companies, with each area interconnected and contributing to the overall financial health and strategic direction of the organization. Financial engineering and risk management, in particular, enhance the decision-making process in corporate finance, investment management, and financial markets, making them indispensable to the effective financial coding and operational success of businesses.

## What Does Financial Management of Companies Mean?

Financial management of companies involves the strategic handling of financial resources to ensure the long-term sustainability, growth, and profitability of businesses. It encompasses the planning, organizing, directing, and controlling of financial activities, specifically tailored to non-financial sectors like construction, trade, industry, and manufacturing. Unlike financial institutions, where the focus is on banking, loans, and investments, company financial management is centered on how firms efficiently manage their internal finances to achieve business goals and maximize shareholder value.

One of the core functions of financial management is "capital budgeting", which involves identifying and selecting investment opportunities that will provide the greatest return to the company over time. Financial managers assess projects based on risk, expected returns, and their alignment with the company's long-term objectives. For example, in industries like manufacturing, companies such as Iran Khodro and petrochemical firms may need to make large investments in machinery or technology. Financial managers play a key role in determining whether these investments will enhance operational efficiency or expand the company's market reach.

Another essential aspect of financial management is "cash flow management". Companies need to ensure that they have enough liquidity to meet day-to-day expenses, such as paying employees, suppliers, and other operating costs, while also keeping reserves for unexpected events. Effective cash flow management requires financial managers to forecast future cash inflows and outflows, helping businesses avoid cash shortages or excessive idle capital. In sectors like trade and construction, where payment cycles may be longer, careful cash flow planning is critical for maintaining financial stability and avoiding disruptions in operations. "Financial forecasting and planning" are other key responsibilities. This involves projecting the company's future financial performance based on historical data and market trends. Financial managers create detailed financial models to anticipate potential challenges or opportunities, allowing businesses to make informed decisions about expansion, cost-cutting, or resource allocation. In industries where market conditions are volatile, such as petrochemicals, having accurate financial forecasts can help companies remain agile and adjust their strategies to stay competitive.

Another crucial component of financial management is "capital structure management". This refers to the balance between debt and equity financing that a company uses to fund its operations and growth. Financial managers must determine the optimal mix of financing sources that minimize the company's cost of capital while maximizing returns. For instance, companies in capital-intensive sectors like manufacturing may rely more heavily on debt to finance large projects, but too much debt increases the risk of financial distress. Striking the right balance between debt and equity is essential for maintaining financial health and avoiding over-leverage.

In addition to managing internal financial operations, financial management also involves "risk management". Companies face various financial risks, including market fluctuations, currency risks, and interest rate changes. Financial managers implement strategies to hedge these risks, such as using financial derivatives or diversifying investments. In industries like construction, where project timelines and costs can be uncertain, risk management is especially important to prevent cost overruns or delays that could impact profitability.

In Iran, many companies face challenges in financial management due to a lack of skilled professionals and limited adoption of modern financial practices. As a result, companies often struggle with issues such as "inefficient capital allocation", where resources are not used optimally, leading to lower profitability, and missed growth opportunities. Additionally, "poor liquidity management" can hinder a company's ability to respond to market opportunities or cover its short-term obligations, putting it at a competitive disadvantage. Improving financial management practices in these organizations is crucial for fostering growth, innovation, and economic resilience, especially in a dynamic market. The financial management of companies involves a broad range of activities, from investment and capital budgeting to cash flow management, risk mitigation, and optimizing the capital structure. It requires financial managers to apply sound financial principles and practices to ensure that businesses can sustain growth, seize new opportunities, and remain competitive in their respective industries. Strengthening financial management in non-financial companies, particularly in countries like Iran, where these practices have often been overlooked, is essential for economic growth and for enabling companies to thrive in an increasingly complex global market.

## What is the Role of Investment in the Financial Management of Companies?

The role of investment in the financial management of companies is crucial, as it directly impacts the company's ability to grow, innovate, and maintain long-term financial stability. When discussing investment in the context of financial management, it is essential to differentiate between "investment in physical assets" (such as machinery, technology, or real estate) and "investment in financial assets" (such as stocks, bonds, or other securities). Both forms of investment are vital for companies, but they serve different purposes in achieving the overall financial goals of the organization.

"Physical investments", often referred to as "capital expenditures", are typically aimed at enhancing the company's operational capacity and efficiency. These types of investments allow a company to expand its production capabilities, improve product quality, or enter new markets. For example, a manufacturing firm may invest in new machinery to increase production efficiency, or a tech company may invest in research and development (R&D) to innovate and stay competitive in its industry. In this way, physical investments directly contribute to the company's long-term profitability and market position. On the other hand, "investment in financial assets" involves the management of securities, such as stocks, bonds, and other market instruments. Financial investments are a key part of a company's overall strategy to manage its surplus capital and generate additional income. By investing in financial assets, companies can diversify their risk, improve liquidity, and potentially earn higher returns than they would through holding idle cash. For instance, a company may invest in short-term bonds to earn interest while keeping its capital relatively liquid, or it may buy equity in other firms to gain strategic advantages or financial returns.

From a broader perspective, "investment management" plays a significant role in aligning a company's financial strategy with its business objectives. Financial managers must evaluate different investment opportunities based on their potential returns, associated risks, and how well they align with the company's long-term goals. This evaluation process typically involves tools such as "capital budgeting", "net present value (NPV)" analysis, and "internal rate of return (IRR)", all of which help determine whether an investment will add value to the company. In addition to evaluating investment opportunities, financial managers are responsible for ensuring that the company's "capital structure" supports its investment strategy. This involves making decisions about how to finance investments—whether through equity, debt, or a combination of both. A well-balanced capital structure allows a company to finance its growth efficiently while minimizing its cost of capital. For example, a company might issue bonds to finance a large capital expenditure while keeping its equity structure intact, or it might reinvest profits into high-potential projects without taking on additional debt. "Risk management" is another key element in the investment process within financial management. Companies face numerous risks related to their investments, including market volatility, interest rate fluctuations, and currency exchange risks. Financial managers must implement strategies to hedge against these risks, such as through the use of derivatives or diversified investment portfolios. For instance, a company that operates in multiple countries might invest in currency hedging instruments to protect against adverse changes in exchange rates that could impact its international profits.

In many cases, financial managers must balance the need for long-term investments with the company's short-term liquidity requirements. This is particularly important for companies in capital-intensive industries, such as construction, manufacturing, or technology, where large investments are often needed to maintain competitiveness. At the same time, these companies must ensure that they have enough liquidity to meet their day-to-day operating expenses. This balancing act requires careful financial planning and the ability to make informed investment decisions that optimize both short-term cash flow and long-term profitability.

In Iran and similar developing markets, the importance of "investment in financial management" is often overlooked in non-financial companies, leading to inefficiencies and missed growth opportunities. Many companies lack the expertise and strategic planning required to effectively manage investments, resulting in poor capital allocation and an inability to compete on a global scale. Strengthening the investment management capabilities of companies in these markets is essential for fostering innovation, competitiveness, and long-term economic growth.

Investment also plays a role in ensuring that companies remain "resilient" in uncertain economic conditions. During economic downturns or periods of financial instability, companies with strong investment portfolios and well-planned capital expenditures are often better positioned to weather the storm. They can rely on their financial investments to maintain liquidity and avoid the need for drastic cost-cutting measures that could harm their operations or market position. Moreover, companies that continuously invest in innovation and capacity building are more likely to emerge from economic downturns stronger and more competitive. Investment is a cornerstone of financial management in companies, serving to enhance operational capabilities, diversify risk, and ensure long-term financial stability. By making informed investment decisions, companies can optimize their capital structure, manage risks effectively, and seize growth opportunities. However, the financial management of investments requires skilled professionals who can navigate the complexities of capital markets, risk management, and financial forecasting (Cheri et al, 2023). Strengthening investment management within non-financial companies, particularly in developing economies, is critical for improving corporate performance and fostering economic growth.

## What is the Difference Between an Investment Company and a Holding Company?

The distinction between investment companies and holding companies is crucial in the realm of finance, particularly in investment management. These two types of companies serve different functions and operate under different principles, despite both being involved in the ownership of securities.

1. **Nature of Operations:**
   - Investment Company: An investment company primarily focuses on securities management, meaning its operations revolve around buying, holding, and selling financial securities, such as stocks and bonds. These companies do not engage in the management of the businesses associated with the securities they own. Instead, their main objective is to generate returns for their investors through various investment strategies. For example, a firm like the National Investment Company may hold a portfolio of stocks from various firms but does not actively manage or influence the operations of those firms.
   - Holding Company: In contrast, a holding company, often referred to as a "group of companies," does own the securities of other companies but

also actively manages those companies. A holding company typically holds a controlling interest in its subsidiaries—often defined as owning a significant percentage of shares (usually 50% or more). This allows it to influence or control the operational and financial decisions of the companies it owns. The holding company's focus is not only on asset appreciation but also on improving the performance and efficiency of its subsidiaries through strategic management and oversight.

2. **Level of Control:**
   - Investment Company: The relationship between an investment company and the firms in which it invests is more passive. Investors in an investment company may own minor stakes (e.g., 3%, 5%, or 8%) in various companies. This level of ownership means that if an investor does not favor a particular stock, they can easily divest their shares without any significant implications for the company's management or operations. The investment company's primary concern is the financial performance of its portfolio, not the operational management of its holdings.
   - Holding Company: Conversely, a holding company holds a more substantial stake in its subsidiaries (e.g., 40% or more). This significant ownership implies a greater responsibility and involvement in the management of those companies. If a holding company wishes to divest from a subsidiary, it cannot do so as easily as an investment company, given its vested interest in the company's performance. Instead, it typically seeks to enhance the subsidiary's value through strategic management, operational improvements, and synergies among its holdings.

3. **Purpose and Goals:**
   - Investment Company: The primary purpose of an investment company is to maximize returns for its investors by managing a diverse portfolio of securities. They may operate mutual funds, hedge funds, or exchange-traded funds (ETFs), which pool money from investors to invest in various securities. Their success is measured by their ability to outperform benchmarks and provide returns to their investors.
   - Holding Company: The holding company's goals extend beyond mere investment returns. It aims to create value by optimizing the performance of its subsidiaries, potentially integrating operations, and realizing cost efficiencies. Holding companies often engage in strategic planning and decision-making processes that drive the long-term growth and sustainability of their owned entities.

while both investment companies and holding companies are involved in the ownership of securities, they differ significantly in their operations, level of control, and objectives. Investment companies focus on managing securities with a passive approach, aiming for financial returns without engaging in the management of the companies they invest in. In contrast, holding companies possess substantial ownership stakes in their subsidiaries and take an active role in their management, striving to enhance overall performance and create long-term value. Understanding these differences is essential for investors and stakeholders in navigating the complexities of the financial landscape.

## Who is the Financial Manager? What is the Duty of the Financial Manager?

It is in non-financial companies that the financial manager means. The title "financial manager" is used for non-financial companies. We do not have the title of financial manager in the bank. CFO is a term for non-financial companies. As we said before, the financial vice president, who is the financial manager under his supervision, also supervises the controller or accounting head according to this diagram. But 90% of the time of the financial assistant is spent on the areas on the left side of this chart, that is, he works in the financial area, although he also monitors the accounting area. Of course, "accounting" did not have to be under his supervision, but accounting could be under the supervision of the information technology department or the CEO himself. Therefore, the fact that the head of accounting is under the supervision of the vice president of finance does not mean that "finance" and "accounting" are in the same scientific field. This article attempted to separate these two areas in your mind. Of course, it is not a coincidence that accounting is under the supervision of the financial manager because the amount of information required by the accounting head is in the "financial" field(Demerjian,2016).

## What is the Position of the Financial Manager in the Company?

The position of a financial manager in a company is pivotal and multifaceted, functioning as a critical link between financial markets and the internal operations of the organization. This role encompasses a broad spectrum of responsibilities aimed at optimizing the management of the company's financial resources, with the overarching goal of maximizing shareholder value and ensuring sustainable growth.

At the heart of a financial manager's duties is the responsibility for raising funds from a variety of sources, including equity investors, debt markets, and financial institutions. This process involves not only identifying the most suitable financing options but also negotiating favorable terms to secure capital at competitive rates.

For instance, if a financial manager successfully negotiates a loan with a low interest rate of 5%, they can allocate those funds into projects that promise higher returns, such as 15%. This strategic allocation not only enhances the company's profitability but also strengthens investor confidence by demonstrating a commitment to effective capital management. In addition to capital procurement, financial managers are tasked with the strategic investment of funds. This requires a deep understanding of the company's operational goals and market conditions to identify high-potential projects. Financial managers utilize various analytical tools and methodologies to evaluate the expected returns and associated risks of potential investments. They work collaboratively with other departmental managers—such as those in marketing, production, and operations—to ensure that the selected projects align with the company's strategic objectives and provide a competitive edge in the marketplace.

Moreover, financial managers continuously monitor and assess the performance of the investments they oversee. This involves analyzing financial statements, cash flow projections, and market trends to make informed decisions about reallocating resources as needed. They must be adept at conducting risk assessments, which involve identifying potential financial threats and developing strategies to mitigate those risks. This proactive approach ensures that the company can respond swiftly to changing market conditions and maintain its financial stability. Another critical aspect of the financial manager's role is ensuring compliance with regulatory requirements and financial reporting standards. This entails preparing accurate financial statements, tax reports, and disclosures that provide transparency to stakeholders, including investors, regulators, and management. By upholding high standards of financial integrity, financial managers contribute to building trust and credibility in the company's financial practices. Furthermore, financial managers play a key role in strategic planning and decision-making at the executive level. They participate in formulating the company's long-term vision and objectives, providing insights based on financial forecasts and analyses. Their expertise is invaluable in evaluating potential mergers and acquisitions, capital investments, and market expansions, ensuring that the company is well-positioned for future growth.

The financial manager's position is integral to fostering a sustainable and profitable business. By effectively balancing the dual objectives of cost-effective capital procurement and efficient project funding, financial managers drive growth and enhance shareholder value. Their role not only influences immediate financial outcomes but also shapes the long-term strategic direction of the company, making them an indispensable asset to the executive team. Through their expertise in financial planning, investment analysis, risk management, and compliance, financial managers ensure that the organization navigates the complexities of the financial landscape effectively, securing its position in a competitive market.

## How is the Financial Balance Sheet of Non-Financial Companies Checked?

The financial balance sheet of non-financial companies is a critical document that provides a comprehensive snapshot of the company's financial health at a specific point in time. It acts as a foundation for evaluating the organization's performance, stability, and capacity for future growth. When examining this balance sheet, several key components must be understood, particularly in terms of asset composition, liabilities, and the hierarchy of claims.

The left side of the balance sheet primarily showcases the company's assets, which typically consist of a mix of non-financial assets, such as property, plant, and equipment, along with financial assets like cash and bank deposits. Non-financial assets are often the backbone of operational capabilities, representing the physical resources the company uses to generate revenue. In contrast, financial assets may only represent a small fraction of total assets, yet they play a crucial role in maintaining liquidity and supporting day-to-day operations.

On the right side of the balance sheet, we encounter the liabilities, which encompass the obligations that the company has towards both shareholders and creditors. Shareholders possess equity claims against the company's assets, reflecting their ownership stake and entitlements to future profits. Creditors, on the other hand, have a legal right to repayment of the loans or debts extended to the company. Importantly, these claims are not distinctly categorized; rather, all assets collectively serve to satisfy the claims of both shareholders and creditors.

One critical aspect of these claims is the concept of priority. In a liquidation scenario, creditors generally have a higher priority over the company's assets compared to shareholders. This means that in the unfortunate event of bankruptcy or liquidation, creditors are repaid before any distributions are made to shareholders. Within the creditor category, certain obligations can also be prioritized over others; for instance, government claims, such as taxes owed, often take precedence over other types of debt. This hierarchy of claims fundamentally impacts the perception of a company's financial health and risk profile.

To effectively check and analyze the financial balance sheet of non-financial companies, stakeholders—including investors, creditors, and analysts—often conduct a thorough examination of its components. This includes assessing the asset composition to evaluate the company's operational efficiency, as well as understanding the financial obligations to determine liquidity and solvency. Key ratios, such as the debt-to-equity ratio and current ratio, are frequently employed to gauge the company's leverage and ability to meet short-term obligations. Additionally, a balance sheet analysis must also consider the trends over time. Comparing current balance sheet figures to those from previous periods can highlight improvements or deteriorations in financial health, offering insights into the effectiveness of the company's management practices.

Ultimately, the financial balance sheet serves as an essential tool for stakeholders to assess the stability and financial management practices of a non-financial company. By understanding the dynamics between assets, liabilities, and the hierarchy of claims, investors and creditors can make informed decisions that align with their risk tolerance and financial goals. This comprehensive evaluation is crucial for guiding strategic choices, such as investment opportunities or lending considerations, thereby fostering a more profound understanding of the company's long-term viability and growth potential.

## What Should Be Done If the Company Goes Bankrupt?

When a company goes bankrupt, the ensuing process of settling its debts and obligations is strictly governed by a legal framework designed to ensure fairness and order among the various stakeholders involved. The bankruptcy process typically unfolds in a series of systematic steps, each aimed at addressing the financial claims against the company in a prioritized manner.

The first step in this process involves addressing the government's claims. These may include unpaid taxes, regulatory fees, and other financial obligations owed to the state. Government debts often take precedence over other obligations due to their legal standing and the societal importance of fulfilling tax obligations. Ensuring that these claims are settled promptly is critical for maintaining the integrity of the legal and financial systems.

Once the government obligations are resolved, the next priority shifts to compensating employees. Workers are considered essential stakeholders in any organization, and their unpaid wages are treated with a higher priority compared to other creditors. This focus on employee compensation reflects the ethical responsibility of the company to honor its commitments to those who have contributed their labor and expertise to its operations. Ensuring that employees receive their due wages not only helps support them during a challenging time but also preserves morale and public confidence in the business community. After fulfilling the obligations to the government and employees, the company's assets are then utilized to settle the claims of creditors. However, it's important to recognize that creditors do not have equal standing; some may have secured claims against the company's assets. Secured creditors hold collateral against their loans, which provides them with a legal claim to specific assets. For instance, if a factory is mortgaged, the creditor with the mortgage has a direct right to that asset in the event of liquidation. As a result, the mortgaged factory cannot be sold or liquidated until the company has settled its obligations to the government and employees.

Following the settlement of these claims, the remaining proceeds from the liquidation of the company's assets are directed toward satisfying the debts of secured creditors. This often involves selling off tangible assets, such as machinery, property, or inventory, to generate funds. Only after the claims of secured creditors are fully addressed do the remaining funds get allocated to unsecured creditors. Unsecured creditors may include suppliers, vendors, and others who provided services or goods without collateral. Finally, any leftover funds, if available, may be distributed to shareholders, but this is rare in bankruptcy situations, as shareholders are typically at the bottom of the priority list in the hierarchy of claims. This hierarchy of claims emphasizes the critical importance of understanding the balance sheet of non-financial companies—such as construction firms, manufacturing industries, hospitals, universities, and retail chains—before a bankruptcy event occurs. The assets recorded on the balance sheet are primarily tangible and real, such as machinery, buildings, and inventory, while the obligations reflect the various claims against these assets. Stakeholders must be aware of these dynamics, as they directly influence the potential for financial recovery and the future operations of the company.

when a company faces bankruptcy, a structured and legally mandated process is followed to address its obligations. This process prioritizes the claims of the government, employees, secured creditors, unsecured creditors, and finally shareholders. Understanding this hierarchy and the underlying principles governing bankruptcy is crucial for all stakeholders involved, as it not only impacts their financial recovery but also shapes their expectations and strategies in the face of potential insolvency. Ultimately, a clear understanding of this process can help stakeholders navigate the complexities of bankruptcy and position themselves for better outcomes in challenging financial circumstances.

## How are Financial Company Balance Sheets Adjusted?

In a financial company, the balance sheet is such that the assets are a set of financial assets. Of course, the financial company has obligations to both equity and debt owners. Equity and debt owners who are money bringers have given money to the company directly or by issuing bonds. Therefore, in financial firms, unlike non-financial firms, both sides of the balance sheet are financial assets. A part is the liabilities of others, which are considered financial assets for the company. Another part is the company's liabilities, which are considered financial assets for others.

For example, consider a bank. This bank gives loans. It has some paper as assets, which are loan contracts or bank credit claims. For example, Housing Bank is a facility that sits on the right side of the balance sheet and is a bank asset. But if this bank has issued bonds, raised money from the market or taken deposits, it sits on the left side. For those who give these deposits, they are a financial asset, and for Housing Bank it is a liability. For those who gave money to the bank and became the owners of the housing bank's capital, that is, the government, the bonds are the financial assets of the government, and like the shares of many companies, the government can sell them. This is an obligation for the bank. So, in financial companies, both sides of the balance sheet are mainly financial assets (Ellul,2018).

## What are the Basic Issues in the Financial Management of Companies?

In financial management, companies face a myriad of basic issues that are crucial for their growth and sustainability. For financial companies, the fundamental concerns revolve around capital acquisition and investment decisions. Specifically, these companies must determine how to source funds—whether through debt, equity, or other financial instruments—and identify the most lucrative financial assets to invest in. This includes assessing various securities, derivatives, and other financial products to optimize their investment portfolios. The decision-making process often involves analyzing market conditions, understanding risk and return profiles, and evaluating the liquidity of potential investments. A financial company must also consider its cost of capital, as the rate at which it can borrow or raise funds significantly impacts its investment strategies.

On the other hand, non-financial companies face distinct but equally important financial management issues. These companies are primarily concerned with where to allocate resources among various real projects that involve tangible assets, such as machinery, real estate, or technology. The key questions here revolve around project selection, which requires a careful analysis of potential returns on investment (ROI), the time horizon for achieving those returns, and the associated risks. Non-financial firms must evaluate whether to invest in new production facilities, expand existing operations, or diversify their product lines. This process often involves capital budgeting techniques, such as Net Present Value (NPV), Internal Rate of Return (IRR), and payback period calculations, to ensure that the selected projects align with the company's strategic objectives and financial capabilities.

Moreover, both types of companies must grapple with cash flow management, ensuring that they have sufficient liquidity to meet operational expenses and financial obligations. This includes forecasting cash flows accurately to avoid potential liquidity crises and strategically managing working capital to optimize operational efficiency. Ultimately, while the specific financial management issues differ between financial and non-financial companies, the overarching goals remain the same: to ensure sustainable growth, maximize returns on investment, and maintain financial health. Effective financial management is essential for making informed decisions that enhance shareholder value and secure the long-term viability of the organization.

## What is the Role of Financing in Investment?

Financing is fundamentally integral to the investment landscape, acting as the lifeblood that fuels various economic activities and initiatives. At its core, financing serves as the mechanism through which individuals, corporations, and governments acquire the necessary funds to engage in investment opportunities, making it a pivotal element in fostering economic growth and stability. This relationship between financing and investment is akin to a complex web, where every thread is interwoven with the other, creating a robust financial ecosystem that supports the movement of capital. From the perspective of investors, financing represents not merely a means of securing assets but a strategic avenue for wealth creation. Investors, whether they are individuals, institutional investors, or venture capitalists, look for opportunities that promise attractive returns on their investments. They purchase various financial instruments—such as stocks, bonds, real estate, or commodities—viewing these assets as vehicles for generating income and building wealth over time. The potential returns from these investments can take multiple forms, including capital appreciation, which reflects the increase in the asset's value over time, interest payments that provide a steady income stream, and dividends that reward shareholders for their investment. Consequently, investors must carefully evaluate not just the potential upside but also the associated risks, as market fluctuations, economic conditions, and geopolitical events can significantly impact asset performance.

On the issuer side, the role of financing is equally critical. Companies, municipalities, and governments rely on financing to fund their operations, expand their businesses, and invest in new projects. The process of raising capital typically involves the issuance of financial instruments, which may include debt instruments like bonds or equity instruments such as stocks. For instance, when a corporation issues bonds, it effectively borrows money from investors, creating a legal obligation to repay that debt with interest over a specified period. This bond issuance enables the company to raise significant capital upfront without immediately diluting ownership, thereby maintaining control over its operations. However, it also entails a commitment to regular interest payments and the eventual repayment of the principal, highlighting the dual nature of bonds as both a financial asset for investors and a liability for the issuer. This interplay between the supply and demand for funds creates a dynamic marketplace where capital flows from those who have excess funds—investors seeking to grow their wealth—to those who require funding to execute their business strategies—issuers seeking to invest in growth and innovation. The competitive nature of financial markets encourages issuers to present compelling value propositions to attract investment, while investors continually seek higher returns on their capital. The balance of this relationship fosters innovation, as companies are incentivized to develop new products, enhance services, and improve operational efficiency, all of which can lead to job creation and economic advancement.

The cost of financing is another critical aspect that influences investment decisions. Interest rates, credit conditions, and overall economic sentiment can significantly affect the cost of borrowing, which in turn shapes corporate and individual investment strategies. Companies must analyze the cost of debt against the expected returns from potential investments, and when financing costs are high, they may choose to postpone or forego projects that do not meet their return thresholds. Similarly, investors assess their risk-return profile in light of prevailing interest rates; lower interest rates often stimulate investment by making borrowing cheaper, while higher rates may deter investment and encourage a more cautious approach. This cost-benefit analysis plays a fundamental role in shaping the decisions made by both issuers and investors.

Moreover, the broader economic implications of financing in investment extend beyond individual entities. The effective functioning of financial markets facilitates the efficient allocation of resources, directing capital toward projects that yield the highest returns and contribute to overall economic growth. In this context, governments also utilize financing to fund essential public projects, such as infrastructure development, healthcare, and education, through mechanisms like public bonds. These government bonds provide a stable and relatively low-risk investment option for individuals and institutions while supplying critical funds for societal development. Financing is not just a background mechanism but a central tenet of the investment process that significantly impacts both microeconomic and macroeconomic landscapes. It acts as the bridge between those who have capital and those who need it, facilitating the allocation of resources that enable businesses to grow and innovate while providing investors with opportunities to earn returns. Understanding the multifaceted relationship between financing and investment is essential for navigating the financial landscape effectively. Both investors and issuers must engage in informed decision-making processes, carefully weighing the risks and rewards involved in their respective choices. As such, the role of financing is instrumental in driving economic growth, supporting innovation, and enhancing the overall efficiency of financial markets, ultimately leading to a more prosperous and dynamic economy.

## A FINANCIAL ASSET BASED ON DEBT OR EQUITY

A financial asset can fundamentally be categorized based on the underlying principles of debt or equity, each offering distinct characteristics, risks, and benefits to both investors and issuers. From an investor's perspective, debt-based financial instruments, such as bonds, play a significant role in portfolio management. When an investor purchases bonds, they engage in a debt-based transaction, effectively lending money to the issuer—whether a corporation, government, or other entity. In return, the investor receives periodic interest payments, commonly referred to as coupon payments, and the promise that the principal amount will be returned upon the bond's maturity. This transaction establishes a financial asset based on debt, where the bond represents a formal promise from the issuer to repay the borrowed amount along with accrued interest. Consequently, this relationship is characterized by a defined timeline, predictable cash flows, and a relatively lower risk profile compared to equity investments.

Conversely, from the perspective of the bond issuer, this transaction creates a liability on their balance sheet. The issuer is obligated to fulfill their commitment to bondholders, managing this financial obligation with care to maintain their financial health. Failure to meet these obligations can lead to severe repercussions, including downgrades in credit ratings, increased borrowing costs, and potential bankruptcy. Thus, the careful management of debt is crucial for sustaining the issuer's operations and financial viability. On the other hand, equity-based financial assets, such as shares or stocks, represent ownership in a company. When a corporation issues shares, it allows investors to acquire a stake in the company's equity, granting them certain rights, such as voting rights and the potential for dividends. From an investor or shareholder's perspective, these shares are valuable financial assets that provide opportunities for capital appreciation—meaning the increase in share price over time—and income through dividends, which are periodic distributions of profits to shareholders. However, for the company that issues these shares, they also represent a liability. The company has an obligation to its shareholders, which may include paying dividends and ensuring the overall performance of the business positively impacts share value. This obligation to shareholders underscores the importance of strategic decision-making within the company, as investors will expect robust performance and sound management practices.

Companies that choose to issue shares as a means of raising capital are effectively entering into a contractual obligation with their investors. By opting for equity financing, they seek to harness the benefits of accessing capital without the immediate pressure of interest payments associated with debt financing. This approach can be particularly advantageous for companies in growth phases or those requiring substantial investment for expansion. However, it comes with the understanding that the company must operate profitably to meet investor expectations and sustain the value of its shares in the market. Any failure to perform may lead to declining share prices and eroded investor confidence.

In the realm of investment decision-making, non-financial firms engage in various business strategies to navigate their capital requirements and optimize their asset compositions. This process is often guided by capital budgeting, which involves evaluating potential investments, estimating future cash flows, and determining the most beneficial allocation of resources. Effective capital budgeting enables companies to prioritize projects that align with their strategic goals while ensuring adequate funding for operational needs. For financial institutions, the investment process operates through asset allocation, where the management of investment portfolios is critical. These institutions must carefully analyze market conditions, risk tolerance, and overarching investment goals to determine the optimal composition of assets. By strategically balancing debt and equity within their portfolios, financial firms aim to maximize returns while managing associated risks effectively. This balancing act is not only crucial for achieving short-term gains but also for ensuring long-term stability and growth.

Moreover, the distinction between debt and equity-based financial assets is fundamental to understanding the broader financial landscape. Both investors and issuers must navigate these instruments with a clear awareness of their respective rights and obligations. Investors must comprehend the risk-return profiles of their choices, recognizing that debt instruments tend to offer lower returns but with reduced risk, while equity investments generally present higher risk with the potential for greater rewards. On the issuer's side, companies must be cognizant of how their financing decisions impact their capital structure, financial health, and ability to attract future investments. The categorization of financial assets based on debt and equity is essential for comprehending the dynamics of financial markets. This classification influences the strategies employed by investors and issuers alike, shaping their decision-making processes and ultimately affecting the overall economy. As such, a thorough understanding of debt and equity instruments and their implications is crucial for anyone engaged in the financial landscape, whether they are seasoned investors, corporate finance professionals, or aspiring financial analysts. The strategic choices made in this context can have far-reaching consequences, not just for individual entities but also for the economy as a whole, as they drive capital allocation, influence market behavior, and foster economic growth and innovation.

## INVESTMENT PORTFOLIO MANAGEMENT

Investment portfolio management is a critical function within financial companies that actively engage in the acquisition of financial assets. Through effective portfolio management, these firms strategically buy and hold a diverse array of assets, enabling them to optimize returns while managing risk. The asset mix—comprising various financial instruments such as stocks, bonds, mutual funds, and other securities—is determined through a structured approach that considers market conditions, investor objectives, and risk tolerance. A portfolio manager plays a pivotal role in this process. Their primary responsibility is to identify and select financial assets that are expected to yield higher returns compared to others available in the market. This requires not only an understanding of financial markets but also the ability to analyze and interpret data, recognize trends, and anticipate shifts in economic conditions. The portfolio manager must employ various techniques, such as fundamental analysis, technical analysis, and quantitative methods, to evaluate potential investments and construct a well-balanced portfolio.

Risk management is a fundamental aspect of portfolio management. The manager's knowledge extends beyond simply selecting high-return assets; they must also understand how to effectively combine different financial instruments to mitigate risk. By diversifying the portfolio, the manager can reduce the impact of any single asset's poor performance on the overall portfolio. This involves a careful analysis of correlations between assets, ensuring that the chosen mix provides a hedge against volatility in the financial markets. IN contrast, the financial manager of a non-financial company faces a different set of challenges. Their focus is on managing non-financial assets, which often include capital projects, physical infrastructure, and operational investments. For instance, if a non-financial manager has a budget of 100 units of currency and is presented with multiple project options, their task is to evaluate and select those projects that promise the highest potential returns relative to their costs and risks.

In this scenario, collaboration between financial managers and technical experts is essential. While financial managers assess projects primarily from a cash flow perspective—considering projected revenues, costs, and profitability—engineers and other specialists evaluate the technical feasibility and operational implications of these projects. Engineers provide insights into the practical aspects of project execution, such as design, construction, and maintenance, which are crucial for ensuring that projects can be delivered on time and within budget. Moreover, in investment portfolio management, sensitivity analysis and financial simulations play a significant role. Managers can use techniques such as Monte Carlo simulations and scenario analyses to predict the impact of various factors on portfolio performance. These tools help managers simulate different market scenarios and assess how the portfolio would respond to market fluctuations and economic changes. Ultimately, the effectiveness of investment portfolio management relies on a combination of financial acumen and technical expertise. By integrating the skills and knowledge of financial managers and engineers, companies can make informed investment decisions that not only maximize returns but also align with their strategic objectives and operational capabilities.

In conclusion, whether in financial companies or non-financial firms, effective portfolio management is vital for navigating the complexities of investment decision-making. By balancing the pursuit of higher returns with prudent risk management and technical evaluation, organizations can enhance their financial performance and achieve sustainable growth. Overall, portfolio management involves not only selecting relevant financial assets but also entails technical and strategic assessments in choosing capital investment projects and managing non-financial assets. This complex and multifaceted process requires collaboration across various disciplines and the ability to make informed decisions.

## FINANCIAL MANAGER OF COMPANIES AND HIS EQUIVALENT IN FINANCIAL INSTITUTIONS

In the realm of corporate finance, the role of the financial officer is commonly designated as the "financial manager." This individual is primarily responsible for managing the financial health of the company, which includes tasks such as budgeting, forecasting, investment analysis, and ensuring efficient use of resources to maximize shareholder value. The financial manager plays a crucial role in strategic decision-making, helping the organization navigate its financial landscape to achieve its objectives. However, the nature of financial expertise differs significantly within financial institutions. In these entities—such as banks, insurance companies, pension funds, and investment firms—the titles and responsibilities of financial professionals are distinct and often specialized. For instance, in an investment fund, the equivalent role is referred to as a "fund manager," who is responsible for making investment decisions that align with the fund's objectives and managing the portfolio of financial assets. In banks, the title "credit manager" is commonly used, focusing on assessing credit risk and managing loan portfolios. In the insurance sector, the role of "insurance portfolio manager" or "insurance product manager" pertains to managing the risk and return of insurance policies and investment products offered to clients.

This distinction highlights that the term "financial manager" is not typically used within financial institutions. Instead, these professionals are primarily engaged in "investment management," which focuses on managing financial assets rather than the financial management of operational businesses. Investment management involves selecting and overseeing a portfolio of investments, including stocks, bonds, and other financial instruments, to meet specific financial goals, such as maximizing returns or managing risk. When discussing their functions in the context of the financial market, it's essential to recognize the different objectives of financial managers and investment managers. A financial manager in a corporate setting primarily seeks to secure funding for various projects aimed at enhancing the company's operations, growth, and profitability. This often involves sourcing funds through equity financing, debt issuance, or retained earnings.

Conversely, an investment manager focuses on optimizing the performance of an investment portfolio by allocating resources among various financial assets. While both roles aim to acquire financial resources, the investment manager typically does not engage in the acquisition of real assets—such as physical property or equipment—but rather purchases financial assets like stocks, bonds, and derivatives. The investment manager's primary goal is to enhance returns on the financial portfolio while managing associated risks, using strategies tailored to market conditions and investor expectations.

While both financial managers and investment managers operate within the broader financial ecosystem, their roles, titles, and areas of focus diverge significantly. Financial managers concentrate on the financial strategy of companies, seeking to drive operational success and shareholder value, whereas investment managers specialize in optimizing investment portfolios, aiming to achieve financial returns through effective asset management. Understanding these differences is crucial for grasping the multifaceted nature of financial management across various sectors.

## What is the Role of the Fund Manager or Portfolio Manager in the Financial Management of Companies?

In the landscape of financial management, the role of the fund manager or portfolio manager is pivotal, particularly within financial institutions. Unlike non-financial companies, where the title "financial manager" is commonly used, financial companies employ a distinct terminology and approach to managing investments. In these institutions, the focus shifts from traditional financial management to a specialized form of investment management, emphasizing the nuances and complexities involved in handling financial assets. Fund managers or portfolio managers are tasked with overseeing investment portfolios on behalf of clients or the financial institution itself. Their primary responsibility is to make informed investment decisions that aim to maximize returns while effectively managing risk. This role involves analyzing various financial instruments—such as stocks, bonds, mutual funds, and other securities—and determining the optimal asset allocation strategy based on market conditions, investment objectives, and risk tolerance.

In the context of banks, the concept of asset-liability management (ALM) becomes crucial. Here, fund managers are responsible for ensuring that the maturity profiles of the bank's loans and deposits are aligned. This means that the timing of cash inflows from loans should correspond with the timing of cash outflows related to customer deposits. Effective ALM is essential for maintaining liquidity, managing interest rate risk, and ensuring the bank's overall financial stability. The title of "credit portfolio manager" is often used in this context, highlighting the specific focus on managing the risks and returns associated with the bank's credit portfolio. In investment funds, the roles of fund managers and portfolio managers are similarly focused but tailored to the needs of investors seeking capital appreciation or income generation. These professionals are responsible for constructing and managing investment portfolios that align with the fund's investment strategy, which could range from aggressive growth to conservative income generation. The fund manager evaluates market opportunities, conducts in-depth analyses of potential investments, and continuously monitors the performance of the portfolio to make necessary adjustments in response to changing market conditions.

Moreover, the role of the fund manager extends beyond mere asset selection; it involves comprehensive portfolio construction and ongoing risk management. Fund managers utilize various financial theories and analytical tools to assess the risk-return profile of different investments, aiming to create a diversified portfolio that minimizes risk while optimizing returns. They also engage in active monitoring and rebalancing of the portfolio, ensuring that it remains aligned with the fund's investment objectives and adheres to regulatory requirements.

The transition from traditional financial management titles to specialized roles such as fund manager or portfolio manager reflects the growing complexity of financial markets and the need for targeted expertise in managing financial assets. In this evolving landscape, fund managers play a critical role in guiding investment strategies, providing valuable insights to investors, and ultimately contributing to the financial performance of the institution they represent.

In summary, the roles of fund managers and portfolio managers within financial institutions are vital components of investment management. Their expertise in analyzing financial markets, managing risks, and optimizing asset allocation enables financial companies to navigate the complexities of investment decision-making while striving to achieve superior returns for their clients or stakeholders. This specialization underscores the importance of strategic investment management in the overall financial health and success of financial institutions.

## What is the Definition of Dedicated Banking?

In private banking, which is banking for high-income and wealthier people, the bank manages the client's wealth. In this case, the person who manages the client's account is called the account manager or wealth manager. "Private banking" is not the opposite of state banking; Rather, in this type of banking, the bank manages the financial lives of those whose wealth is above a threshold, who have high expertise, and who do not want to spend their time buying and selling stocks or real estate transactions. If a high-income surgeon, scientist, football player, actor, or electronic engineer wants to preserve his savings and not spend his time learning the capital market by running a construction project and wants to focus on his professional work, He is looking for a trusted expert to entrust him with managing his financial life.

For example, an actress should not have to open a restaurant to save her savings; Or a good football player should not have to open a sports store to preserve his wealth. Financial institutions can help these people manage their wealth properly and beyond wealth, their financial life can be managed effectively. They are looking for an institution that will pay their child's school tuition, buy 1000 dollars in currency for their trip, rent their second home or rent a place in the north for their vacation, prepare their financial contracts, and give them advice. pay their salaries and taxes and finally invest their savings effectively.

## CONCLUSION

Many politicians use the services of dedicated bankers for other reasons to avoid conflict of interest. When we talk about dedicated banking, it is not only about managing the client's wealth but also about financial services. In some countries, wealth management has been mentioned in some banks, but in these banks, wealth management has been limited to the establishment of investment funds for customers, and there has been no news of financial services. Therefore, it is true to say that private banking has not yet taken root in some countries. Therefore, those interested in the field of financial management can enter the field of private banking and provide valuable services to various organizations (Cenciarelli, 2018).

# REFERENCES

- Cenciarelli, V.G. (2018). Research seminar: Bankruptcy Prediction and EarningsManagement. Research seminar. Cerovic, S., Gerling, K., Hodge, A., &Medas, P. (2018). Predicting fiscal crises. IMF Working Paper, WP/18/181.

Chiaramontea, L, & Casu, B. (2017). Capital and liquidity ratios and financial distress. Evidence from the European banking industry. *The British Accounting Review*.

-. (2023). Investigating the effects of Information and Communication Technology (ICT) on capital market uncertainty by considering its impact on the textile industry: A case study for Iran. *Industria Textila*, 74(6), 667–687. DOI: 10.35530/IT.074.06.2022136

Christensen, H. B., Nikolaev, V., & Wittenberg-Moerman, R. (2016). Accounting information in financial contracting: The incomplete contract theory perspective. *Journal of Accounting Research*, 54(2), 397–435. DOI: 10.1111/1475-679X.12108

Cohn, J. B., Liu, Z., & Wardlaw, M. I. (2022). Count (and count-like) data in finance. *Journal of Financial Economics*, 146(2), 529–551. DOI: 10.1016/j.jfineco.2022.08.004

Demerjian, P. R., & Owens, E. L. (2016). Measuring the probability of financial covenant violation in private debt contracts. *Journal of Accounting and Economics*, 61(2-3), 433–447. DOI: 10.1016/j.jacceco.2015.11.001

Ellul, A., & Panayides, M. (2018). Do financial analysts restrain insiders' informational advantage? *Journal of Financial and Quantitative Analysis*, 53(1), 203–241. DOI: 10.1017/S0022109017000990

- Hasler, M., Khapko, M., & Marfe, R. (2019). Should investors learn about the shape of the term structure of equity risks? Journal of Financial Economics, 132(3), 182–204. -https://www.lsbf.org.uk/blog/news/importance-of-financial-management/117410-https://www.netsuite.com/portal/resource/articles/financial-management/financial-management.shtml

Li, K., & Xu, C. (2023). Asset pricing with a financial sector. *Financial Management*, 52(1), 67–95. DOI: 10.1111/fima.12407

Pourmansouri, R., Fallah, M. F., Birau, R., Spulbar, C., & Cinciulescu, D. (2023). Investigating the relationship between ownership structure, board composition, and company performance: An extensive overview of companies in the textile industry in Iran. Industria Textila, 74(5). DOI: 10.1111/fima.12407

Pourmansouri, R., Fallah, M. F., Birau, R., Dekamini, F., & Nioata, R. M. (2024). *Exploring Governance, Ownership, and Auditor Impact on Company Risk: A Comparative Analysis Before and After COVID-19 pandemic. Multidisciplinary Science Journal.* Accepted Articles.

# Chapter 5
# Financial Concepts for Non-Financial Managers

## ABSTRACT

*Today, according to the increasing development of management science, in every economic enterprise, including production, service and commerce, of any nature, including government, private and quasi-government, managers need to have the ability to control and supervise various aspects of that business. Regardless of the content of different branches of management science, what is their current vital need is to have common monitoring and control tools. Financial science somehow translates all the different branches of management science and the big decisions of managers into the common language of financial numbers and gives managers the possibility to make decisions based on this information. Investment decisions, performance evaluation, evaluation of investment plans, risk management and even human resource management.*

## INTRODUCTION

In today's competitive landscape, the success of a business heavily depends on its ability to achieve sales objectives and expand market share. Sales planning, as a structured and strategic process, provides the essential tools needed to meet these goals. This process encompasses key steps such as market analysis, identifying target customers, designing a sales team, setting financial objectives, and defining actionable strategies, all aimed at enhancing sales performance.

An effective sales plan not only guides and motivates the sales team but also helps businesses make better decisions by gaining a deeper understanding of the market, customers, and competitors. It creates a framework where every team member has a clear understanding of their responsibilities, ensuring that their efforts are aligned toward common objectives. Additionally, sales planning enables organizations to

DOI: 10.4018/979-8-3693-9415-1.ch005

adapt to changing market conditions by identifying weaknesses and implementing solutions for improvement. The goal of this chapter is to explore the essential steps involved in designing and executing an effective sales plan. These steps range from defining the business's mission and objectives to identifying the target market, crafting marketing and sales strategies, and monitoring the performance of the sales team. Moreover, the chapter will emphasize the importance of leveraging modern tools such as Customer Relationship Management (CRM) software to optimize sales processes and increase efficiency. Given the complexity and significance of sales planning, understanding this concept is essential not only for sales managers but also for every member of the sales team. This knowledge empowers businesses to seize available opportunities, address emerging challenges, and move toward sustainable growth.

## FINANCIAL CONCEPTS FOR NON-FINANCIAL MANAGERS

Today, according to the increasing development of management science, in every economic enterprise, including production, service and commerce, of any nature, including government, private and quasi-government, managers need to have the ability to control and supervise various aspects of that business. Regardless of the content of different branches of management science, what is their current vital need is to have common monitoring and control tools.

Financial science somehow translates all the different branches of management science and the big decisions of managers into the common language of financial numbers and gives managers the possibility to make decisions based on this information. Investment decisions, performance evaluation, evaluation of investment plans, risk management and even human resource management. The financial management course for non-financial managers seeks to answer this key need of non-financial managers. In this section, we will try to provide non-financial managers with a tool to measure the financial status of an economic enterprise. Some of these tools are also used in personal financial management (Heath, 2023).

1. **What is financial planning?**

Financial planning is a critical process that involves creating a comprehensive strategy to manage one's financial resources effectively to achieve long-term goals related to personal well-being, savings, and investment. At its core, a financial plan serves as a roadmap, guiding individuals or organizations toward their desired financial future. This plan can be developed independently or with the assistance of a financial advisor, who brings expertise and insights that can enhance the planning process. Regardless of the approach, the foundation of any sound financial plan is a thorough assessment of the current financial situation, which includes analyzing income, expenses, assets, liabilities, and future prospects.

Financial planning can be divided into short-term and long-term planning, each serving distinct purposes but ultimately interconnected. "Short-term financial planning" focuses on immediate financial needs and operational decisions that impact current assets and liabilities. This type of planning is essential for managing day-to-day operations, ensuring that an organization can meet its short-term obligations while efficiently allocating resources to achieve operational goals. It typically involves identifying priorities and determining how to allocate available resources effectively, setting the stage for the organization's ongoing activities.

In contrast, "long-term financial planning" takes a broader perspective, influencing key areas such as capital budgeting, financial structure, and profit-sharing policies. It involves strategic decisions that align with the organization's long-term vision and objectives. Long-term planning considers various factors, including projected revenues, investment opportunities, and market trends, to determine how resources should be allocated for sustainable growth. This planning typically starts from the insights gained through short-term planning, forming a foundation for more comprehensive strategies that guide the organization toward achieving its long-term goals.

The interplay between short-term and long-term planning is crucial. Effective short-term planning ensures that operational needs are met, thereby providing the necessary resources and stability to pursue long-term objectives. When senior management approves short-term plans, it fosters a sense of ownership and accountability among managers, supervisors, and operational staff, encouraging their active participation in the long-term planning process. This collaboration is vital for aligning the organization's mission, functions, ideals, and goals with its strategic vision, enabling a holistic approach to financial management.

"The importance of financial planning" cannot be overstated, as it encompasses several key aspects that contribute to the overall health and sustainability of an organization. First and foremost, efficient liquidity management is essential for maintaining a healthy cash flow. Financial planning helps establish an acceptable balance between cash inflows and outflows, ensuring that the organization can meet its financial obligations without running into liquidity crises.

Moreover, sound financial planning attracts financiers and investors, as it demonstrates a company's commitment to prudent financial management and sustainable growth practices. When investors see that an organization prioritizes financial planning, they are more likely to invest, knowing their funds are being managed responsibly and strategically. Additionally, effective financial planning facilitates the implementation of growth and development programs, which can significantly enhance the organization's long-term performance. By forecasting financial needs and market conditions, organizations can make informed decisions about expanding operations, launching new products, or entering new markets. Furthermore, financial planning helps mitigate uncertainties associated with changing market trends. By anticipating potential challenges and having sufficient cash reserves, organizations can navigate fluctuations in the economic landscape more effectively. This proactive approach reduces the risks that may hinder growth and development, allowing organizations to remain agile and adaptable.

## The Importance of Financial Planning

1. Liquidity must be efficient.
2. Financial planning helps to establish an acceptable balance between cash inflows and outflows.
3. Financial planning ensures that financiers invest in companies that focus on this practice.
4. This action has helped in the implementation of growth and development programs that have a positive effect on the long-term performance of the organization.
5. This reduces uncertainties by taking into account the changes in market trends that can be faced with sufficient cash.
6. This practice helps to reduce the uncertainties that can be an obstacle to the growth of the organization.

## Knowing the Financial Plan

Regardless of whether the financial plan is developed individually or with the help of a financial expert, the first step in preparing a financial plan includes the preparation and collection of all financial documents, including bills, savings accounts, bills and certificates of investments. and debts, so that the summary of the current situation is entered in a spreadsheet like Excel.

**Key Features**
- The financial plan establishes individual long-term goals and provides a commitment for future strategy.
- The financial plan should be flexible based on the current financial situation, risk tolerance level, future expectations, and investment horizon.
- The plan starts with calculating net present value and cash flow.

The following steps can be used to create a financial plan, although it can be developed individually or as a group:

### Calculation of Net Worth

You should estimate your net worth and list the following:

- **Your Assets:** This includes your home, car, cash, bank account, invested money, insurance, and any other financial assets.
- **Your Debts:** Including loan installments, credit card debt, student loans, housing, or cars.

Your total assets minus your liabilities equals your net present worth.

## Determination of Cash Flow

Understanding your daily expenses is fundamental to effective financial planning. Without a clear grasp of your cash flow, it becomes nearly impossible to create a sustainable financial plan that encompasses savings and investments. Documenting your expenses allows you to assess how much money you need to allocate each day, identify your savings rate, and determine your investment capabilities. This awareness can lead to strategic adjustments—whether it means increasing or decreasing your spending, saving, or investing in response to your financial situation.

To accurately document your expenses, consider utilizing various methods. For instance, printing bills or reviewing microtransactions from your bank account online can provide a comprehensive overview of your spending habits. It's essential to maintain a detailed record of your expenses over time. If you notice significant fluctuations in your expenses throughout different seasons, a more effective strategy may be to compile your expenses on an annual basis. By summing up all your expenses for the year and then dividing that total by 12, you can calculate your average monthly expenses. This approach ensures that all costs, from utility bills like water, electricity, and gas to occasional expenses like holiday gifts, are accounted for, giving you a clearer picture of your financial landscape.

A robust financial plan encompasses several critical elements, including:

1. **Retirement Strategy:** A plan for accumulating the necessary funds to support your lifestyle after you stop working. This includes determining how much to save annually, understanding retirement accounts (such as IRAs or 401(k)s), and projecting the income needed in retirement.
2. **Risk Management Plan:** An assessment of potential risks to your financial stability, such as unexpected medical expenses, job loss, or market fluctuations. This plan typically includes insurance coverage (health, life, property) and emergency funds to mitigate these risks.

3. **Tax Management Strategy:** A comprehensive approach to understanding your tax obligations and identifying ways to minimize your tax liability. This includes leveraging deductions, credits, and tax-advantaged accounts to optimize your tax situation.
4. **Estate Planning:** Planning for the distribution of your assets after your passing, ensuring your wishes are honored, and minimizing potential taxes and legal complications for your heirs. This often involves creating wills, trusts, and designating beneficiaries for accounts.

When preparing your financial documents, meticulously track your annual spending. This should encompass housing-related expenses, such as maintenance, mortgage payments, and costs associated with home purchases, including appliances and furnishings. Break down your expenses into various categories, such as healthcare, clothing, education, and investment. Additionally, account for entertainment expenses—this includes travel, dining out, and leisure activities—ensuring no detail is overlooked. Even minor purchases, like toiletries, should be included, as these can add up over time.

By maintaining this level of detail in your financial records, you can identify personal spending patterns and categories that may need attention. For instance, you might discover that a particular hobby is costing more than you realized, prompting you to reassess its impact on your overall budget. After compiling and categorizing your expenses, you can sum them up and divide by 12 to determine your average monthly cash flow. This analysis will illuminate your financial habits, allowing you to make informed decisions about your spending, saving, and investing. Ultimately, determining your cash flow is not just about tracking numbers—it's about creating a comprehensive view of your financial health. By understanding where your money goes, you can develop a solid financial plan that aligns with your long-term goals, enhances your ability to save and invest, and ultimately leads to a more secure financial future.

## Considering Individual Preferences

At the heart of any effective financial plan lies the careful consideration of individual preferences and aspirations. Each person's financial journey is unique, shaped by their life experiences, values, and long-term objectives. The core of the financial plan is therefore determined based on these individual goals, which can vary widely from one person to another. For instance, many individuals prioritize their children's education, envisioning a future where their kids have access to quality education, whether it be for primary schooling or advanced post-secondary studies. This goal often necessitates setting aside substantial funds to cover tuition fees, extracurricular activities, and other related expenses, which can be quite significant in today's educational landscape.

Similarly, the desire to buy a bigger house often reflects a need for more space, whether due to a growing family or the aspiration for a more comfortable lifestyle. This goal involves not only the financial aspects of saving for a down payment but also considerations around mortgage options and long-term housing market trends.

Starting a business is another common goal that many aspire to achieve. This ambition requires careful planning, as it involves not just capital investment but also a thorough understanding of the market, business operations, and the potential risks involved. A well-thought-out financial plan can help individuals allocate the necessary resources to turn their entrepreneurial dreams into reality. Retiring early is yet another aspiration that many people hold dear. This goal necessitates a proactive approach to savings and investments, as individuals must build a substantial nest egg to ensure financial independence during their retirement years. It involves evaluating current expenses, estimating future living costs, and strategically investing to create a sustainable income stream. Leaving an inheritance is a significant consideration for some individuals, as it reflects a desire to provide for future generations. This goal often requires careful estate planning, including wills, trusts, and understanding tax implications to ensure that wealth is transferred effectively and in accordance with one's wishes.

While individuals may have their unique set of priorities, it is crucial to acknowledge that no one can dictate how to rank these goals. Each person's situation is different, influenced by their financial circumstances, values, and life stages. This is where the expertise of a professional financial advisor becomes invaluable. They can help individuals navigate the complexities of financial planning, assisting in the prioritization of goals based on personal values and circumstances. Moreover, a financial advisor can provide guidance on asset allocation, helping clients determine how much to set aside in savings accounts versus investments. They can offer insights into different investment positions, advising on the potential risks and rewards associated with each option. This tailored approach ensures that individuals can pursue their goals with a structured financial strategy, optimizing their chances of success.

In conclusion, the foundation of any financial plan should be a reflection of individual preferences and goals. By considering personal aspirations—be it funding education, buying a home, starting a business, retiring early, or leaving a legacy—individuals can create a financial roadmap that aligns with their unique journey. With the assistance of a professional financial advisor, they can make informed decisions about asset allocation and investment strategies, empowering them to achieve their dreams while securing their financial future.

## Special Considerations of the Financial Plan

When embarking on the journey of financial planning, it's important to recognize that financial plans do not follow a one-size-fits-all approach. Each individual's financial situation, goals, and circumstances are unique, and a professional financial advisor can create a tailored financial plan that reflects these distinct factors. This personalized plan may necessitate adjustments to your short-term objectives to align them with your long-term aspirations. In developing a robust financial plan, several key elements must be considered or modified:

- **Retirement Strategy:** Regardless of your immediate priorities, a comprehensive financial plan must incorporate a strategy for generating income during retirement. This aspect is crucial because retirement often spans several decades, and having a reliable income source is essential for maintaining one's lifestyle. Your retirement strategy should address various income streams, such as Social Security benefits, pensions, retirement accounts, and potential investment income. A clear understanding of your anticipated expenses in retirement will also guide your savings strategy and help you determine how much you need to set aside to achieve financial security in your later years.
- **Comprehensive Risk Management Plan:** A thorough financial plan should include a comprehensive risk management strategy, which encompasses various types of insurance to protect against unforeseen events. This plan may include life and disability insurance to safeguard your family's financial future in the event of an untimely death or inability to work due to illness or injury. Additionally, personal liability coverage is essential for protecting your assets in the case of legal claims. Ensuring adequate housing and fire insurance is also critical to safeguard your property against damage or loss. By proactively addressing these risks, you can provide peace of mind for yourself and your loved ones.
- **Long-Term Investment Plan:** An effective financial plan incorporates a long-term investment strategy tailored to your specific goals and risk tolerance. This customized plan should consider factors such as your investment time horizon, desired asset allocation, and personal comfort level with market fluctuations. By aligning your investments with your long-term objectives, whether it's saving for a home, funding education, or building wealth—you can create a strategic approach that enhances your potential for growth while managing risk appropriately. Regular reviews and adjustments to your investment portfolio will help ensure it remains aligned with your evolving goals and market conditions.

- **Tax Reduction Strategy:** Taxation can significantly impact your overall financial well-being, making a well-crafted tax reduction strategy a vital component of your financial plan. This strategy should focus on minimizing your income tax liability while adhering to legal requirements. Various techniques may be employed, such as tax-advantaged accounts, tax-loss harvesting, and strategically timing income and deductions. By optimizing your tax situation, you can retain more of your hard-earned money, which can then be reinvested into your financial goals.
- **Property:** When managing your finances, it's essential to include planning for property maintenance as part of your overall financial strategy. This involves budgeting for regular upkeep, repairs, and improvements to your property, which can help maintain or enhance its value over time. Whether it's routine maintenance for your home or considerations for rental properties, having a clear plan ensures that you are financially prepared for these expenses. Additionally, understanding the potential costs associated with property ownership, including property taxes and insurance, will help you develop a more comprehensive view of your financial obligations.

## Six Important Factors in Financial Planning for Businesses

As you know, the main goal of starting any business or commercial activity is to obtain a minimum profit, of course, the efforts to increase this level are minimal. Therefore, in order to obtain the determined profit and achieve other business goals, a detailed plan for all activities must be developed, and the most important part of this plan is the financial plan.

In simpler terms, financial planning deals with the analysis of current and future costs and revenues to determine the activities that should be considered for business growth and development. The costs that should be considered in the financial plan include the calculation of employee salaries and wages, the cost of training the workforce, marketing and research and development costs.

By calculating the costs and revenues of the companies, you can better decide to allocate your resources in order to implement the program and activities. Always remember that the financial plan for the business changes along with the competitive environment of that business and it needs to be re-examined in different time frames and changes should be considered for it if necessary. It is recommended that the following items must be included in the financial plan so that it has significant efficiency and effectiveness in achieving the goals:

- The amount of capital required to implement the operation
- Plans determined to use the proceeds

- Projected revenues
- Balance sheet
- Cash flow

## What is a Financial Plan?

Financial plan is defined as the process of documenting the current financial situation of a person or a business unit, setting financial goals for it and how to achieve these goals. To be more precise, the financial plan is considered as a road map for the growth of the business or the growth of the individual in terms of finance and in a way, it expresses the long-term goals of a business or an individual.

Although the definition of personal financial plan or business financial plan is the same, these two financial plans have many differences. As an example, a person's financial plan can include planning for retirement and a source of income for the expenses of that time, investment and property purchase. While the financial plan of a business includes other things such as adding human resources, increasing inventories through increasing purchases, expanding the production line and increasing the market share of the business.

Here, it is necessary to emphasize that budget and financial plan are two separate concepts, and contrary to public opinion, budget and financial plan cannot be used interchangeably. Of course, the financial plan includes the budget (determining the budget needed to achieve the goals). But besides that, it covers other very important financial information such as detailed analysis of the business's cash flow, its tangible and intangible assets, forecasting the amount of income and capital, and more (Peyravan,2020).

## Why does my Business Need a Financial Plan?

Let us continue the discussion with the premise that:
No business needs a financial plan, but all businesses can benefit from it.

Developing a financial plan for your business forces you to think about where you would like to be in the future in addition to your current position and determine the path to reach it. Always remember that growth and success do not happen by accident, but success is the result of hard work. And of course, without having specific goals, hard work will not bring any results.

The financial plan[1] for the business is actually a kind of guide to achieve all its goals, especially the financial goals. Because the main purpose of starting a business is to make a profit and achieve financial goals. Important factors should be taken into account when developing a business financial plan, the three main components of which are the balance sheet, cash flow and income statement. In the following, we have listed the important factors and components for developing a financial plan.

1. **Sales Forecast in the Financial Plan**

A business owner should estimate his sales for the month, season and year. Identifying patterns in the sales cycle of a business helps with its growth. Advertising programs and growth strategies can also be determined. For example, a business that has seasonal sales can set the main goal of increasing sales in other seasons. Therefore, the sales forecast can be considered as the basis for determining the company's growth goals.

2. **Determining Expenses in the Financial Plan**

The financial plan should cover all expenses such as general and financial expenses of the business. General expenses include current business expenses such as property rent, water and electricity, employee salaries, and other expenses that must be paid regularly.

Another type of expense under the title of anticipated expenses should be included in the financial plan of the business. As an example, we can mention the prediction of an increase in the tax rate, an increase in wages and salaries of employees based on the approved rate in the new year, or expenses related to unforeseen events such as fire.

3. **Determining the Financial Status of the Company in the Financial Plan**

The balance sheet, which is one of the most important financial statements in accounting, lists and displays the company's assets and liabilities. Reviewing the company's assets and liabilities will help you assess the improvement in the value of your business. The profit and loss statement also shows the financial status and the way the company operates in a certain period, through which the net profit from economic activity can be calculated for some time. The balance sheet report provides a clear view of the company's financial situation at a specific moment.

4. **Determining the Cash Flow of the Business in the Financial Plan**

In order to be successful in your business, it is necessary to forecast your cash flow for the month, quarter and year in addition to forecasting expenses. In fact, by predicting the cash flow, you will be more prepared for possible financial challenges, and you can make better decisions.

5. **Break-Even Analysis in the Financial Plan**

In this section, you should calculate the fixed costs related to the increase in production and, as a result, the increase in sales per unit. This analysis is necessary to have a correct understanding of the income and costs of increasing your production. In fact, break-even analysis can be a good way to determine the competitive price of your products. Because in this way, you evaluate that you need to sell at least a few products to cover your fixed costs, what price can you set for sales that will meet your costs and attract customers' attention in comparison to the prices of other competitors. attract you.

6. **Developing an Operational Plan in the Financial Plan of the Business**

For business activities to be effective, it is better to have a clear vision of your operational needs. It is necessary to know what job titles you need to achieve the set goals, what is the job description of each employee and how can the output of the employees be maximized, or information about the costs related to each stage of the supply chain. It can help you make an informed decision.

Business owners have been advised to determine their financial plan for one year at the beginning of the year, just as they take care of the accounts at the end of the financial year and close the financial accounts in the accounting books and accounting software. In this program, they should create a clear and accurate picture of financial affairs and reach a realistic view of the growth and expansion of the business throughout the year. This financial program helps managers to make more informed decisions regarding expenses, amount of purchases, debts, cost control, and other activities. For financial plans to be more effective, it is better to compare the actual performance based on the financial data recorded in the accounting software at the end of the year with what is considered in the financial plan, and your strengths and weaknesses in Finding the performance and use them to improve the financial plan and implement it.

## The Importance of Preparing the Annual Financial Plan

Preparing an annual financial plan is a fundamental step in achieving financial stability and success. A strategic approach to managing your finances involves regularly engaging in activities that relate to the financial management of your personal life. However, even the most disciplined individuals often find it challenging to dedicate the time necessary to develop and monitor a comprehensive financial plan throughout the year. Thus, the importance of preparing an annual financial plan cannot be overstated.

- **Establishing Long-Term Goals**

Establishing long-term financial goals is a crucial aspect of personal finance management, and the earlier one starts, the better. Ideally, individuals should begin this process around the age of 12, a time when they are still impressionable and open to learning new concepts. At this formative stage, young people are well-positioned to start setting clear, achievable financial goals that can guide their financial decisions for years to come. These objectives can encompass a variety of aspirations, such as saving for higher education, purchasing their first car, or even investing in a business venture. By focusing on long-term goals, young individuals can cultivate healthy financial habits early in life. For instance, if a student aims to save for college, they can learn the importance of setting aside a portion of their allowance or earnings from a part-time job. This practice not only promotes saving but also teaches them the concept of delayed gratification, where they learn to prioritize their future needs over immediate desires. Similarly, the goal of purchasing a car can inspire them to create a budget, track their spending, and identify areas where they can cut back to increase their savings.

Creating an annual financial plan serves as an essential roadmap for achieving these long-term objectives. This plan should outline specific goals, timelines, and actionable steps to reach each financial aspiration. By breaking down larger goals into manageable milestones, individuals can stay motivated and track their progress. For example, if their goal is to save a specific amount for college, they can set smaller, monthly savings targets that are easier to achieve. This systematic approach fosters a sense of accomplishment as they meet each milestone, reinforcing positive financial behaviors.

Understanding the significance of budgeting, saving, and investing is another crucial component of this process. Budgeting allows individuals to gain insight into their income and expenses, enabling them to allocate funds effectively towards their goals. Learning to save regularly instills a sense of discipline and responsibility, while investing introduces the potential for their money to grow over time. As they become more familiar with these concepts, they will develop a deeper understanding of how financial decisions impact their overall well-being.

As young individuals progress through life, the foundational skills they acquire during this time will not only empower them to achieve their financial aspirations but also instill confidence in their ability to manage money effectively. These skills are vital for navigating various life stages, whether it's managing finances in college, entering the workforce, or planning for retirement. Moreover, by establishing long-term goals early on, they will be better prepared to make informed decisions regarding loans, credit, and investments, ultimately leading to greater financial stability and success. In addition, establishing long-term financial goals can also foster a sense of purpose and direction. When young individuals have clear objectives, they are more likely to stay focused and motivated, even when faced with challenges or setbacks. This goal-oriented mindset encourages them to persevere and find creative solutions to financial obstacles, whether it's finding ways to increase their income or adjusting their budget to accommodate unexpected expenses.

Furthermore, these early experiences in financial management can lay the groundwork for a lifetime of sound financial practices. As they grow older, they will carry these lessons into adulthood, influencing their financial behaviors, investment strategies, and overall financial literacy. They will become more adept at analyzing financial opportunities, understanding risk and return, and making informed choices that align with their long-term goals. Ultimately, the process of establishing long-term financial goals at a young age is a powerful tool for personal development. It teaches young individuals the value of planning, the importance of financial literacy, and the necessity of proactive financial management. By fostering these skills early on, they can navigate the complexities of personal finance with confidence and competence, setting themselves up for a prosperous future.

- **Enhancing Financial Awareness**

Even if you feel content with your current financial situation and believe your financial plan is sufficient, taking the time to prepare an annual financial plan can significantly enhance your financial awareness. Engaging in this process allows you to analyze your income, expenses, and savings patterns in detail. By reviewing your financial situation annually, you can identify areas where adjustments may be necessary. This proactive approach leads to improved financial decisions, as you gain a clearer understanding of your financial health and the factors influencing it. Increased awareness also equips you with the knowledge needed to recognize financial opportunities and threats, enabling you to respond strategically.

- **Improving Financial Decision-Making**

An effective annual financial plan can greatly enhance the accuracy of your financial decisions. By adopting a strategic approach to your finances, you can align your spending and saving with your overall goals. The planning process encourages you to evaluate potential investments, consider the implications of major purchases, and weigh the benefits of different savings options. For instance, when contemplating a significant expenditure, such as a home or vehicle, having a well-structured financial plan allows you to assess whether this investment aligns with your long-term objectives or if it may jeopardize your financial security. With a solid financial foundation in place, you'll be better equipped to make informed decisions that support your aspirations, ultimately enhancing your overall financial well-being.

- **Adapting to Life Changes**

Life is dynamic, and your financial situation can change significantly due to various factors such as job transitions, family dynamics, or broader economic conditions. An annual financial plan provides the flexibility to adapt to these changes. By regularly reviewing and updating your financial plan, you can ensure it reflects your current circumstances and future aspirations. This adaptability is crucial for navigating unexpected expenses or shifts in income, allowing you to respond effectively and maintain control over your finances. For example, if a family member faces a medical emergency, having a solid financial plan enables you to allocate resources quickly and responsibly, alleviating stress during challenging times.

- **Tracking Progress and Accountability**

Another key benefit of preparing an annual financial plan is the ability to track your progress toward your financial goals. By setting measurable objectives and regularly reviewing your performance, you can hold yourself accountable for your financial decisions. This accountability fosters a sense of responsibility, motivating you to stay committed to your financial goals. Tracking your progress can provide valuable insights into your spending habits and savings behavior, helping you identify patterns that may require adjustment. For instance, if you notice that your entertainment expenses are consistently higher than planned, this insight allows you to make informed decisions about cutting back in that area to stay on track with your overall financial objectives.

- **Leveraging Resources and Tools**

In today's digital age, numerous resources and tools are available to assist in creating and managing an annual financial plan. From budgeting apps to comprehensive financial planning software, these tools can simplify the process and make it more accessible. By leveraging technology, you can streamline your financial management, allowing for more efficient tracking and planning. Furthermore, seeking guidance from financial advisors or attending workshops can provide additional insights and strategies for enhancing your financial plan. These resources can also help demystify complex financial concepts, empowering you to take control of your financial future with confidence.

In conclusion, the importance of preparing an annual financial plan lies in its ability to provide clarity, direction, and structure to your financial journey. By establishing long-term goals, enhancing financial awareness, improving decision-making, and adapting to life changes, an annual financial plan serves as a vital tool for achieving financial success. Whether you are just starting your financial journey or looking to refine your existing plan, taking the time to develop an annual financial strategy will undoubtedly yield significant benefits. This effort will lead to greater financial stability and a more secure future. Ultimately, the sooner you begin this process, the more prepared you will be to navigate the complexities of personal finance and work toward achieving your dreams. Through careful planning, you not only set the stage for financial success but also cultivate a mindset that values proactive financial management, equipping you to thrive in an ever-changing economic landscape.

## What is the Annual Financial Plan?

The annual financial plan is a map or guide of your current financial situation, what your financial goals are and what approaches you need to reach your goals. This plan takes into account every aspect of your financial life, from investments to taxes and retirement savings. While the starting point of an annual financial plan can vary according to age, income, assets and liabilities, the most important components of an annual financial plan are always the same.

### Life Events

Reaching special events in life, such as marriage and the birth of a child, are clear reasons that the financial plan should be reviewed. For example, if your children are in their teens, you should have seen their education savings in your financial plan. By the time your children reach adulthood, their college expenses will need to be paid for. On the other hand, if you are newly married, you should consider more cash for initial purchases and home repairs and improvements.

What kind of financial situation you have been in during the past year, according to the events that happened in your life and work, affects your financial plan. Also, retirement is another special life event that should be considered.

## Retirement and Investment

In fact, saving for retirement should be a priority in any age's financial plan, but unfortunately, this issue is often overlooked. However, a very small percentage of people have saved for their retirement. However, savings is not a financial plan but one of its components.

Retirement savings and how to use it effectively should be reviewed in the financial plan. For example, if you are currently paying pension insurance premiums, you should consider whether this will be enough for you when you retire. If you don't have a retirement account, you can use self-employment plans to pay insurance premiums or investment options in multi-year bonds. Your account balance, both in the savings account and the amount of your investments, should be mentioned in the financial plan. Obviously, retirement accounts should also be specified in the plan (Utami, 2017).

Beyond whether you have a retirement account or not, you need to see how your assets are allocated to different options. It is important to pay attention to what you spend your money on. Pay attention to upcoming or completed investment options. It may be time to sell OTC bonds, or you may need to increase your premiums. In addition, if you have a brokerage account in the stock market, you should review the diversity and balance of your investment portfolio.

Finally, you should consider increasing your retirement account balance with other investment options. For example, you can buy a property and save the rent received in your account or expand your business if you can increase the income through a side business or part-time business.

Savings for emergencies. While saving for retirement is a big part of financial planning, you can't ignore your other savings goals. If you don't have an emergency savings account or its amount is not enough, open a deposit account for this purpose or increase its remaining balance.

## Financial Planning Tools

In today's digital age, various financial planning tools and software are available in the market, designed to help individuals effectively manage their finances. These tools range from free budgeting apps to more comprehensive paid financial planning software, catering to different needs and preferences. If you are currently utilizing one of these programs for your financial planning, it's essential to evaluate whether it meets your specific requirements.

Start by assessing the features offered by the software you're using. Does it provide a clear overview of your income and expenses? Can it help you set and track your savings goals? Look for tools that offer budgeting capabilities, cash flow analysis, and investment tracking. You should also consider whether the software allows for customization, enabling you to tailor it to your unique financial situation and goals. Comparing different financial planning software can also be beneficial. Review the performance of various applications, considering factors such as user interface, ease of navigation, and available resources for financial education. Free budgeting apps may be suitable for individuals looking for basic tracking and planning functionalities, while paid options often provide more advanced features, such as tax planning, investment portfolio management, and financial forecasting. Additionally, consider the level of customer support and resources that come with the software. Some programs offer tutorials, webinars, and direct customer service, which can be invaluable for users who may need assistance in navigating the features. Ultimately, the right financial planning tool for you will depend on your personal financial goals, preferences, and the complexity of your financial situation. By investing time in selecting and utilizing the appropriate software, you can enhance your financial planning process, leading to more informed decisions and better overall financial management.

### Savings Goals for Next Year

When planning for your financial future, it's crucial to take a holistic view that encompasses your past, present, and future. Begin by reflecting on your financial history—analyzing past spending habits and savings patterns will provide valuable insights into your current financial situation. Next, consider your financial outlook: think about your expected income, potential expenses, and any upcoming financial commitments. By estimating your future expenses based on historical data, you can create a more accurate picture of the savings you need to achieve your goals.

To establish your savings goals for the coming year, start with the total amount you wish to save. Whether it's for a specific purchase, an emergency fund, or long-term investments, defining this target is the first step. From there, break down this annual savings goal into manageable monthly or weekly increments. This approach not only clarifies how much you need to set aside regularly but also offers a clearer view of your current savings status in relation to your future aspirations.

While developing a comprehensive financial plan can be time-consuming, it's a valuable investment in your financial well-being. You may find yourself confronting financial realities you've been avoiding, but addressing these truths is essential for growth. Once your financial plan is complete, you can make informed decisions regarding your spending and saving habits, ensuring that you stay on track to meet your goals. Ultimately, setting savings goals and formulating a financial plan empowers you to take control of your financial destiny. By committing to regular evaluations and adjustments of your plan, you position yourself for long-term success and financial stability.

## A Comprehensive Guide to Writing a Sales Plan

Designing a sales plan is a fundamental aspect of the sales management process, serving as a strategic blueprint that outlines how a business will achieve its sales targets and drive revenue growth. A well-structured sales plan not only provides direction for the sales team but also aligns the organization's resources and efforts towards common objectives. In an increasingly competitive marketplace, the importance of having a detailed sales plan cannot be overstated, as it allows businesses to identify opportunities, address challenges, and optimize their sales strategies effectively. The principles and techniques involved in sales planning encompass a range of essential elements, including market analysis, sales forecasting, target setting, and the formulation of strategies tailored to specific customer segments. These components work together to create a comprehensive approach that ensures all stakeholders are on the same page and that the sales team is equipped with the necessary tools and insights to succeed. This article will delve into the intricacies of creating an effective sales plan, exploring each element in detail and providing actionable insights to help businesses enhance their sales performance. Whether you are a seasoned sales professional or new to the field, understanding the nuances of sales planning is crucial for achieving sustained success and maintaining a competitive edge in your industry.

## What is Sales Planning?

Sales planning is a structured and systematic process designed to enhance an organization's ability to meet its sales targets and drive revenue growth. This process encompasses various key components, including sales forecasting, demand management, and the establishment of profit-based sales goals. Additionally, it involves the formulation of a sales promotion plan, which outlines specific strategies and tactics to boost sales performance. Essentially, sales and marketing planning involves organizing the activities and resources necessary to achieve the business objectives set forth by an organization. A well-crafted sales plan acts as a strategic document that not only identifies and defines these business goals but also outlines the various resources—such as personnel, budget, and technology—needed to achieve them. At its core, the sales planning process is about aligning an organization's sales efforts with its overall strategic objectives. It requires a deep understanding of the market, customer needs, and competitive landscape, which enables businesses to tailor their sales strategies accordingly. This comprehensive approach ensures that all aspects of the sales function are well-coordinated and focused on driving results.

## The Importance of Sales Planning

Sales planning is crucial for several reasons, as it lays the foundation for successful sales operations and overall business performance:

1. **Define a Set of Sales Goals:** Sales planning helps organizations establish clear and measurable sales goals, which serve as benchmarks for performance. These goals can range from increasing overall sales revenue to expanding market share or launching new products. By having specific objectives in place, sales teams can stay focused and motivated to achieve their targets.
2. **Choose Sales Strategies that Fit Your Target Market:** Understanding the target market is essential for developing effective sales strategies. Through the sales planning process, businesses can analyze customer demographics, preferences, and buying behaviors to select the most suitable approaches. This alignment between strategy and market needs increases the likelihood of success.
3. **Define Sales Tactics for Your Sales Team:** A well-structured sales plan breaks down high-level strategies into actionable tactics that sales teams can implement. These tactics may include lead generation techniques, customer engagement methods, and follow-up processes. By providing clear guidelines, sales planning ensures that team members know exactly what steps to take to achieve their objectives.
4. **Activate and Motivate Your Sales Team:** A comprehensive sales plan serves as a motivational tool for the sales team. By involving team members in the planning process and communicating the goals and strategies effectively, organizations can foster a sense of ownership and accountability. Motivated sales personnel are more likely to perform at their best and contribute to the organization's success.
5. **Determine the Steps to Achieve Goals and Budget Requirements:** Sales planning outlines the necessary steps to reach the defined sales goals, ensuring that all activities are organized and prioritized. Additionally, it allows businesses to allocate resources effectively, including budgeting for marketing initiatives, training, and other sales-related expenses. A clear budget helps manage costs and maximize return on investment.
6. **Periodically Review Goals and Improve Sales Approaches:** The sales planning process is not a one-time activity; it requires regular review and adaptation. By periodically assessing sales performance against the established goals, organizations can identify areas for improvement and refine their sales approaches

as needed. This continuous feedback loop ensures that the sales plan remains relevant and effective in a changing market environment.

In summary, sales planning is a critical function that provides structure and direction to an organization's sales efforts. By setting clear goals, selecting appropriate strategies, and implementing effective tactics, businesses can significantly enhance their sales performance and achieve sustainable growth in a competitive landscape.

## Why Does Having a Sales Plan Leads to Increased Sales?

Having a well-structured sales plan is paramount for driving increased sales and ensuring a seamless transaction process for all stakeholders involved, including sales teams, customers, and other participants in the buying process. A sales plan serves as a strategic blueprint that not only delineates the necessary steps for successful sales but also provides a comprehensive framework for managing these steps effectively. In a world where transactions can become increasingly complex, the likelihood of errors rises significantly; however, a well-crafted sales plan mitigates this risk by breaking the overall sales process into smaller, manageable components. This segmentation minimizes potential mistakes and enables more efficient management of sales activities, ultimately leading to improved performance and outcomes.

Introducing new products or consistently selling existing ones can often present considerable challenges for sales teams. The complexities and uncertainties associated with these tasks can deter some individuals from taking the necessary actions to drive sales. However, a well-defined sales plan equips salespeople with the tools, resources, and strategies they need to navigate these challenges confidently. By framing the sales plan as an investment opportunity, sellers are motivated to take proactive steps rather than remaining passive. This perspective encourages them to showcase their products effectively, aligning their selling techniques with customer needs and market trends. As a result, the sales team can accelerate sales activities, foster stronger relationships with clients, and ultimately boost overall sales figures.

Moreover, a sales plan serves as a diagnostic tool that helps identify weaknesses within the sales process. By pinpointing areas of underperformance, sales teams can implement targeted strategies to address these shortcomings. For instance, if data reveals that certain products are not performing as expected in a particular market segment, the sales plan can guide the team in revising their approach, such as adjusting pricing strategies, enhancing marketing efforts, or providing additional training to sales representatives. This cycle of continuous evaluation and improvement fosters an environment where the sales plan evolves and adapts over time, ensuring it remains relevant in a constantly changing market landscape. With a refined sales strategy, businesses can expect not only enhanced sales performance but also sustained growth in revenue, allowing them to stay competitive.

An important consideration in this process is the alignment of sales goals with the overall vision and mission of the business. Each organization must establish clear objectives regarding the value and usability of their sales program, ensuring these align with the features and benefits of the products they offer. This alignment is crucial because it helps ensure that every sales effort contributes to the broader goals of the organization. By regularly assessing the weaknesses in their sales plan and seeking expert guidance to address these issues, companies can develop a more robust sales strategy that responds effectively to market demands. Additionally, having a sales plan fosters accountability within the sales team. When specific goals and metrics are established, each team member understands their responsibilities and the expectations set for them. This clarity not only enhances individual performance but also promotes a sense of teamwork and collaboration. Sales representatives are more likely to support one another and share best practices when they are all working towards a common goal. Furthermore, periodic reviews of sales performance against the established plan can help motivate the team to stay focused and engaged, celebrating successes and learning from setbacks together. A sales plan is not merely a document; it is a critical framework that facilitates better transaction management, empowers sales teams, and drives ongoing improvement in sales performance. By investing in a comprehensive sales strategy, organizations create a proactive culture that embraces challenges and maximizes opportunities, ultimately leading to increased sales and long-term business success. The benefits of a well-executed sales plan extend beyond just improved sales figures; they include enhanced customer satisfaction, stronger team dynamics, and a sustainable competitive advantage in the marketplace. Therefore, every organization, regardless of size or industry, should prioritize the development and implementation of a robust sales plan to navigate the complexities of modern sales effectively and achieve their growth aspirations.

## When is it Necessary to Design a Sales Plan?

Designing a sales plan is an essential step for any business seeking to enhance its sales process or launch new initiatives. Whenever your organization defines or revises its sales process, it is crucial to create a tailored sales plan that aligns with your specific goals and strategies. This plan should comprehensively outline all products or services intended for sale, as well as the range of activities necessary to facilitate those sales. By providing a clear framework for the sales process, a well-structured plan ensures that every team member understands their roles and responsibilities, ultimately fostering better collaboration and execution.

One significant factor that highlights the necessity of a sales plan is whether your customers understand the buying process associated with your offerings. If the answer is negative, it is imperative to develop a detailed sales plan that articulates how customers can navigate the purchasing process. This plan should not only outline the steps involved in making a purchase but also include strategies for addressing common questions or concerns that potential buyers may have. Clearly communicating the purchasing process helps to reduce any potential confusion and reassures customers that they are making informed decisions. Additionally, the sales plan should focus on effectively convincing potential buyers that your product or service is the best option to meet their needs. To do this, you should emphasize the unique features and benefits of your offerings, showcasing how they can solve specific problems or enhance the customer's experience. Introducing similar projects or products that have proven successful can also help build credibility and increase the likelihood of a sale. By presenting customers with compelling evidence of your product's value, you create a persuasive narrative that encourages them to choose your offerings over competitors.

In scenarios where customers are already familiar with your brand and products, the necessity for an elaborate sales plan may seem less pressing. These customers likely have a clear understanding of your offerings, know whom to contact for purchases, and are accustomed to the transaction process. However, even in these familiar contexts, it remains essential to acknowledge that customers still value your expertise and guidance. Your sales plan should reflect this by positioning your sales team as knowledgeable partners who can assist customers in navigating their options. By demonstrating your industry expertise and providing tailored recommendations, you reinforce customer trust and increase the likelihood of repeat business. Moreover, identifying issues within the sales cycle is a crucial indicator that signals the need to revisit your sales plan. If you frequently encounter situations where potential customers express interest in your products but ultimately delay or avoid making a purchase, this serves as a clear sign that your sales plan may require refinement. These challenges may stem from misunderstandings about the product, concerns about pricing or quality, or a lengthy and cumbersome purchasing process. By thoroughly analyzing your sales plan, you can pinpoint the underlying weaknesses and implement necessary adjustments to enhance the buying experience.

Addressing these weaknesses proactively is essential in reducing delays and improving overall customer satisfaction. By taking the time to identify and rectify any issues in the sales process, you not only streamline the purchasing journey but also reinforce a positive customer experience. This, in turn, leads to increased customer loyalty and ultimately drives sales growth. For instance, if feedback indicates that customers find the purchasing process cumbersome, you might consider simplifying the steps involved or offering additional support, such as personalized consultations or online resources. Continuous evaluation and refinement of your sales plan are critical to adapting to market changes, evolving customer preferences, and the dynamic nature of your business environment. Regularly soliciting feedback from your sales team and customers can provide valuable insights into what is working well and what areas may need improvement. This iterative approach enables you to stay ahead of potential challenges and seize new opportunities, ensuring that your sales strategy remains effective and relevant.

## Sales Planning Steps

The sales planning process consists of 10 main steps, which are as follows:

1. **Determine the Purpose and Vision of the Business**

Start planning your sales team with your business goals and vision in mind. Write a brief history of your business, with this overall goal in mind, you won't get sidetracked in the next steps and designing the details of the sales plan.

2. **Designate Your Sales Team**

Define your sales team structure and then explain who is on your sales team and what their roles are. Perhaps you are responsible for managing 5 sales professionals or working with professional sales professionals. If you intend to make changes and increase the number of employees, job promotion or the timing of their start, include all these things in the sales plan.

3. **Getting to Know the Target Market of Your Business**

Regardless of whether you are writing your first or fifteenth sales plan for your business, you need to know the demographics of your target market. What are your best customers like? Do they all have the same business? Is the size of their organization similar? Do they have the same problems and challenges?

Keep in mind that different products and services may have different buyers. This part of your sales plan can change dramatically over time as your business solutions and strategies evolve and find the right market. In the early stages of the business, when your product was new and the prices of products and services were lower, you had successful sales to startups. Now that products and services are more stable and their prices are higher, middle markets are probably more suitable for your business. That's why it's important to constantly review and update your target market.

4. **Description of Tools, Software and Resources**

You should also include a description of your sources. Which software do you intend to use? Have you budgeted for sales and marketing campaigns? Do you have a plan to use CRM software?

In this stage of product sales planning design, you determine what tools your sales experts can use to succeed in their activities. (training, documentation, sales enablement tools, etc.).

5. **Business Positioning and Competitor Identification**

One of the important and basic steps in designing a sales plan is to identify competitors. Provide a comparison of your products with the products of the competing company and identify their strengths and vice versa. Also specify how their services and products are priced compared to yours. You should also be fully aware of market trends. If you offer advertising services, keep in mind that mobile programmatic advertising is a growing business. Try to anticipate how these changes will affect your business.

6. **Marketing Strategy**

In this section, which is also called strategic sales planning, specify the pricing and promotions you have planned for your products or services. What key actions are you taking to increase customer brand awareness and lead generation? Apply the influence of these factors in planning your sales increase.

7. **Prospective Customer Conversion Strategy**

How does your sales team evaluate the leads generated by your marketing strategy? Determine the necessary criteria and conditions for your potential customers so that if they are qualified, sales experts will contact them, and determine what introvert and extrovert sales methods your team should use to close the sale more successfully.

8. **Action Plan to Achieve Goals**

After determining the goal and sales plan, the ways and methods of achieving these goals are also important. Here are some examples for designing a referral sales program:

Goal: In these three months, increase the referral rate (collaboration in sales) by 30%.
- Conduct a referral techniques workshop.
- Hold a sales contest for referral sales.
- Increase referral sales commission up to 5%.

Goal: Add 20 new companies to your customers.
- Identify 100 prospects and assign the right sales professionals to convert these prospects.
- Hold two executive level events.
- Offer a bonus for the sales team that adds three new companies to existing customers.

9. **Goals**

Most sales goals are based on revenue. For example, you might set an annual gross income goal of $900. Alternatively, you can set a sales goal based on the number of sales. This goal can be attracting 100 new customers or 450 closed sales. Make sure the goals you set are realistic, otherwise your entire sales plan will be for naught. Factor in your product price, total reachable market, market penetration, and your resources (including sales volume and marketing budget).

Your goal should also be close to your business's strategic goals. To give you an idea, if the company is trying to gain more market share, your goal might be to "attract 20 large organizations rather than sell X number of products to new businesses" (because the latter encourages you to focus rather than focus). Just look for deals in the right type of customers) (Utami, 2018).

Of course, you will probably have more than one goal. Determine the most important, then prioritize the rest. If you have several areas covered, set specific goals for each of these areas. This makes it possible to evaluate the performance of each of these areas. Set your own schedule as well. Having regular benchmarks reassures you that you are on track to achieve your goals or that you need to work harder.

10. **The Budget**

Describe the costs associated with achieving your sales goals. which usually includes the following:

- Payment (salary)

- Sales training
- Sales tools and resources
- Marketing and sales campaigns
- Team activities
- Mission expenses
- Food

## How to Create a Functional Sales Program?

Designing a good and practical sales program is a complex and very basic task. Below are some questions that help design a practical and comprehensive sales program.

Questions related to the purpose of the collection in order to increase sales

In this section, some questions related to the goals of your collection are examined. If there is a clear definition of the collection's goals, the sales process can be improved.

- **What are your goals?**

People who don't have a goal can't expect their collection to increase sales. Your job as a sales representative is to define clear and big visions for your portfolio. In this way, the number of your customers will increase every day. If you have clearly defined your sales goals, you can use methods to increase sales and reach your desired result as quickly as possible.

- **What is your reason for customers?**

Usually, people don't buy for logical reasons. Rather, they buy a product for emotional reasons. Your product is a logical means to an end, but that end is often influenced by emotion. Your customer has a picture of the future in mind, and your product can help them get there. Creating a vision to talk about that future will help them understand why they should invest time and money in your solution.

- **Following this purchase plan, what changes will be made in the performance of your collection?**

With the help of this question, you can get clear visions for the future. If I sell my product to customers and they use it successfully, what major changes will need to be made to my portfolio business? Is it necessary to add to the number of troops? Is it necessary to hold regular training sessions? Is it necessary to make changes in the way of budget allocation? The important point for designing a sales plan is that all these questions must be answered. So, if you can answer these questions accurately and attainably, you will experience an increase in sales in your future work.

**Questions related to the process.**

These questions will help improve your sales process. The proper sales process plays a prominent role in increasing sales. Try to answer all the following questions in accordance with the group's vision and goals and clearly. Having a practical sales process is one of the main pillars of increasing sales.

- **Who is responsible for sales?**

The answer to this question depends on who your buyers are. On the other hand, the sales range of the collection will also be effective. In some cases, with the increase in sales, it is necessary to assign someone to the position of sales management to implement the sales process. One of the tasks of the sales manager is to identify competing companies and groups. If some of your customers tend to switch from your products to other products, you must identify the competing company and add their competitive advantages to your collection. This will improve the performance of your collection and thus increase sales.

- **What are your biggest challenges in sales?**

It is suggested that you identify the barriers to sales as soon as possible. With the help of this method, you will be able to fix your sales weaknesses and do all the necessary work to improve the sales process and, as a result, increase the sales of your products.

**What are the reasons why your customers do not complete this purchase?**
With the help of this question, you can prepare a secondary program for yourself. Ask your customers what makes them not buy from your collection. By doing this, you will identify the weaknesses in your services. Also, user feedback helps you to improve your app and compete with others to increase sales.

- **What is the personal goal of your customers?**

One of the most important questions that every person should ask their customers is what their purpose for is buying. By knowing this question, you can highlight the motivating factors of the deal. By doing this, you can assure your customers that this deal is in their favor and meets their needs. The longer the sales process is and the closer the buyer is to the end of the buying cycle, the more likely he is to get tired. By knowing motivational tips, you can convince him to accompany you to the end of the sales process.

**Necessary actions after designing a sales plan**

After you have created a sales plan for your collection, you need to do the following four steps:

- Ask your potential customers to review the prepared plan. It is necessary to present your sales plan to your customers and ask them how you can help them buy. In other words, make the shopping process easy and pleasant for them.
- Check the views of all the stakeholders of this sales plan and ensure that the interests and values of all the people will be preserved.
- Answer people's questions. Check all the weaknesses that people have in this sales program and try to answer them in the best way.
- Define the sales process by asking questions like the following:
    1- Who is your real buyer?
    2- Does the purchase process include signing a contract and other legal matters?
    3- Is there a need for excess information to be available to customers?
    4- What is the pricing method and how will it change over time?
    5- If additional documents or checks are required, how long will these procedures take?

A successful sales program will make your sales process as simple and fast as possible. The sales plan covers your collection prospects. By answering the above questions, you can strengthen your sales process at the most critical point and enjoy the increase in sales of your collection in the future. To implement each of the techniques mentioned above, you need a powerful sales tool, namely customer relationship management software. This software works from the initial stages of sales, i.e. evaluation of leads to the review of successful sales and the presentation of periodic sales reports, and makes your sales process agile, optimized, and effective.

## Sales Planning Manager Job Description[2]

A sales planning manager fulfills a leadership position by providing overall direction for a company's sales department and is expected to improve the sales department's performance by a certain percentage within a certain time. These managers define short-term and long-term sales plans for the team and help implement these plans, and then create goal frameworks to accurately measure these processes. They also monitor the performance of the entire department and provide reports to determine whether plans are being met or need to be modified. Based on the overall performance of the team, sales planning managers may change their sales planning principles or think of ways to increase efficiency and quality. They should analyze the strengths and weaknesses of their department to identify areas for improvement. They must also ensure that all the right tools are available to the sales team and forecast future performance by reviewing current performance and market trends that may affect sales team performance.

The Sales Planning Manager may work directly with customers, especially high-end customers, so strong customer service skills and strong marketing/sales skills are essential for success. To hire a sales planning manager, the minimum education required is a bachelor's degree and sufficient experience in the field of sales. It is also very important to have management skills (Anderson, 2016).

### Duties of Sales Planning Manager

- Managing and facilitating cooperation between different departments and divisions
- Performance evaluation of the sales program
- Development and analysis of advertising and commercial launch

One of the first steps in proper sales management is to determine the company's expectation level and make it clear to all team members. In CRM software, you can specify sales goals quarterly or monthly and efficiently advance your sales planning process and transform your team's sales.

# REFERENCES

Ha, K.-M. (2018). Changing the emergency response culture: Case of Korea. *International Journal of Emergency Services*, 7(1), 60–70. DOI: 10.1108/IJES-12-2016-0026

Heath, D., Ringgenberg, M. C., Samadi, M., & Werner, I. M. (2023). Reusing natural experiments. *The Journal of Finance*, 78(4), 2329–2364. DOI: 10.1111/jofi.13250

Anderson, D. (2016). *Organization development: The process of leading organizational change. Translated by SeyedNaghavi MA, Masoud Sinaki S, Kosar Z &Khosravi SH*. Koohsar Publication. [Book in Persian]

Peyravan, L. (2020). Financial reporting quality and dual-holding of debt and equity. *The Accounting Review*, 95(5), 351–371. DOI: 10.2308/accr-52661

- Utami, C. W. (2017). Attitude, Subjective Norms, Perceived Behavior, Entrepreneurship Education and Self-efficacy toward Entrepreneurial Intention University Student in Indonesia. European Research Studies Journal, 20(2), 475–495. - https://hbr.org/1996/11/the-questions-every-entrepreneur-must-answer

# ENDNOTES

[1] https://www.forbes.com/uk/advisor/investing/what-is-a-financial-plan/

[2] https://climbtheladder.com/sales-planning-manager/

# Chapter 6
# Financial Markets and Its Tips

## ABSTRACT

*Financial markets are one of the important sectors in the economy of any country as well as the global economy. Buying and selling is the most important event that happens in a financial market and causes money to flow. Financial markets are one of the important sectors in the economy of any country as well as the global economy. Buying and selling is the most important event that happens in a financial market and causes money to flow. Almost all countries have at least one formal financial market where stocks of certain companies are bought and sold. Of course, there are different types of financial market that we decide to learn about in this article. The stock market, the bond market, the foreign exchange market and the derivatives market are among the most important financial markets in the world, and hundreds of billions of dollars of money are moved in them every day.*

## INTRODUCTION

Financial markets form the backbone of both national and global economies, acting as critical hubs for the exchange of assets and the flow of capital. These markets, driven by the fundamental process of buying and selling, enable the movement of money from investors to businesses and governments, fostering economic activity and growth. Almost every country boasts at least one formal financial market, such as a stock exchange, where companies' shares are traded. Additionally, the financial market ecosystem comprises diverse categories, including bond markets, derivatives

DOI: 10.4018/979-8-3693-9415-1.ch006

markets, foreign exchange markets, commodities markets, and the rapidly emerging cryptocurrency markets, each playing a unique role in the financial system.

The scale of financial markets is staggering, with transactions amounting to trillions of dollars daily across various sectors. Traditional markets like the stock market and bond market remain foundational, facilitating corporate growth and government financing. Simultaneously, innovative sectors such as the cryptocurrency market are reshaping the financial landscape with decentralized technologies like blockchain.

Understanding financial markets is essential for participants at all levels—whether governments, corporations, or individual investors. These markets not only provide liquidity and investment opportunities but also play a pivotal role in shaping economic policies and business strategies. However, participation in these markets requires knowledge, training, and strategic planning to navigate their complexities and inherent risks.

This chapter explores the types of financial markets, their key features, and their critical functions. By examining major markets such as stocks, bonds, derivatives, and currencies, as well as emerging trends in digital currencies, we aim to provide a comprehensive understanding of how financial markets operate and their significance in the broader economic framework. This foundational knowledge will equip readers with the insights needed to engage effectively with these markets, leveraging their opportunities while managing associated risks.

## FINANCIAL MARKETS AND THEIR ESSENTIALS

Financial markets[1] are one of the important sectors in the economy of any country as well as the global economy. Buying and selling is the most important event that happens in a financial market and causes money to flow. Financial markets are one of the important sectors in the economy of any country as well as the global economy. Buying and selling is the most important event that happens in a financial market and causes money to flow. Almost all countries have at least one formal financial market where stocks of certain companies are bought and sold. Of course, there are different types of financial markets that we decided to learn about in this article.

The stock market, the bond market, the foreign exchange market, and the derivatives market are among the most important financial markets in the world, and hundreds of billions of dollars of money are moved in them every day. The digital currency market is also one of the emerging financial markets in the world that is growing rapidly and depends on decentralized technologies and blockchain. Stay with us to get acquainted with the types of financial markets and to better understand the uses and features of each one.

## What is the Financial Market?

A financial market is a place where buyers and sellers gather and buy and sell various assets. Financial markets allow money to flow from investors to businesses.

The financial market is a physical space or virtual platform where it is possible to buy and sell stocks, goods or other valuable assets. The nature of what is transferred between buyers and sellers and how it is done determines the type of financial market. For example, in the stock market, the shares of a few specific companies are publicly bought and sold among people, or in the "Foreign exchange market", what is exchanged between buyers and sellers, the currency of different countries. Is. In the following sections, we will talk in detail about each type of financial market.

Financial markets play an important role in facilitating economic affairs in countries that have a "Capitalist Economy" and provide the necessary resources and liquidity for businesses and entrepreneurs. Market participants, known mostly as buyers and sellers, can easily circulate their funds in these markets and invest in various assets. In simpler terms, financial markets allow money to flow from investors to businesses. In this way, after a few months or a few years, businesses prosper, and investors' property increases (Abdo, 2022).

Let's not forget that the stock market is only one example of the financial market, and buyers and sellers can operate in all financial markets such as bonds, currencies, derivatives, etc. Financial markets are highly dependent on information transparency. This information means sales reports, loans, debts, profits, spot prices, etc., which are reported on different platforms and analysts and traders make decisions based on them. We should also note that:

The price of stocks or other assets that are bought and sold in a financial market does not necessarily reflect the real value of that asset and can vary.

Due to the existence of financial circulation and the high volume of funds in such markets, each country has established specific and relatively strict rules regarding financial markets. Organizations implementing these platforms are required to submit regular periodic reports and comply with defined standards. If any violation of the rules is observed by companies, investors, brokers, banks, financial institutions, etc., heavy fines and restrictions will be applied.

For stock exchange and financial markets training, refer to stock exchange and investment training course.

## Types of Financial Market

As mentioned, there are different types of financial markets, some are small and limited to one country and some are international with trillions of dollars in turnover. In the following, we will get acquainted with the most important types of financial market.

## Stock Market

The stock market is one of the oldest and most common types of financial markets in the world. In this type of market, shares of certain companies are bought and sold publicly by different investors. The stock market is one of the oldest and most common types of financial markets in the world. In this type of market, shares of certain companies are bought and sold publicly by different investors. The purpose of selling shares of a company is to increase the amount of capital and liquidity of companies in order to develop their business. When a company's shares are offered for sale in the stock market for the first time, an "initial stock offering" or (IPO) is held and investors who believe in the activity of that company buy these shares. With the activity of the company and the provision of services or goods and the development of that business, the value of that company's shares will gradually increase, and the investors will benefit in this way (Ahlström,2021).

In general, buying stocks is a simple task, but distinguishing the desired stocks from among hundreds of companies, as well as the right time to buy, is a relatively difficult task. For this reason, working in the financial markets requires training, skills, and experience; Otherwise, it may cause irreparable financial losses to people.

Stocks are bought and sold on special platforms. Traders can operate in the stock market both in person at the stock exchange organization and offline using intermediary platforms called "Brokers". The broker provides an infrastructure so that buyers and sellers can easily access the information of the list of companies, the current price of shares, participate in the initial offering of shares, etc. and carry out their transactions. The broker receives a percentage of the transaction volume as a fee for each transaction.

New York Stock Exchange (NYSE), Chicago Stock Exchange (CHX), Nasdaq and IRAs are some examples of the world's largest financial markets in the United States. Tehran Stock Exchange is the largest stock market in our beloved country, Iran, which is about 45 years old.

## Bond Market

The bond market is a critical component of the financial system that facilitates the issuance and trading of bonds, which are a form of debt security representing a loan made by an investor to a borrower, typically a corporation or government entity. In essence, bonds are formal agreements that outline the terms of the loan, including the specified maturity date, which indicates when the principal amount will be repaid, and the interest rate (or coupon rate), which determines the periodic interest payments that the bondholder will receive. Bonds are primarily issued by large corporations seeking to raise capital for various purposes, such as expansion or operational funding, but they can also be issued by municipalities, states, and government agencies for projects like infrastructure development. The main purpose of the bond market is to provide the necessary capital for these projects and operations, allowing issuers to tap into a broad pool of investors. This access to capital helps diversify funding sources and potentially secures lower interest rates compared to traditional bank loans.

Operating much like a marketplace, the bond market enables the buying and selling of these securities, making them accessible to a wide range of investors—from individual retail investors to large institutional players like pension funds and mutual funds. Investors are drawn to the bond market for its fixed-income securities, which provide steady income and the preservation of capital, particularly in uncertain economic conditions. The bond market is often referred to as the debt market, credit market, or fixed-income market, reflecting the nature of bonds as instruments of debt where issuers incur liabilities while bondholders have claims to interest payments and principal repayment. It is important to note that the relationship between bond prices and interest rates is inversely proportional; when interest rates rise, existing bond prices tend to fall, and conversely, when rates decrease, bond prices usually rise.

While bonds are generally considered safer investments than stocks, they come with their own set of risks, such as credit risk (the possibility of issuer default), interest rate risk, inflation risk, and liquidity risk. Investors must carefully assess these risks when considering bond investments. The bond market is also segmented into various categories based on the type of issuer, credit quality, and maturity, including government bonds, corporate bonds, municipal bonds, high-yield bonds, and investment-grade bonds, each catering to different investor needs and risk appetites. Furthermore, the bond market is subject to regulatory oversight, ensuring transparency and protecting investors. Regulatory bodies, such as the Securities and Exchange Commission (SEC) in the United States, enforce rules governing bond issuance, trading, and disclosures. Overall, the bond market serves as a vital mechanism for raising capital and generating investment opportunities, contributing to economic growth and stability in the financial landscape.

## Derivative Market

The derivative market is a sophisticated segment of the financial system that deals with contracts whose value is derived from the performance of underlying assets, which may include stocks, commodities, currencies, interest rates, and market indices. Unlike traditional asset markets where actual assets are bought and sold, the derivatives market involves trading contracts that speculate on or hedge against the price movements of these underlying assets. As a result, derivative assets themselves do not possess intrinsic value; their worth is entirely dependent on the value of the assets they are linked to. This characteristic allows traders to engage in a variety of strategies that can amplify their exposure to price fluctuations without necessarily owning the underlying assets.

One of the primary advantages of the derivatives market over conventional stock trading is the ability to engage in more complex financial instruments, such as "Options Contracts" and "Futures Contracts." These contracts allow traders to bet on the future price movements of assets, providing opportunities for hedging risks and enhancing profit potential. For example, options contracts give the holder the right, but not the obligation, to buy or sell an underlying asset at a predetermined price before a specified expiration date. This flexibility enables traders to capitalize on both bullish (rising) and bearish (falling) market conditions, effectively profiting in a wide array of scenarios. Futures contracts, on the other hand, obligate the parties to transact at a predetermined price at a future date, allowing for price lock-in and risk management for both producers and consumers of commodities.

The derivative market also plays a crucial role in providing liquidity and facilitating price discovery in the broader financial markets. It enables participants to hedge against potential losses in their portfolios, thereby enhancing overall market stability. This is particularly significant for entities exposed to fluctuations in commodity prices, foreign exchange rates, or interest rates. By using derivatives, companies can manage their financial exposure and protect their profit margins against adverse market movements. One of the most notable venues for trading derivatives is the Chicago Board Options Exchange (CBOE), recognized as a leading platform in the United States. The CBOE provides a regulated environment for trading various derivative products, including options on individual stocks and indices. The existence of such exchanges helps standardize contracts, increases transparency, and ensures regulatory compliance, thus fostering a trustworthy trading environment. The derivative market is an essential aspect of the financial landscape that allows traders to engage in complex contracts, manage risks, and speculate on price movements without directly owning the underlying assets. With the potential for significant leverage and flexibility, it attracts a wide range of participants, from institutional investors and hedge funds to individual traders. However, trading in derivatives also comes with its own set of risks, including market risk, credit risk, and liquidity risk, necessitating a thorough understanding of the instruments and careful risk management strategies.

## Foreign Exchange Market

The Foreign Exchange Market, often referred to as "Forex" or "FX," is a vast global marketplace dedicated to the trading of national currencies against one another. Operating as one of the most significant components of the international financial system, this market facilitates the exchange of currencies such as the U.S. dollar, euro, British pound, Japanese yen, and Swiss franc. The sheer scale of the Forex market is staggering, with daily trading volumes exceeding $5 trillion. This volume not only eclipses that of all other financial markets combined but also highlights the market's pivotal role in global economic interactions. By enabling seamless currency exchanges, the Forex market supports international trade, investment, and travel, thereby underpinning the global economy.

One of the defining characteristics of the Forex market is its decentralized nature. Unlike traditional financial markets that operate through centralized exchanges, the Forex market relies on a vast network of electronic trading platforms, brokers, and financial institutions dispersed across the globe. This structure facilitates 24-hour trading, allowing participants from various time zones and regions to engage in currency trading at any time. The continuous nature of trading means that market participants can respond promptly to news and economic events that may influence currency values, making Forex one of the most dynamic and fluid financial markets available. Key participants in the Forex market include a diverse array of entities, each contributing to the market's depth and liquidity. Major banks, including financial powerhouses such as JPMorgan Chase, Citibank, and Deutsche Bank, are among the largest players, executing significant amounts of currency trading on behalf of their clients or for their own accounts. These institutions engage in transactions that can reach billions of dollars, influencing currency values and providing liquidity to the market. Additionally, central banks play a crucial role in the Forex market. They manage their countries' currency reserves and implement monetary policy, which can directly impact exchange rates. For example, when a central bank adjusts interest rates, it can lead to fluctuations in currency values, affecting both domestic and international economic conditions.

Beyond banks and central banks, capital management firms and hedge funds actively participate in Forex trading. These entities utilize sophisticated trading strategies to capitalize on currency fluctuations and manage risk. They often employ advanced algorithms and high-frequency trading techniques to identify opportunities in the market, aiming to generate profits from even the smallest price movements.

Furthermore, brokers serve as intermediaries, facilitating trades for individual investors and enabling access to the Forex market without requiring substantial capital or complex trading infrastructure. This democratization of Forex trading has opened up opportunities for ordinary individuals, allowing them to engage in currency exchange through accessible online platforms equipped with educational resources and trading tools.

The significance of the Forex market extends beyond its liquidity; it plays a crucial role in shaping global economic conditions. Currency fluctuations can influence trade balances, inflation rates, and economic growth. For instance, if the value of the U.S. dollar appreciates against the euro, American exports may become more expensive for European buyers, potentially leading to a decline in demand for U.S. products. Conversely, a depreciation of the dollar could enhance the competitiveness of U.S. goods in international markets, stimulating exports and supporting economic growth. Therefore, understanding currency movements is essential for businesses and investors alike, as these fluctuations can have profound implications for profitability and market positioning.

The foreign exchange market serves as a vital infrastructure for the global economy, enabling currency exchanges and supporting international financial transactions. Its decentralized structure, exceptional liquidity, and participation from a diverse range of stakeholders underscore its complexity and significance. As global trade continues to expand, the Forex market will remain an essential platform for managing currency risk and facilitating economic growth worldwide. The continuous evolution of this market, driven by changes in global economic conditions, technological advancements, and regulatory developments, ensures its relevance and importance in the ever-changing financial landscape. As investors and businesses navigate the complexities of international finance, a comprehensive understanding of the Forex market will be paramount for successful engagement in the global economy.

## Commodities Market

The "Commodities Market" represents a critical and dynamic sector of the global financial landscape, facilitating the trading of physical assets and goods that are essential for everyday life and economic development. Commodities, which are broadly classified into several categories, play a foundational role in global supply chains and economies. These categories range from agricultural products to energy resources, precious metals, and soft goods, each influenced by a distinct set of factors that contribute to the market's complexity.

"Agricultural products", for instance, form a major segment of the commodities market, with staple crops like wheat, corn, soybeans, and livestock such as cows and sheep representing key items. These commodities are essential for food supply chains globally, but their prices are highly sensitive to external variables like seasonal cycles, climate conditions, and global demand trends. Unpredictable weather patterns, such as droughts or floods, can drastically affect yields, leading to significant price volatility. Additionally, geopolitical factors, trade policies, and shifting consumer preferences further complicate the pricing of agricultural commodities, creating an environment where market participants must constantly monitor global events. "Energy commodities", including oil, natural gas, and coal, are another critical component of this market. These commodities are the lifeblood of modern economies, fueling industries, transportation, and households. The energy market, however, is known for its inherent volatility. Oil prices, in particular, can swing dramatically in response to geopolitical tensions, changes in government regulations, technological advancements in energy production, and supply-demand imbalances. For instance, conflicts in major oil-producing regions, such as the Middle East, or policy decisions by influential organizations like the Organization of the Petroleum Exporting Countries (OPEC), can lead to sudden price spikes or drops. Additionally, the ongoing global transition toward renewable energy sources is introducing new dynamics to this segment, as market participants must now consider long-term shifts in energy consumption patterns.

"Precious metals"—such as gold, silver, and platinum—occupy a unique space within the commodities market. These metals serve both as valuable investment vehicles and as hedges against inflation, currency devaluation, and economic instability. Historically, gold, in particular, has been regarded as a safe-haven asset, especially during periods of market turmoil or when confidence in fiat currencies declines. Investors flock to precious metals during uncertain times, driving up their prices as they seek to preserve wealth. Moreover, precious metals are widely used in industrial applications, from electronics to automotive industries, further influencing their demand and price movements. Another significant sector of the commodities market is "soft goods", which includes products like coffee, cotton, and sugar. These goods are essential in consumer markets and are heavily influenced by agricultural yields, climate conditions, and evolving consumer preferences. For example, changes in dietary trends, such as the growing demand for organic or fair-trade coffee, can directly impact market prices. In addition, events like poor harvests or disease outbreaks in key producing regions can disrupt supply and create price fluctuations, making the soft goods market particularly sensitive to global economic and environmental changes. While many transactions in the commodities market occur through the "Spot Market"—where traders exchange physical goods for cash, taking immediate possession—an even larger volume of trade happens in the "Derivatives Market". In this market, participants trade contracts based on the future prices of commodities rather than the physical assets themselves. This approach provides a more accessible and flexible way for traders to speculate on price movements without the logistical complexities of owning and managing the actual commodities. For example, a trader speculating on the price of oil in the derivatives market does not need to worry about the costs associated with transporting and storing barrels of oil. Instead, they can profit from price fluctuations through futures contracts or options, making the derivatives market a vital tool for hedging and speculative activities.

Major global exchanges, such as the "Chicago Mercantile Exchange (CME)" and the "Intercontinental Exchange (ICE)", play a pivotal role in facilitating commodity trading, both in the spot and derivatives markets. These platforms offer a structured and regulated environment for traders to engage in transparent transactions, contributing to price discovery, liquidity, and market stability. The existence of these exchanges also provides a standardized framework for pricing commodities, enabling market participants to hedge risks and speculate on future price movements more effectively.

The commodities market, with its vast array of goods and intricate price dynamics, is an essential component of the global financial system. It not only affects individual sectors but also influences broader economic trends, making it a critical area of focus for investors, policymakers, and businesses alike. From food security to energy supply, and from inflation hedging to industrial production, the commodities market underpins many of the fundamental aspects of modern life. Understanding its mechanisms, drivers, and potential risks is crucial for those looking to navigate this complex and often volatile environment.

## OTC Market

The OTC (Over the Counter) market is an essential and multifaceted segment of the global financial landscape, offering a decentralized and flexible environment for the trading of a wide range of financial instruments. Unlike traditional stock exchanges, which operate within a centralized and regulated framework, the OTC market functions without a designated physical location. Instead, it is conducted electronically, allowing participants to interact directly, facilitating the buying and selling of assets through a network of dealers. This decentralized nature distinguishes the OTC market from formal exchanges, such as the New York Stock Exchange (NYSE) or Nasdaq, where transactions are more structured and subject to stringent listing requirements.

One of the main advantages of the OTC market is its capacity to accommodate a broad array of securities and financial products, many of which are not listed on major exchanges due to their size, risk profile, or other factors. These securities can include stocks from smaller or emerging companies that do not meet the listing requirements of major exchanges, as well as penny stocks, which often trade at low prices and represent companies with high growth potential but also significant risks.

The OTC market provides a platform for such companies to raise capital and for investors to access potentially lucrative opportunities. However, the lower levels of regulation and transparency associated with these securities make them inherently riskier. Investors must conduct thorough due diligence to assess the viability and financial health of these companies before investing. Beyond equities, the OTC market is a key venue for trading derivatives such as "options, swaps, and forward contracts. These financial instruments are often customized to meet the specific needs of the participants, providing a high degree of flexibility that is not typically available on more formal exchanges. For example, a company might enter into a customized interest rate swap agreement through the OTC market to hedge against future interest rate fluctuations, tailoring the terms to suit its particular financial situation. This ability to customize financial contracts is one of the OTC market's greatest strengths, enabling investors and institutions to manage risk more effectively. However, the complexity and bespoke nature of OTC derivatives can also introduce significant challenges, as they are often harder to price and may lack the liquidity found in standardized exchange-traded derivatives.

Liquidity, or the ease with which assets can be bought and sold, is another critical feature that distinguishes the OTC market from traditional exchanges. The decentralized structure and lower trading volumes in the OTC market often result in lower liquidity, which can create wider bid-ask spreads. This means that the difference between the price at which a buyer is willing to purchase an asset and the price at which a seller is willing to sell it can be significant, making it more expensive and difficult for investors to execute trades quickly and efficiently. The implications of this reduced liquidity are particularly pronounced during periods of market stress or volatility, when it can become even harder to enter or exit positions without causing substantial price fluctuations. This stands in contrast to the more liquid environments of formal exchanges, where large volumes of standardized assets can be traded with greater ease.

The regulatory environment in the OTC market also differs considerably from that of formal exchanges. OTC markets are generally less regulated, with fewer reporting and disclosure requirements. While this lighter regulatory framework can offer greater flexibility to issuers and participants, it also increases the risk of transparency issues. Investors may find it more difficult to obtain accurate and reliable information about the securities being traded, making it harder to assess their true value. This lack of transparency can also open the door to price manipulation and fraudulent activities, as unscrupulous actors may take advantage of the reduced oversight to artificially inflate prices or mislead investors. As a result, those trading in the OTC market must be particularly vigilant and proactive in conducting their own research and due diligence to mitigate these risks.

Despite the inherent challenges, the OTC market continues to play a vital role in the financial ecosystem by providing liquidity and trading opportunities that may not be available on more regulated platforms. Institutional investors, hedge funds, and high-net-worth individuals frequently utilize the OTC market to execute complex trading strategies, hedge risk, or gain exposure to niche sectors and asset classes. For example, a hedge fund might use the OTC market to trade in emerging market bonds or exotic derivatives that are not available on mainstream exchanges, allowing it to diversify its portfolio and pursue returns that are not correlated with the broader market. In this sense, the OTC market serves as a "barometer of investor sentiment", offering insights into trends and market conditions that may not be immediately visible in more formal trading environments.

Furthermore, the OTC market provides access to a diverse range of securities, from foreign exchange (FX) and fixed-income products to commodities and structured financial products. Many companies and governments around the world rely on the OTC market to issue bonds, particularly in regions or industries where the infrastructure for formal exchanges is less developed. Similarly, the foreign exchange market, the largest OTC market in the world, operates around the clock, facilitating trillions of dollars in currency transactions each day. The FX market is a key component of international trade and investment, enabling businesses, governments, and investors to convert currencies and hedge against foreign exchange risk.

## Cryptocurrency Market

The cryptocurrency market has evolved dramatically in recent years, with more than 10,000 different projects now existing within the broader block chain ecosystem. Each of these projects is typically associated with a digital asset or "coin" that can be bought, sold, and traded on a variety of exchanges. This dynamic and rapidly growing market has become a crucial part of the financial world, reshaping how people perceive and interact with money, investment, and decentralized technology. At the heart of the cryptocurrency market is Distributed Ledger Technology (DLT), with block chain being its most prominent example. Block chain serves as the underlying platform for implementing a vast array of cryptocurrency projects, where digital currencies like Bitcoin and Ethereum are the most well-known. These currencies are built on decentralized networks, which allow transactions to be recorded and verified without the need for a central authority, such as a bank. This innovation has led to the development of new financial products and services, as well as greater opportunities for investors seeking to participate in the cryptocurrency space.

The backbone of the cryptocurrency market is composed of numerous crypto exchanges, which serve as platforms for trading these digital assets. These exchanges enable users to convert one cryptocurrency into another or exchange them for fiat currencies—traditional government-backed currencies like the U.S. dollar or the euro. Centralized exchanges (CEXs) are the most commonly used platforms for such transactions, where users' assets are held in wallets controlled by the exchange itself. While this model offers convenience and ease of use, it also poses certain risks, particularly in terms of security. Centralized exchanges have historically been vulnerable to hacking attempts, resulting in significant losses for users when security breaches occur. High-profile incidents like the Mt. Gox and Coin check hacks serve as reminders of the potential dangers of storing assets on centralized platforms.

In response to these concerns, Decentralized Exchanges (DEXs) have gained popularity. DEXs operate without a central authority, facilitating peer-to-peer (P2P) trading between users directly on the block chain. This structure eliminates the need for intermediaries to hold users' funds, thus reducing the risk of hacking or fraud. One of the key innovations enabling the smooth operation of DEXs is the use of Automatic Market Makers (AMMs), which rely on liquidity pools to facilitate trades. In this system, users provide liquidity by depositing their assets into smart contracts, which are then used to execute trades in a decentralized manner. This model has democratized access to liquidity and empowered individual users to participate in the trading process.

In addition to spot trading, where cryptocurrencies are bought and sold for immediate delivery, the cryptocurrency market also supports more complex financial products, such as options and futures contracts. These instruments allow traders to speculate on the future price movements of digital currencies, providing opportunities to hedge risk or amplify potential returns. The availability of such products has attracted more sophisticated traders and institutional investors to the cryptocurrency market, further solidifying its place within the broader financial landscape. However, despite the immense growth and innovation within the cryptocurrency space, the market remains highly volatile and speculative. Prices of cryptocurrencies can fluctuate dramatically within short periods, driven by factors such as market sentiment, regulatory developments, technological advancements, and macroeconomic conditions. For instance, Bitcoin's price has experienced multiple boom-and-bust cycles, surging to all-time highs only to crash soon after, reflecting the inherent risks associated with cryptocurrency investments. Moreover, regulatory uncertainty continues to be a significant factor influencing the cryptocurrency market. Different countries have adopted varying approaches to regulating cryptocurrencies, with some embracing them as legitimate financial instruments, while others impose strict restrictions or outright bans. Regulatory scrutiny is particularly focused on anti-money laundering (AML) and know-your-customer (KYC) requirements, as governments seek to ensure that cryptocurrencies are not used for illicit activities. The future of cryptocurrency regulation will likely shape how the market evolves, particularly as it becomes more integrated with traditional financial systems. As a result, navigating the cryptocurrency market requires a solid understanding of both its technological underpinnings and the associated risks. While the potential for significant returns is appealing, it is essential for investors and traders to remain cautious and well-informed about the projects they invest in, the platforms they use, and the broader market conditions. The market's decentralized nature, rapid pace of innovation, and evolving regulatory landscape make it both exciting and challenging, offering vast opportunities for those willing to engage with its complexities) Fallah, et al, 2024).

## THE STORY OF THE COLLAPSE OF FINANCIAL MARKETS IN THE ECONOMIC CRISIS OF 2008

In 2008 and early 2009, a major financial crisis occurred in the world, which is known as the "Global Financial Crisis". A set of various factors caused this to happen, one of the most important of which was the "Mortgage-Backed Security" (MBS) issue. MBS is actually a type of bond-like investment that pays investors periodic interest. In this method, the bank, as an intermediary, takes the money from the investor and pays it as a loan to the home buyers. MBS form a type of OTC market and generate a cash flow of loan repayments to investors.

According to some experts, the roots of this economic crisis go back to 1970. Because since then, banks were forced to allocate part of their credit in the form of "subprime mortgages" to support low-income groups.

The amount of credit considered for sub-loans increased over time. On the other hand, in 2000, the Federal Reserve (or the Central Bank of America) decided to reduce the bank interest rate to prevent economic recession. The set of these factors caused the banks' capital to decrease and, as a result, the credit required for sub-loans also decreased sharply, and on the other hand, with the increase in housing prices, a big bubble was created in the real estate sector.

This process continued for several years and due to the sharp increase in housing prices, the demand for such loans became more and more until the bubble burst and suddenly investors and borrowers realized that the amount of money they had to pay for the loan was much higher than the value of the property. is an opinion with the decrease in property prices, more people canceled loans, and every moment the credit of banks decreased more, and a phenomenon called "liquidity outflow" occurred in banks. The two big banks, Lehman Brothers and Bear Stearns, went completely bankrupt as a result of this crisis, and about 450 banks went bankrupt in the next 5 years. Some important banks were also able to survive this predicament by receiving the government's support package.

# CONCLUSION: FINAL WORDS

Financial markets play an important role in the world economy and individual countries and are a space for the flow of people's capital. In this section, we tried to introduce the types of financial market and examine their most important features. Trading in financial markets mostly takes place on platforms provided by brokers.

The largest volume of transactions is related to the foreign currency exchange market and the purchase and sale of common currencies of countries. The stock market is the most famous financial market and is a place for buying and selling shares of different companies. The purpose of the public sale of a company's shares is to provide the necessary capital for the development and advancement of that company's goals, and traders try to buy the shares of companies that are more likely to grow and, as a result, the price of their shares will increase in the future in order to achieve more profit.

Other financial markets include commodity market, bond market, OTC market and digital currency market. The digital currency market is only a decade old and growing rapidly. Most of the projects in this market are decentralized and based on blockchain technology(Arner,2020).

## Twelve Golden and Secret Tips for Success in the Financial Market

In general, to be successful in the financial markets, how to manage capital is one of the topics that every investor must learn and use in his transactions in order to succeed in the financial markets. In addition, he must know the risks of these markets in order to preserve the value of his capital, protect them from negative shocks and leave behind a successful performance in the financial markets by earning additional income. To achieve this goal, acquiring the necessary knowledge and training, capital management, and understanding market behavior and psychology are the three main things that should be paid attention to. Every person should know that success in financial markets requires years of training and practice and focus on personal psychology and analytical knowledge. We review some fundamental tips for success in the financial markets.

1. **Let's Learn**

Before entering any market, and especially entering the capital market, the investor must first receive the necessary training from reputable training centers and experienced consultants. It is only in this way that activity in the financial markets turns from a high-risk activity into an almost predictable and analyzable activity.

Through the training he receives, the investor learns to focus on capital preservation, i.e. survival (especially at times when the investor is looking to fluctuate from the market) and at the next stage, think about making a profit from the market. This is while non-professional investors prioritize profitability and therefore fail, but professional traders increase their capital by focusing on minimizing losses. In markets such as forex or the coin futures market, where the investor can trade with multiples of his capital, the sensitivity of the issue is much higher. Therefore, receiving training and equipping with the necessary expertise will make the investor to succeed in a financial market without getting involved in the excitement of transactions and try to make regular and logical transactions.

2. **Relaxation and Acceptance of Responsibility for Each Transaction**

Emotional performance in the market often causes investors to fail. In addition, fear and greed cause the biggest losses to investors' capital. A professional investor enters the market with knowledge and calmness, making success in the financial market of his choice more likely. This issue is very important for investors in the financial markets due to the risks we mentioned earlier.

3. **Estimate the Amount of Profit and Loss in Advance**

Before making any transaction, the investor must evaluate the amount of investment return as well as possible loss and determine how much loss he can bear for each unit of profit. Actually, before making the transaction, the investor has not yet taken any risk and can check the various profit and loss parameters. Not considering the loss limit and not monitoring the accounts will allow the loss to progress and a large part of the investor's capital will be lost. Using technical analysis is one of the useful tools to determine profit and loss limits.

Paying attention to Warren Buffett's inverse investment strategy says, "In the stock market, you pay a high price for something that everyone is bullish on." Professional investors know that, for example, when the value of a fundamental stock falls unrealistically, other market participants must have made a mistake in their analysis. They take advantage of this opportunity and start buying instead of selling to succeed in the financial market. It should be kept in mind that reverse investment is associated with risk, and in this way, the role of serious and specialized research should not be ignored. If a professional investor realizes that there is a solid fundamental reason behind the fall and decline and that this investment will not have a good outcome, he will not enter his capital into the market.

4. **Setting a Journal File**

Setting up a journal file and recording the monthly balance of the account can monitor the success rate of the investor in financial markets such as the stock market. This action will prevent past mistakes from being repeated. Successful investors never make the same mistake twice. In addition to this, the continuous record of profits and losses helps the investor to constantly perfect and improve the strategy and system he has chosen for trading.

5. **Adopting a Strategy and Continuously Improving It**

Investors and professional traders constantly use the feedback they get from their strategies to improve it in order to succeed in the financial market. They test different systems and patterns, estimate risk and profit, and focus on building their account. An effective strategy in the long run increases the percentage of successful and winning bets. Otherwise, if the strategies are not suitable, there is nothing capital management can do. An effective strategy should know why it wants to enter the trade and be able to estimate the profit relative to the risk. This strategy allows the investor to determine how much risk he is willing to take in order to make a profit and determine in advance how long he intends to trade. A professional investor knows that short-term strategies cannot be traded for a long period of time, and he has a plan for himself if he encounters a problem during the trade, and finally knows when to exit the trade.

6. **Writing the Market Exit Strategy and Acting on It**

One of the common mistakes of investors is insisting on holding a losing trade. They want to give the losing trade a chance to make a profit, while the so-called "first loss is the best loss". In fact, you should not be biased on a transaction or a share.

7. **Daily Schedule**

It is very important for investors to plan and develop detailed plans for how to operate. Professional planning means being ready to trade at specific times. Investors and professional traders usually follow a specific time table for trading. In addition, before starting to trade, it is necessary to have a glimpse of the news and an understanding of the market situation, because the regular control of the market situation and its use in order to identify suitable investment platforms can bring more success in the financial markets.

8. **Backup Budget**

Another important point is to allocate a part of your capital as a backup budget. This can ensure the security of your financial and economic activities during economic crises and its impact on the stock market.

9. **Borrowed Capital**

Small investors usually do not take the risk of trading with money that does not belong to them!

10. **Reliable Sources of Information**

Sometimes inaccurate and wrong information given to investors is due to ignorance. But sometimes people knowingly lead novice investors to the bottom of losses to achieve their own benefits. Currently, there are sites, Telegram groups and other media, which in some cases even have many followers. Investors should be aware that they cannot solely rely on these sources because they may provide incomplete information. So, what is important is that you, as an investor, be careful in choosing your advisor and know who the advisor you are looking for helps and in which part of the capital market he/she specializes in. The consultant should pay attention to the amount of capital that you want to enter into the market and determine which direction is suitable for you.

11. **Profits of Professional Traders**

People with access to inside information (Inside Information), middlemen and basket makers and the like earn is not representative of the profit that ordinary people earn, this should not be considered as an indicator of profitability and success in the financial markets. Besides, the excess profit (that is, beyond the profit proportional to the risk in the long term) in the stock market is a "zero sum game", that is, one person will win and one person will lose; As in a bet on a horse race, not everyone will win. Many studies show that early movers and early exits are likely to be winners and those who enter the market during asset bubbles are likely to be losers. Non-professional and untrained traders active in financial markets eventually exit this market with a loss on average. so try to win out of the game.

12. **Choosing the Right Option in the Stock Market**

To choose the best trading position in any market, one should have economic studies and high analytical power and be aware of the mechanism of that market. For example, in the stock market, the pressure of demand or the influx of hot money in the paper market can raise the value of a company's stock higher than its intrinsic value in the short term, but this happens in the short term because the value of the company's stock in the long term cannot increase. The real value of the tangible and intangible assets of the company is far away. In the case of large companies active in mature stock market industries such as petrochemicals, this issue is more tangible because these companies are usually so mature that their growth capacity has reached the lowest level and their stock value in the long term is close to the current value of tangible assets. However, companies active in growing industries and relying on new technologies, such as Internet service providers and pharmaceutical companies, since they have more growth options, their stock value in the long term can stand at a higher level than the current value of assets (Banga,2019).

## Increase Income with 8 strategies That Fill Your Pocket with Money

Zig Ziglar, an American author and professional seller believes: "All life is not money, but the importance of money is something like oxygen." When it comes to money and increasing income, most people start chanting and mention spirituality, of course spirituality has its place, but the issues should not be mixed. So read this article to see how you can easily increase your income.

Money does not bring happiness, but lack of money creates a thousand and one problems. When we don't have enough money to live, water and electricity bills... on the one hand, house rent on the other hand, and a thousand and one other expenses bend our backs... Yes, money and income are an important part of life. We must stop chanting. Many people believe that money is the root of corruption, the rich are greedy, money does not bring happiness and... All these are clichéd and repetitive statements that are violated by numerous examples. There are many rich people in the world who with their financial ability have led to the flourishing of talents, treatment of diseases and creation of facilities for their fellows. So, money in itself is not a bad thing, but the approach and way of using it has created these edges and a negative image for it. Increasing income and becoming rich requires hard work, effort and thought. A valuable process that helps your talents grow and flourish in life. We all have 24 hours in each day, so how do some people get rich and increase their income more and more day by day? The differences are in people's approach and way of looking. Here are some ways to increase your income.

1. **Quit What You Don't Like**

If your job doesn't pay much and doesn't suit your dreams and lifestyle, leave it. What makes you do something that is painful for you? It is true that the state of the job market is not encouraging but admit that efforts and ideals together have an amazing result. If you do what you love, you will find more income and success.

2. **Your Value is Not Worth Your Money**

Financial issues have nothing to do with your values. Never let the number of zeros in your bank account be the proof of your character and respect. An increase in income and wealth is not a sign of your personal and spiritual values. Tie yourself to strong and important values in your life. If your pocket is empty, it could be because of your circumstances or lack of work, but with a little effort and persistence, you can improve the situation. Whatever economic situation you are in, it is only your lifestyle that shapes your life and it has nothing to do with your pocket.

3. **Prioritize Income Generating Activities**

When you plan your weekly schedule, prioritize profitable and profitable activities. According to Pareto's law, 80% of events come from 20% of events. In simpler words, 80% of your income comes from 20% of your activities. Think about this 20%. Which economic activities generate the most income for you? If you are on a good career path, don't let anything stop you from increasing your income.

4. **Know the Value of Time**

Time is gold and it is worth much more than money. The lost money may be put back in the safe, but the lost time will never be returned. Do not underestimate the value of time. Get up early in the morning, have a precise schedule for your work. When you have a detailed plan, you are several steps ahead of others and you will get more done during the day. Don't leave things from today to tomorrow, don't say that I will start tomorrow, there is still time and... Especially in today's competitive market, you will only win if you move early.

5. **Practice Saying No**

Steve Jobs said: "The secret of Apple's success has been our ability to say no to unnecessary things." Practice the art of saying no. If you see that increasing your responsibilities does not contribute to increasing your income, do not accept them. Invest in a job that will increase your income. Say no on time and don't waste your time.

6. **Hang Out with the Rich**

Our behavior becomes like the people we hang out with. If you hang out with the rich, you will understand their thinking system better. You will learn their attitude and you will find better and more opportunities to increase your income and work. Hang out with the rich, sit and stand and try to learn their tricks to increase income and generate money and wealth.

7. **Stop Making Excuses and Making Excuses**

Instead of making excuses for your low income and making excuses that blame the earth and time for your lack of money, just act. Your energy is depleted by negativity and making excuses. Put your focus and energy to achieve your goals, make your determination and move forward with effort.

8. **Change Your Look**

It is accepted that the economic situation is bad and there are a thousand and one other problems. But try to change your perspective. Don't think you are a victim. If you want, you can take control of your situation. Do not think about the past and your previous mistakes. Don't point the blame so much at the boss and this and that. Look at the world a little kindlier. The moment you take full responsibility for your life is the moment you begin to succeed.

The difference between low income and increased income is in action. Be a man of action. Think about getting rich, think about increasing your income and try. Get rid of negative energies. There is definitely a way to improve. You just have to find it. make a decision A little more persistence and difficulty is needed to increase income. But the result will definitely be sweet and desirable. At whatever level of literacy and skill you are, there is a way ahead of you. Think about your skills and abilities and strengthen them if necessary. By trying and being in the environment of activity and work, more opportunities will arise for you. Put aside laziness and fear. In most cases, the fear of starting work is the main obstacle to success (Battiston,2021).

## Sixteen Suggestions to Increase Income During Recession

McGill University's research on 600 companies working in different fields showed that companies that improved their advertising and marketing budget during the recession were more than 255% more successful in their sales than companies that did not spend this part of the budget. They cut or reduced them. The superiority of these companies has mostly continued in the post-recession era. It is important to be able to perform at your best at all times. The new life literacy lesson suggests 16 very important ways to work and earn money during the recession:

1- During recession, your company's strategy should be "survival" before anything else and not "maximum profit"; Until you accept this fact, you will not be able to have a good life during the recession. So, in the first step, redefine your strategy realistically.

2- Review the company's expenses again and very obsessively and see which expenses can be cut or reduced; Cost management has far more value than increasing income; Act decisively on this matter.

3- Customers of businesses during the recession usually do not stop their shopping but limit it. Therefore, selling becomes more difficult than before.

In such a situation, you should try to adapt to the limitations of the customers and maintain their loyalty by serving them more, otherwise they will go to the competitors. Things like these can help you retain loyal customers:

- Providing appropriate and even long-term discounts (instead of reducing the price)
- Leasing
- Sale with bonus
- Presenting offers

4- Diversify your product portfolio and include cheaper goods and services. For example, if you own a supermarket, bring cheaper pasta, or if you are a language teacher who gives private lessons, from now on accept classes of 5 people so that the costs are divided among your students, or if you are a consultant, you can In addition to the usual one-hour consultations, include limited 20-minute consultations at a low price (for example, in such a way that the client gives you his problem in advance on a typed page so that you have more time to give advice in a limited time Of course, this is just an example and maybe the regulations and requirements about counseling require a different way). Obviously, the meaning of cheap and expensive is different in every business. If you are a seller of luxury watches, you may be able to retain some of the previous customers by bringing 5 million dollars watches alongside the existing 10-20 million dollars watches, but in a sandwich by including cheap falafel next to hamburgers. Think customer.

5- During the recession, people pay more attention to the prices and compare them with the balance of their bank cards than they pay attention to the appearance and beautiful packaging. Therefore, if you are a manufacturer - especially in general items - try to lower the cost by reducing the cost of packaging.

6- Never fall into the trap of reducing prices by reducing quality. This decision will destroy your brand, and even if you manage to survive the recession, you will no longer be trusted.

7- Ask your company's staff to share with you if they have creative suggestions to improve the situation and reduce costs. Consider a suitable reward for actionable suggestions.

8- During the recession, the morale of your forces may decrease. As a compassionate leader, you need to have real—not show—companion and empathy with your troops. Humane treatment of troops as members of a family can keep them together and by your side.

In some places, it is necessary to tell them some parts of the problems so that they do not have the misunderstanding that you are confiscating the fruits of their work unfairly, but the problem should not be presented in such a way that it scares them about the future and disappoints them. slow

9- Check how you can use virtual space to develop your sales; This point is very important and vital.

10 - The first thing many managers do when faced with a recession is to cut or reduce advertising and marketing budgets.

McGill University research on 600 companies working in different fields showed that companies that improved their advertising and marketing budget during the recession were more than 255% more successful in their sales than companies that did not spend this part of the budget. They cut or reduced them. The superiority of these companies has mostly continued in the post-recession era.

Effective advertising and marketing can help during a recession when customers are confused and confused, especially since many competitors have mistakenly reduced or cut their advertising and marketing budgets, and you can be seen better and easier.

11 - Strengthen communication with customers. We suggest you use a CRM software. CRM means customer relationship management and in order to manage this relationship well, there are software in the market that if you choose and act well, you can increase your sales.

12- If normally your sales in one city meet the needs of your company, check if you can expand the geographical range of your products during the recession?

13 - Numerous researches show that during the recession, family solidarity increases (for example, instead of buying new shoes for himself, the father buys one of the family necessities, or instead of going to a restaurant four times alone, once he goes to a restaurant with his family or his mother prefers to replace their broken refrigerator instead of buying gold). So focus on family values instead of individualism in your ads.

14- Support your distribution network more so that they have more motivation to distribute your product. They are your frontline troops.

15 - During the recession, many competitors lose their efficient forces, if you can attract them, you have made a long-term investment for your company. So be aware of the dismissals of competitors and of course keep your key forces.

16- Update your work and business knowledge. Also, learn about marketing, branding, advertising, etc. You will definitely find attractive ideas for the prosperity of your business and get ahead of your competitors.

# REFERENCES

AL-Barakani, A., Bin, L., Zhang, X., Saeed, M., Qahtan, A. S. A., & Hamood Ghallab, H. M. (2022). Spatial analysis of financial development's effect on the ecological footprint of belt and road initiative countries: Mitigation options through renewable energy consumption and institutional quality. *Journal of Cleaner Production*, 366, 132696. DOI: 10.1016/j.jclepro.2022.132696

Ahlström, H., & Monciardini, D.: The regulatory dynamics of sustainable finance: paradoxical success and limitations of EU reforms. J. Bus. Eth. (2021). DOI: 10.1016/j.jclepro.2022.132696

Arner, D. W., Buckley, R. P., Zetzsche, D. A., & Veidt, R. (2020). Sustainability, FinTech and financial inclusion. *European Business Organization Law Review*, 21(1), 7–35. DOI: 10.1007/s40804-020-00183-y

Banga, J. (2019). The green bond market: A potential source of climate finance for developing countries. *Journal of Sustainable Finance & Investment*, 9(1), 17–32. DOI: 10.1080/20430795.2018.1498617

Battiston, S., Dafermos, Y., & Monasterolo, I. (2021). *Climate Risks and Financial Stability* (Vol. 54). Elsevier.

Fallah, M. F., Pourmansouri, R., & Ahmadpour, B. (2024). Presenting a new deep learning-based method with the incorporation of error effects to predict certain cryptocurrencies. *International Review of Financial Analysis*, 95, 103466. https://www.forbes.com/uk/advisor/investing/what-is-a-financial-plan/. DOI: 10.1016/j.irfa.2024.103466

# ENDNOTE

[1] https://www.investopedia.com/terms/f/financial-market.asp

# Chapter 7
# Financial Intelligence

## ABSTRACT

*It has happened to many of us that in the economic conditions we are in, we cannot make the right decision where to invest so that we can get a good profit? Or at least how can we maintain the value of our money? The answer to all these questions is one word: financial intelligence. It is the ability of financial intelligence that can give us the power to know when and where to invest, so most of us are losing out by not having the knowledge of financial intelligence in our lives. In this section, we tried to explain the topic of financial intelligence to you in detail. One of the types of intelligence is called financial or economic intelligence, which is related to financial issues. In fact, this type of intelligence is used to diagnose and provide solutions to improve economic and financial problems.*

## INTRODUCTION

In today's challenging economic environment, many of us struggle to make informed decisions about where to invest or how to preserve the value of our money. Questions such as, "How can I ensure a good return on investment?" or "How can I prevent the devaluation of my savings?" often arise. The answer lies in developing financial intelligence. Financial intelligence is the ability to analyze economic conditions, understand financial systems, and make sound decisions that enhance financial stability and growth. This capability enables individuals to navigate complex financial landscapes, mitigate risks, and seize opportunities, thereby improving their overall financial well-being. Without a solid foundation in financial intelligence, people often miss out on maximizing their wealth potential. In this section, we delve deep into the concept of financial intelligence, exploring its various dimensions, significance, and practical applications. By enhancing your financial intelligence, you can make smarter choices about earning, saving, bud-

DOI: 10.4018/979-8-3693-9415-1.ch007

geting, leveraging, and improving financial literacy, ultimately leading to greater financial security and prosperity.

## FINANCIAL INTELLIGENCE

It has happened to many of us that in the economic conditions we are in, we cannot make the right decision where to invest so that we can get a good profit? Or at least how can we maintain the value of our money? The answer to all these questions is one word: financial intelligence.

It is the ability of financial intelligence that can give us the power to know when and where to invest, so most of us are losing out by not having the knowledge of financial intelligence in our lives.

In this section, we tried to explain the topic of financial intelligence to you in detail. One of the types of intelligence is called financial or economic intelligence, which is related to financial issues. In fact, this type of intelligence is used to diagnose and provide solutions to improve economic and financial problems.

### High or Excellent Financial Intelligence

High or excellent financial intelligence refers to a heightened ability to analyze financial situations and make informed decisions that enhance one's financial well-being. People with high financial intelligence are adept at understanding complex economic conditions and can make sound decisions that lead to improved financial stability and growth. They possess the skills to allocate resources efficiently, manage risks effectively, and seize investment opportunities that align with their long-term financial goals. Financial intelligence encompasses the ability to analyze market trends, grasp the intricacies of cash flow management, and leverage financial tools to make strategic moves. Those with high financial acumen not only thrive in stable financial environments but are also resilient in the face of economic challenges such as inflation, market volatility, and fluctuating interest rates. Their enhanced decision-making ability enables them to navigate these challenges with greater confidence, making adjustments to their financial strategies as necessary.

Moreover, high financial intelligence involves long-term planning and the ability to create effective financial strategies for various life stages, such as retirement, higher education, or major investments. People with this level of intelligence can forecast financial outcomes, set realistic financial objectives, and adjust their actions to meet these goals. They tend to have a comprehensive understanding of how different financial factors, such as taxes, investments, savings, and debt, interact and affect overall wealth creation.

Ultimately, financial intelligence allows individuals to optimize their wealth-building potential, minimize financial risks, and achieve greater financial security over time. Whether it's managing personal finances or guiding business-related decisions, a high level of financial intelligence empowers individuals to take proactive measures to safeguard and grow their wealth.

## Low or Poor Financial Intelligence

It means that you are taking irresponsible measures in front of your financial issues. This article contains the methods and advice of Robert Kiyosaki, the great self-made billionaire investor and the author of the enduring book "Rich Dad, Poor Dad". His thought about the concept of financial or economic intelligence has helped many people around the world to create wealth using their creative ideas and experience getting rich in life(Zhang,2019).

For example: when you don't have a way to increase your income, or on the contrary, when you have enough money and capital, but you don't have enough knowledge to use it, you can solve these problems by using "financial or economic intelligence" correctly. Find the right solution for generating income. It is a fact that money and capital are the needs of every person to have a peaceful life.

For this reason, one of the most important issues in life that should be paid attention to is financial intelligence. Therefore, you should try to strengthen the financial intelligence that exists within everyone to be able to generate more and better income.

For example, the:

I will describe one of the things that people with high financial intelligence do.

Suppose you are buying and selling a certain commodity, then you will be called a trader. Merchants pay more commissions to brokers, in the meantime, individuals and property management allocate part of the transaction profit according to the law. If you have good tax intelligence, you can reduce a significant percentage of these costs.

If you properly understand the concept of capital, debt, income and expenses in a financial flow, your chances of becoming rich will increase greatly. "Robert Kiyosaki" divided human intelligence into several parts in modern psychology. One of the human intelligences, which many professors all over the world have recently highlighted its importance and use, is financial intelligence.

Financial or economic intelligence, or in our own language, economic intelligence

The definition of financial intelligence from Mr. Robert Kiyosaki's point of view "is the set of diagnosis, decision and actions that a person uses in order to financially manage his life and his business"

The quality of your financial situation today depends on the quality of growth and development of your financial intelligence from childhood until now. It is interesting to know that a child's financial intelligence is a copy of the financial intelligence of parents and relatives. Later, a person's financial and economic investment intelligence changes in response to future experiences, positive or negative, which finally takes a personal and special form in adulthood. It means that each of us at any age has a specific financial personality and we act based on our financial belief system.

## Definition of Financial or Economic Intelligence

Robert Kiyosaki in his book "Increase Your Financial Intelligence" writes: "It is not real estate, stocks, savings funds, businesses or money that make people rich. It is information, knowledge, reason and thought that make people rich. Or in other words, it is financial intelligence that makes people rich.

He reminds that, for example, if you want to gain enough skill in doing a certain sports activity. Buying the equipment will not help you but you must be trained to be successful. Education plays a very important role in this process.

## Classification of Financial or Economic Intelligence

Robert Kiyosaki divides financial or economic intelligence into 5 things, which we ask you to pay attention to:

1. **Earning More Income**

This is measured by the amount of money you earn.

2. **Saving Money**

Once you earn an income, you need to keep it. Protecting money, especially against taxes, is the second aspect of financial or economic intelligence.

3. **Money Budgeting**

Kiyosaki writes, "The ability to live a good life while investing regardless of how much money you make requires a high level of financial intelligence." This area of financial or economic intelligence is measured by the amount of money you have left over after paying your expenses.

4. **Leverage for Money**

This area of financial or economic intelligence is measured based on investment returns. How have you allocated your surplus money to get more wealth? "

5.  **Improving Financial Information**

Financial intelligence doesn't just mean knowledge of financial concepts – it also includes detailed information about your investments. Financial or economic intelligence is a bridge to getting rich. Do you have financial or economic intelligence? Does money make you rich?

We all know that people who work very hard every day earn more money, but they never become rich! Even many of them become more in debt and have more financial problems. We've all heard the stories of winning the lottery, where people become rich completely by accident.

Some others make a profit and become rich by buying a house or buying various places in a short period of time. On the other hand, we hear that many people make losses by buying securities or gold coins and lose all their profits and capital at once. But there are many other people whose wealth increases every day.

Although they may spend even less time on their work, their wealth is increasing day by day and their lives are becoming more prosperous and luxurious. what?

Financial intelligence is the answer to all these phenomena and these developments. Those whose lives suddenly change did not do magic or witchcraft. In this section, we want to introduce you to our financial intelligence. So that you can do great things and welcome the society of the rich. Many people who are looking for money and wealth think that getting rich has a magic or magical methods and formulas, but I tell you it is not like that at all. The only thing that makes you rich is your financial intelligence, how much and to what extent you have recognized it and been able to strengthen it. There are different ways to strengthen financial intelligence, which are different for each person depending on the type of life conditions and personal skills of that person(Qin,2020).

- But what are these ways of strengthening financial intelligence?
    Can it be trusted?
    Is financial intelligence enough to get rich?

## The First Area of Financial Intelligence: Making More Money

Robert Kiyosaki says: "Many people fail to build wealth and earn more because they want money without work. What many people don't understand is that it's the process that leads them to wealth, not money.

You can increase your money only by learning how to earn money.

For each person, this process will be different. Each of us has different goals, dreams and ambitions. The important thing is to find the best way to earn more money and set your goals accordingly. To earn more money, you also need to control your emotions.

You must learn to force yourself to be content. Do not waste your financial future for a few dollars. Never give up. Moving forward may seem very difficult at times, but if you have confidence along the way, you can also solve your problems. Focus your mind on your goal and find a way to achieve it.

## The Second Area of Financial Intelligence: Saving Money

Once you start earning, you need to protect it from "financial predators". Kiyosaki says you should protect your money against these 6 things:

1. **Government Officials**

Robert Kiyosaki acknowledges the need to pay taxes (legally) with government officials. His only emphasis is to pay as little tax as possible.

2. **Bankers**

Banks are constantly trying to take your money as deposits bit by bit.

3. **Stockbrokers**

Similarly, stockbroker fees can end up being your wealth. Often, the purpose of buying and selling stocks for brokers is to earn more commissions.

4. **Businesses**

"All businesses always have something to sell you," says Kiyosaki. Their job is to get you out of your money, and your job is to keep your money. Robert Kiyosaki advises you to ask yourself when buying a device: "Does having it make you poorer or richer?!" "

5. **Relationships**

Money plays a key role in any relationship. You need to trust your partner and reach a mutual understanding of finances.

6. **Lawyers**

Finally, it's important to keep your money out of legal trouble.

*Some Guaranteed Methods to Strengthen Financial Intelligence*

Most people don't start trying until they hit a dead end in life. Like the famous phrase that says: "You don't appreciate something until you lose it", I am one of these people. I usually don't think about it until there is a problem.

I remember when I was studying, I didn't study until the night of the exam. The night of the exam was a nightmare for me, I had to stay up until midnight and study. In my sophomore year of high school, when I received my report card, I had failed several courses. I remember that in the summer of the same year, I studied calculus so that I could get good grades. After seeing the results, my father turned to me and said you could get such grades, why didn't you get these results in June? My father was right, I was not far-sighted.

## The Third Area of Financial Intelligence: Money Budgeting

There are two ways to solve the budgeting crisis:

1. You need to cut your expenses
2. Increase your income

Both methods address the budget deficit. But like many people, Robert Kiyosaki believes that in the long run, increasing income is the better solution.

Robert explains that allocating an amount of budget to a fixed cost is very important. If you decide to save 10% of your income, then make this 10% a fixed amount in your budget. First, allocate an amount to yourself. Kiyosaki writes: "You can predict people's future by looking at the amount of time and money they spend." He continues: "Time and money are your most important assets. Use them wisely." He notes that when things don't go their way, people choose not to spend money instead of spending it. But if they have the right prioritization to spend money, they can improve the situation. Reduce spending on snacks and extra food expenses and instead add to the costs of education and upgrading your knowledge.

## The Fourth Area of Financial Intelligence: Leverage for Money

In Robert Kiyosaki's book on increasing financial intelligence, this chapter is the longest and most sensitive section in the entire book. This section represents the main part of his financial philosophy.

*Leverage*

Borrowing money to increase your liquidity is a very good thing if you have the power to control your investment according to Robert Kiyosaki. But if you are poor in controlling the investment, leverage will become very dangerous. He writes: "Many of the people who faced failure with the real estate crash were people who had counted on the increase in the value of their properties through the real estate market."

They borrowed money against the high value of their home, but they have no control over the ups and downs of the housing market. This shows poor financial intelligence. Instead, he argues, you should use leverage for low-risk investing, invest in a way that you can master.

*4 Guaranteed Ways to Improve Your Financial or Economic Intelligence*

1. Let's be honest, most of us haven't started doing anything about our finances
2. We will be sticking a fork in our eye soon, so we need to learn about finances.
3. You are an expert in your business, so why are you anxious?
4. You are likely to say: If finances are one of my weaknesses, why is there no attention paid to the development of my strengths?

## The Fifth Area of Financial or Economic Intelligence: Improving Financial Information

Warren Buffett is the most successful investor of all time. But he never gambled. Buffett (and his partner, Charlie Munger) do extensive research for their decisions. Before they buy a company's stock, they need to know everything about it. Having this information allows them to invest with confidence.

In contrast, Robert Kiyosaki has made some of his investments out of ignorance. He had bought stocks that he hoped would go up. These types of decisions are not based on information, but on emotions.

To improve your financial information, it is important to:

Separate reality from thoughts. Many elders happily offer their opinions, "The price of gold is going up," but it would be foolish to base our financial decisions on these. Make your decisions based on reality. Verify the information. Don't just believe one source of information and verify it from other sources.

Know the rules. If you don't know what your investment is like, don't do it. "Rules are valuable sources of information about how to play with money," Kiyosaki writes in his book. Understand trends. Trends and trends are important facts.

Smart investors can use trends and trends to make informed decisions. However, note that this process does not lead to future realities; However, they are valuable sources of financial information.

Robert Kiyosaki writes: "Ultimately, it's not your possessions that make you rich, but your information." Here are some quotes from Robert Kiyosaki:

In his new book, "Second Chance: Your Money, Your Life, Our World", Robert Kiyosaki once again points out the importance of financial intelligence and says: When you have many financial problems, you should go for those products that will lead you in the right direction. Getting rich leads. Not those goods that cause other costs. so look for wealth building products. Robert Kiyosaki on people who go to court to get their fortunes

He made important recommendations, which are not bad to mention a few of them:

1- Keep your property documents in a very safe place.
2- When you write a contract: make all the necessary and necessary provisions for withdrawing from it.
3- Instead of receiving a fixed salary, if you have high financial intelligence, try to participate in the work and use your own dividends or take a share of the royalties for yourself. Because in this case, you will not be charged income tax.
4- This researcher believes that you should not transfer valuable property to your own name. He says that due to the high rate of divorce in societies, it is better for people who have financial intelligence not to name their valuable property. It will not be useful to change the business system that has not been developed for years; In this case, we should see the necessary training to change our people. From the thoughts and habits, we had in childhood to other characteristics, this is not impossible at all.

Therefore, learning to see in any work will be one of the secrets of success. In fact, the ignorance of people in a society is one of the things that make the rich richer day by day. So, to succeed in the financial field, first identify your talent and know in which field your abilities are, then provide a suitable working environment and allow yourself to grow in that field. This is one of the characteristics of people with high financial intelligence. Anyone can improve their financial intelligence, and you don't need to be educated at Harvard University, you just need to be fully committed to improving your financial situation. Regardless of how you earn money, you can improve your financial intelligence right now. These recommendations will give you high financial power. are you ready?

# WHERE ARE YOU IN THE PYRAMID OF FINANCIAL INTELLIGENCE?

In this section, you will get an understanding of exactly which level of financial intelligence you are at. This information will help you to easily increase your level of financial intelligence and if you are one of the financially conscious people, it will not decrease your level of awareness.

Next, be careful to know what level of financial intelligence you are in order to reach the highest level in terms of financial understanding. In the following, pay attention to the categories of the pyramid of financial intelligence:

Financial unconscious people in the pyramid of financial intelligence

Unemployed people with no income: The first category that we will deal with at this stage are the financially ignorant, most of these people are currently unemployed in Iran and have no income. Those born in the 60s and 70s mostly fall into this category. The main reason for this is that they have been turned into weak, unwilling and self-confident people by their families.

Features of financial unconscious:

- They have problems and conflicts with their families.
- These people are very degraded and humiliated.
- Many of these people are extremely confused.
- They haven't even found their talents yet.
- They have not been trained to set goals.
- Have not worked on personal improvement.
- They don't have a suitable idea and always say: "There is no work, we don't have capital."

Often these people are hopeless and depressed.

- They are more afraid of being humiliated and because they have not taken action, they have become lazy and fat.
- The dream of these people is financial independence, and they like to be valuable and needless people.
- They even recognize the obstacles to their growth, for example according to the financial unconscious 1) lack focus and open mind 2) lack information 3) lack partners 4) lack motivation and limited mind 5) lack self-confidence.
- The financially uninformed blame others for their unemployment and low income.

Solutions provided for the financially unwary:

- Learn to be responsible.
- Write down a list of all your abilities.
- Discover ways to earn money through your talents and abilities.
- Appreciate your abilities and try to earn money from them.
- If you have few abilities, create them within yourself and use them.

## Financial Intelligence, Average Economy

Low income: Most of the people who fall into this group are either employees or their business is like a taxi driver. Their income is low. These people are the largest group in the pyramid of financial intelligence. Most of these people are engaged in repetitive tasks for a long time and work in one place. These people create money but very little.

The problems of these people are the habit of their current conditions and they have become accustomed to everyday life and things are always repetitive for them. Most of these people don't work for themselves and are employees of others and just do repetitive tasks over and over again. People with average financial intelligence are mostly not satisfied with their income and are disappointed that their needs are not met.

These people do not even have job security, every day they are threatened by the fear of being unemployed. The dream of these people is often to be among the rich people and live in a better environment. People with average financial intelligence like to be their own manager and not work for others.

## Characteristics of People with Average Financial Intelligence

- People with average financial and economic intelligence think that all conditions must be perfect when starting a business, and they make decisions based on perfectionism.
- Often they do not consult with experts and professional financial advisors, and if they share their decisions with ordinary people, they will be hindered.
- These people are always afraid of being humiliated and failing.
- Risk power is very low among these people.

## Solutions for People with Average Financial and Economic Intelligence

The first solution is that if you are an employee, learn how to get a second job for yourself. Increase the power of risk in yourself; The solution to this issue is to reduce the risk of what you intend to do. Contrary to what many people think, great entrepreneurs and self-made billionaires never took dangerous risks.

Instead, they reduce the risk to their work. For this, use techniques such as increasing information in your business, complete your information in that field if you intend to start any business. Ask about your work from professionals who are engaged in the job you want.

If they tell you that business is bad, it's definitely not bad, you just need to work harder. The reason for this answer is that they compare their current income with their prosperous business past and that they never expanded their business. Another way to help you is even if you don't have any financial problems.

Reduce your expenses as much as possible to start a business. Fears and doubts betray you. Don't let fear stop your growth and progress; Be a perfectionist.

## Good Financial Intelligence

These people earn well. They have a good place in the pyramid of financial intelligence and are self-made people. Their income depends a lot on market conditions. If these people have a lot of experience, they will have better conditions than the newbies.

## Characteristics of People with Good Financial or Economic Intelligence

People who are in the good category in the pyramid related to financial or economic intelligence, mostly work in a traditional and old way.

## Five Types of Financial Intelligence That If You Don't Know, Your Financial Future Will Be At Risk

One of the human intelligences, which many professors around the world have recently highlighted the importance and application of, is financial intelligence. Without the development of financial intelligence, even a successful person or a person who has earned a lot of money, no matter how much he has financial support, will fail.

You have an IQ, which stands for "intelligence quotient", and evaluates your overall level of intelligence, and you also have an emotional IQ, which measures your ability to control your emotions.

Your Financial Intelligence Quotient (IQ) is measured by your financial intelligence and shows how well you handle financial matters.

Financial intelligence is a part of our general intelligence that we use to solve financial problems. Common financial problems in today's world are the mismatch between income and living expenses, not having a private house, debt, car expenses, healthcare expenses, etc., which can be solved by using financial intelligence. If we do not strengthen our financial intelligence, the problems will become more serious day by day and the conditions will become more difficult day by day. The fact is that money has a significant impact on lifestyle and quality of life. Money brings comfort, freedom of time and freedom of choice. But getting money alone will not lead to wealth if not using financial intelligence. It should be kept in mind that if you can solve financial problems, your financial intelligence will grow, and when financial intelligence grows, you will become richer, and if you do not solve financial problems, you will become poorer day by day (Westhead, 2016).

## Financial Intelligence Compared to Financial Intelligence

Most of us know that a person with an IQ of 130 must be smarter than a person with an IQ of 95. The same ratio can be considered in financial intelligence. You can be a genius in terms of academic intelligence, but your financial intelligence is that of an idiot. It is often asked: What is the difference between financial intelligence and financial intelligence? The answer is:

Financial intelligence is a part of our mental intelligence that we use to solve financial problems.

Financial Intelligence Quotient is the measure of this intelligence or the way to determine the quality of our financial intelligence. For example, if my income is $100,000 and I pay 20% of it in taxes, I have more financial savvy than someone who makes $100,000 and pays 50% of it in taxes. In this example, someone whose net income after taxes is $80,000 has a higher financial IQ than someone whose net income is $50,000 after taxes. Both of them have financial intelligence; But the person who keeps more money for himself has a higher financial IQ.

## Five Main Coefficients of Financial Intelligence

There are five factors to financial intelligence, which include making more money (income), protecting money, budgeting money, leveraging money, and improving financial literacy.

### Financial Intelligence #1: Earn More money

We all have enough financial intelligence to earn money. The higher your income, the higher your financial IQ number 1; In other words, someone who earns 1 billion dollars a year has a higher financial intelligence than someone who earns 300 dollars a year.

If each of them earns $1 billion a year, the person who pays less tax than the other is the person who has a higher financial intelligence. Because he is closer to the goal of achieving financial integrity by leveraging Financial Intelligence #2, money protection. We all know that someone may have a high academic IQ and be a genius in the classroom, but not be able to make much money in the real world.

Robert Kiyosaki says that my father was a great teacher and a hard-working man, he had a high scientific IQ, but a low financial IQ. He performed very well in the scientific world, but was poor in the business world.

### Financial Intelligence #2: Protecting Money

There is a simple truth that everyone wants to take your money; But not everyone who takes your money is a fraud or a law breaker. One of the biggest financial predators of our money is taxes. Governments legally take our money away from us. If a person's financial IQ number 2 is low, he will pay more taxes and have more expenses on his shoulders.

This financial intelligence quotient states that the net profit should be increased as much as possible.

### Financial Intelligence #3: Budget Money

Budgeting money requires a lot of financial intelligence. Many people budget their money like a poor person rather than like a rich person. Many people make a lot of money but can't keep a lot of money for themselves because they budget poorly. For example, a person who earns 200 million dollars a year and spends all of it, compared to someone who earns 100 million dollars a year and can live well with a budget of 30 million dollars and invest 70 million dollars. It has a lower financial

IQ number 3. It requires a high level of financial intelligence to be able to live well despite our income and still invest.

## Financial Intelligence # 4: Leveraging Money

After a person budgets his surplus income, his next challenge is to invest his surplus income. Most people invest their surplus income in the bank.

This was considered smart when inflation was lower than bank interest rates. But when the inflation is higher than the interest paid by the bank, keeping money in the bank will only make your money worthless and you will not get real interest.

For example, if annual inflation is 35% and the bank pays 20%, you will lose 15% of the value of your money.

Millions of people in Iran do not know where to invest their money, so they invest their excess income in fixed income mutual funds or leave it in the bank, hoping to make their money profitable. Although saving and investing in diversified portfolios of mutual funds is a form of leveraging money, there are better ways to make your money work. Any honest person must admit that saving money in the bank and investing in mutual funds does not require much financial intelligence. Saving money and investing it in mutual funds is not difficult and does not require high financial intelligence. Financial Intelligence Quotient No. 4 is evaluated based on the ratio of profitability to investment.

For example, a person who receives 50% of his money as interest has a higher financial IQ number 4 than someone who receives 5% interest; And the person who pays less tax for the profits he has earned has a higher financial intelligence.

## Financial Intelligence #5: Improving Financial Knowledge

There is a very wise point in this sentence:

Before you can run, you have to learn to walk. This applies to financial intelligence. Before people can learn how to make significant profits from their investments (Financial Intelligence Factor #4: Leveraging Money), they must learn how to walk, which means they must learn the principles and rules of financial intelligence.

One of the reasons many people have trouble with Financial IQ #4, Leveraging Money, is that they have learned to put their money in the hands of financial "experts" like banks and mutual funds. The problem with entrusting your money to financial experts is that you stop learning yourself and you cannot increase your financial intelligence, and as a result, you cannot become a financial expert. If someone else manages your money and solves your financial problems, you cannot increase your financial intelligence. In fact, with your own money, you are making others smarter! If you have a solid foundation of financial knowledge, it is easy for you to improve your financial intelligence; But if your financial IQ is weak, new financial knowledge can be confusing and of minimal value to you.

One of the benefits of acquiring financial knowledge is that over time you will gain a better understanding of more complex financial information, just as mathematicians can solve complex equations after years of solving math problems. But you still need to learn to walk before you can run. Most of us have been in a class, lecture session, or conversation centered around such information. Or we attended a class where the information discussed was so complex that we couldn't understand it no matter how hard we tried. This means either the teacher is not teaching well, or the student needs more basic information.

The thing is, we all have to start somewhere. Of course, if I try to sit in on a class (say nuclear physics) that I have no background in, I'll get a headache; Because before someone wants to learn nuclear physics, he must learn its basics. Many financial issues remain unresolved; And instead of using financial knowledge to solve them, we inject them with low-backed money. We have used old ideas to solve the problems of modern life. Using old ideas to solve new problems will only cause bigger and newer problems. For this reason, I believe that the five financial intelligences are important. If you develop these five financial intelligences, you are more likely to succeed in a rapidly changing world. In this way, you can better solve your problems and improve your financial intelligence(Usman, 2019).

## 4 Ways That You Can Build Your Financial Intelligence From Today

1. **Engage Yourself in Work:**

How long do you think your boss will keep you at work if you refuse or ignore the duties of your job that you really don't like to do? It won't take long, rest assured! Your job is your financial source and actually your money. When you pay proper attention to your money or finances then you can see the change. Practicing improving your relationship with money will increase your financial intelligence.

2. **Educate Yourself:**

We're not suggesting you go back to school to learn about finance or enroll in stocks and bonds classes. As long as you can hire a trusted advisor to help you make financial decisions and choices, you don't need to know all the ins and outs of investing yourself.

Understanding how to change the way you behave with your money is important. Be aware of how you treat your money and what decisions you make on a daily basis that make your finances better or worse. Commit to only acting in a way that is in your best interest. This will increase your financial intelligence.

3. **Change Your Thinking:**

Most of the time it is our thinking that keeps us where we have no intellectual growth. To increase financial intelligence and feel financial success, change your way of thinking. Instead of thinking that life without buying something expensive is absurd for you, think more about building wealth.

When you focus on spending, your financial intelligence is kept low, but when you think about how you can make more money, your financial intelligence increases and you start making decisions that change your thinking. Being smarter means thinking smarter.

4. **Spend Your Time Wisely:**

Increasing financial intelligence involves allocating your time to doing the things you really need to do to live a healthier life with money. In order to have a better relationship with money, you need to do better things with it. Freeing yourself from debt will increase your financial intelligence, so keep a strict check on your daily spending. Instead of waiting around to see if you can afford it, set aside time each month to write a financial plan that outlines exactly how much money you'll earn and how you'll spend it. Doing so gives you more control over your money. Does money make you rich? The answer to this question is no, money alone cannot make you rich. We all know that people who work very hard every day earn more money but never become rich. Even many of them become more in debt than before and...

## REFERENCES

https://corporatefinanceinstitute.com/resources/wealth-management/financial-plan/

Qin, L.: 2020 China Intelligent Finance and Taxation Management Summit Forum, keynote speech-Liu Qin: Accounting Future under the Application of Intelligent Technology_Revolution (sohu.com). Accounting Future under the Application of Intelligent Technology (2020)

Usman, B., &Yennita. (2019). Understanding the entrepreneurial intention among international students in Turkey. *Journal of Global Entrepreneurship Research*, 9(10), 1–21.

Westhead, P., & Solesvik, M. Z. (2016). Entrepreneurship education and entrepreneurial intention: Do female students benefit? *International Small Business Journal*, 34(8), 979–1003. DOI: 10.1177/0266242615612534

Zhang, J.: Financial analysis of the implementation of intelligent methods. Financ. Manag. Res. (03), 1–7 (2019)

# Chapter 8
# Financial Management During the Crisis

## ABSTRACT

*How to manage the financial crisis? Nowadays, the speed of economic and political changes is so high that sometimes economic and political events surprise us all between sleeping at night and waking up in the morning. leads to a financial crisis, in this article we seek to find a suitable answer to the question of how to manage the financial crisis? we will be At the beginning, it is emphasized that the best strategy is to prevent any financial crisis, but the fact is that despite following all business principles and proper financial planning, sometimes factors beyond our control (such as the emergence of (corona disease) is so urgent and strong that its effects take us all by surprise. I will address this issue by presenting some questions and answering the questions (Anderson et al, 2016).*

## INTRODUCTION

In an era where economic and political changes occur at lightning speed, the financial stability of individuals and businesses is often challenged overnight. Events ranging from global pandemics to economic recessions can lead to unexpected financial crises, making it crucial to understand how to manage such challenges effectively. Financial management during a crisis involves identifying potential risks, implementing preventive measures, and adopting adaptive strategies to maintain stability. While proactive planning is always the best defense, unforeseen circumstances—like the COVID-19 pandemic or sudden market crashes—can disrupt even the most carefully designed financial plans. This section explores the concept of financial crises, their causes, and practical strategies for overcoming them. From effective cost management and innovative financing methods to leveraging technology and workforce optimization, we discuss actionable steps that can help

DOI: 10.4018/979-8-3693-9415-1.ch008

individuals and businesses navigate financial challenges, ensuring resilience and preparedness in an unpredictable world.

## HOW DO I MANAGE THE FINANCIAL CRISIS?

Nowadays, the speed of economic and political changes is so high that sometimes economic and political events surprise us all between sleeping at night and waking up in the morning. leads to a financial crisis, in this article we seek to find a suitable answer to the question of how to manage the financial crisis?

At the beginning, it is emphasized that the best strategy is to prevent any financial crisis, but the fact is that despite following all business principles and proper financial planning, sometimes factors beyond our control (such as the emergence of (corona disease) is so urgent and strong that its effects take us all by surprise. I will address this issue by presenting some questions and answering the questions (Anderson et al, 2016).

First, let's define the financial crisis? Financial crisis means any situation where a person (real or legal) faces problems in terms of paying current expenses and current debts of his business. In other words, if you cannot pay current expenses such as salaries, rent, necessary purchases, etc., or your check is due and you are unable to pay it, you are facing a financial crisis. Perhaps it is better to use the term working capital, a company that faces a serious problem in providing its working capital has faced a financial crisis. It should be noted that the financial crisis does not necessarily mean when the company's workers go on strike and creditors gather in front of the company's door. If you have to go to banks to finance your current expenses and working capital, and you are willing to finance at any price, you are facing a financial crisis (Walid Mensi,2019).

Basically, why does the financial crisis occur? The financial crisis is caused by controllable and uncontrollable variables, some of the controllable variables can be prevented by using correct financial planning and in other words by coordinating income and expenditure, but our main problem is with unpredictable variables such as the outbreak of Corona disease, embargo, Extreme changes in currency, war, etc. Therefore, in the first step, we must manage all the controllable variables and prevent the creation of controllable financial crises with proper financial planning and budgeting, but how can we prevent the creation of a controllable financial crisis or control it if we have a financial crisis?

1. **The First and Most Necessary Tool to Control the Financial Crisis is Proper Cost Management**

In other words, most of the time we need to use strict cost management strategies to overcome the crisis. Applying the cost management strategy is the missing link of many Iranian companies. The company should adopt the right strategy at any time. A company that has a severe decrease in sales and cash flow compared to the previous year should not spend as much as the previous year. In the first step, it should quickly Expenses that can be removed, for example, travel expenses, unnecessary missions, luxurious receptions, unnecessary welfare expenses, etc. be deleted.

Controllable costs should be managed quickly and reduced as much as possible, the costs of water, electricity, gas, telephone, overhead, waste, etc. Be carefully managed. Applying the cost management strategy may include reducing personnel costs such as reducing bonuses, efficiency, overtime, etc., but it is the duty of the management to assure the personnel that immediately after passing the crisis and returning to normal conditions, all these items will be compensated for the personnel. will be. Unfortunately, I have seen a lot of wrong management of reducing personnel costs, which not only does not lead to a reduction of personnel costs, but also leads to a decrease in efficiency, an increase in waste, and in general leads to an increase in company costs. Reducing personnel costs has very important differences with overhead costs. In relation to the reduction of personnel costs, it must be ensured that all these cases and cost management are necessary for the survival of the company and maintaining the working conditions of the personnel, and immediately after the crisis, compensation for all of them will be taken. In general, unfortunately, human resources management in Iran does not have its real position, and usually the position of human resources management is a ceremonial position where non-specialists are employed in this position.

2. Using the correct methods of financing to overcome the crisis, it has been abundantly observed that companies that have a financial crisis, by taking heavy loans with high financial interest, only seek to transfer the crisis from one time to another and practically They are not looking for a solution to the crisis, a company that has problems in terms of paying current expenses cannot afford to pay heavy interest expenses, what should be done? All the correct and principled financing methods should be checked, maybe sometimes by handing over a percentage of the company's shares, we can actually get past the crisis safely, of course, all these issues should be carefully checked by the financial team. The management of the company should check all the financing methods of the company using the experienced financial team. Remember that the bank is only one of the financing methods and we can finance in other ways as well. But safe from uncontrollable variables such as corona disease, embargo, currency problems, etc.

How should a company prepare for a recession in advance and what actions should it take when the recession comes? The research and studies that were conducted during the Great Depression clarify the answers to these questions. In some cases, these answers are consistent with conventional logic; In some cases, they challenge it. The most interesting findings relate this issue to three areas: debt, workforce management, and digital transition. The main message from all these areas is that the recession is an exercise in managing change with a lot of pressure to find a way to succeed and that a company must be flexible and ready to adapt.

## Financing Before the Recession

Rebecca Henderson (of the Harvard Business School) likes to remind her students that "the first rule is: Don't let the company fail." This means, first and foremost, don't run out of money. Because recession is often associated with a decrease in sales and, as a result, less liquidity for operational financing, surviving in recession requires agile financial management. If Amazon hadn't made all that money before the dot-com bubble burst, it would have had far fewer options, and if it had, it would have had to take huge losses in its other startups and sell its marketplace platform to resellers for over a year. Then he presented. But this did not happen, and the company expanded its markets (kitchen, travel and apparel) along with new markets (Canada) during and after the recession. Companies with a lot of debt are especially vulnerable during a recession.

In a study conducted in 2017, Xavier Grod (MIT School of Management) and Holger Müller (NYV's Stern School of Business) examined the relationship between business closures and resulting unemployment and housing price declines in different US states. In general, as housing prices fell, so did consumer demand, which led to more business closures and deeper unemployment. But research showed that this effect was more visible among companies with higher debt. They classified companies based on whether their debt-to-equity ratio increased or decreased during the recession, and their criterion for this classification was the change in the debt-to-equity ratio in these companies. In the majority of businesses that were closed due to the decrease in demand, the ratio of debt to capital was much higher. "The more debt you have, the more cash you need to make your principal payments and turn a profit," Mueller explains. When a recession hits and there's less cash coming into the system, "it puts you at risk of slacking off."

Companies with more debt have to cut costs more aggressively to make payments, often through layoffs. These deep cost cuts can affect the productivity of these companies and reduce their ability to finance new investments. A high ratio of debt to capital significantly limits the options of companies and makes them much less able to use opportunities. The risk that high debt can bring to companies during a recession depends on various factors. Shai Bernstein (Stanford Business School), Josh Lerner (Harvard Business School), and Filippo Mezzanotti (Northwestern University of Management) found that privately held firms outperformed non-privately held firms during recessions. Companies that have a lot of debt are in trouble because the lack of access to capital destroys their agility to transition from recessionary conditions.

Privately owned companies are in a better situation because, according to research, the owners of these companies are able to provide financing for these companies when needed. Issuing shares is another way that companies can take the burden of debt obligations off their shoulders. "If you issue shares during a recession, the problem of neglect and neglect will be less," says Mueller. Of course, the reality is that many companies have some level of debt when the recession hits. Muller's research showed that the average ratio of debt to capital among companies that had an increasing level of debt during the Great Recession was 38.3%. Among the groups that were financed, this amount was 19.5%. Although there is no magic number, having a moderate level of debt is not necessarily a sign of a problem. Still, Mueller's view is that if a company thinks a recession is coming, it should think about financing (Jiang, 2019).

Recent McKinsey research on the recession bears this out: Companies that emerged from the Great Recession in better shape had lower debt-to-equity ratios from 2007 to 2011 than less successful companies. When it comes to financing, according to Mackenzie consultants, it is better to do it earlier and in the early stages. It means reducing the level of debt before it becomes clear that the economy is in recession. Messiur says you should "take a hard look at the securities you're holding" because divesting assets can be a way to lower your debt-to-equity ratio without necessarily cutting costs in core operational areas.

## Looking Beyond Employee Layoffs

Some layoffs are inevitable during a recession; During the Great Depression, 2.1 million Americans were laid off in 2009 alone. However, the companies that made it through the crisis at their strongest considered fewer layoffs to cut costs and instead relied on operational expansion. The reason for this is that layoffs are not only detrimental to employees; It is also costly for the company. Hiring and training are expensive, so companies prefer not to have to rehire when the economy picks up, especially if they think the downturn will be short. Layoffs can also hurt morale and reduce productivity when companies themselves are struggling. Fortunately, layoffs are not the only way to reduce labor costs. Companies can consider methods such as reducing working hours, giving time off and paying wages based on efficiency.

Many countries and more than half of the states in the U.S. have some form of "short-term" compensation package program in which workers whose hours are reduced receive a portion of their unemployment benefits. In France, 4% of workers and 1% of companies benefited from this short-term program in 2009, and this program paid both employees and companies. In a study at the Center for European Economic Policy Think Tank, Pircaho, Frances Kraharz and Sandra Nod found that companies that took advantage of the short-time work schedule laid off fewer employees and were more likely to survive the Great Recession. This effect was more pronounced among firms that were hit harder by the recession than others and those that had more debt.

According to these researchers, the short-term work approach allowed vulnerable companies to retain more labor in their company. Without this approach, they would be more likely to lay off large numbers of employees, making it more difficult for them to recover from the recession, or to go out of business altogether. The researchers estimated that one job was saved in the form of short-term work for every five workers, and they calculated that the cost per job saved was lower than other similar programs that had been implemented, because the alternative scheme would have paid full unemployment benefits. However, this program actually saved money for the French government (Coombs et al,2018).

One of the interesting things about both furloughs and short-term work is that companies know that layoffs affect employees. On the other hand, reducing the costs of salaries and wages or stopping the contract of employees, if the issue of productivity is not taken into account, it can have the opposite result and cause damage to the morale of the employees and destroy the motivation of the best employees. Similarly, stopping a contract without evaluating potential hires can undoubtedly affect all units. Performance-based pay (that is, pay based on productivity measurements or results) is another way to control labor costs without hurting productivity. There is a lot of debate about performance-based pay for managers and senior employees, and there are many pros and cons around this issue. But a new study by Christo Makridis (of the White House Council of Economic Advisers) and Marie Gitelmann (of the US Bureau of Labor Statistics) reveals an important truth.

Using responses to salary surveys from 2004 to 2014, this study shows that U.S. companies used performance-based pay more during the recession. Although these researchers cannot confirm whether this strategy is beneficial for companies, they have shown that during tough times, jobs with performance-based pay are more likely. According to their hypothesis, the reason for this problem is that paying wages based on efficiency makes companies more flexible because they can adjust employee rewards according to changing conditions.

## Investing in Technology

We all like to think that in times of recession we will get through all the crises and reach our destination safely. However, recession is the perfect time to adapt to new technologies. In a 2018 study, Brad Hershbein (of the VPjohn Institute for Employment Research) and Lisa Beacon (of the University of Rochester) compared more than 100 million online job listings posted from 2007 to 2015 with economic data to see how the Great Recession affected them. It focused on the types of skills that employers were looking for. They found that American cities that were less affected by the recession had a higher demand for higher skills, such as computer skills. Alisha Sacermodestino (of Northeastern), Danielle Shaung (of Harvard University) and Joshua Ballance (of the Center for Urban Policy, UK) argued that part of the increase in demand is due to employers having wider choices during the recession due to rising unemployment. have. Their research found that the demand for technology-oriented skills returns to a more normal level when the labor market grows. But according to Hershbein and Kahn, it was not the case that companies only had wider choices; They also became more digital (Heath,2023).

In areas of the United States that were less affected by the recession, companies also increased their investment in information technology and included IT skills in their hiring. But why do companies invest in technology in times of recession and when money is tight? Economists' theory is that because their opportunity cost is lower than in boom times. When the economy is at its best, a firm will use every incentive to reach its maximum output. If the company spends its resources on investing in new technologies, there may be some extra money left over. But when people want to buy what you're selling, you don't have to operate at full capacity. Therefore, operating budget can be spent on purchasing IT solutions without harming sales. Therefore, adapting to technology during a recession is less expensive.

Of course, this opinion is correct in theory, but there are other reasons that can make managers act. Technology can make your business more transparent, flexible, and efficient. According to Cathy George, who is a senior partner at Mackenzie, the first reason to prioritize digital transformation before or during a recession is that advanced analytics can help management better understand the business, how the recession affects it. and situations where performance improvement can be achieved. The second reason is that digital technology can help reduce costs. George says companies should prioritize projects that "fund themselves," such as automation or adopting data-driven decision-making. A third reason is that investing in IT makes companies more agile and thus better able to weather a period of instability and adapt to the rapid changes that occur during a recession. He says: "In the field of production, we are finally seeing the understanding of the adaptation of digital and advanced analytics".

It used to be that manufacturers could either be the cheapest on the market or remain agile, not at the same time. Flexibility came with huge costs. However, digital technologies have "created much greater flexibility around changes in product, changes in production volume, etc., and the movement of supply chains around the world has undergone many changes." This was the opinion of George, who believes that this is proof that the next recession will probably be different from the past recessions. Companies that have already invested in digital technology, analytics and agile business methods may be better able to understand the threat they face and respond to it more quickly. As we have seen, recessions can create deep and large efficiency gaps between companies. Research has shown that digital technology can do the same. Companies that have neglected the digital transition may find it out of reach during the next recession (Sun, 2020).

# REFERENCES

Coombs, W. T., & Laufer, D. (2018). Global Crisis Management- Current Research and Future Directions. *Journal of International Management*, 24(3), 199–203. DOI: 10.1016/j.intman.2017.12.003

Heath, D., Ringgenberg, M. C., Samadi, M., & Werner, I. M. (2023). Reusing natural experiments. *The Journal of Finance*, 78(4), 2329–2364. DOI: 10.1111/jofi.13250

Jiang, L., Levine, R., & Lin, C. (2019). Competition and bank liquidity creation. *Journal of Financial and Quantitative Analysis*, ●●●, 1–50.

Sun, H., Ni, W., Teh, P. L., & Lo, C. (2020). The Systematic Impact of Personal Characteristics on Entrepreneurial Intentions of Engineering Students. *Frontiers in Psychology*, 11, 1–15. PMID: 32581939

Anderson, D. (2016). *Organization development: The process of leading organizational change. Translated by SeyedNaghavi MA, Masoud Sinaki S, Kosar Z &Khosravi SH*. Koohsar Publication. [Book in Persian]

- Walid Mensi . (2019) 'Global financial crisis and co-movements between oil prices and sector stock markets in Saudi Arabia: A VaR based wavelet' Borsa Istanbul, Review 19-1, pp. 24 -e38.

# Chapter 9
# Business Intelligence for Financial and Non-Financial Managers

## ABSTRACT

*Familiarity with financial or economic intelligence and the need to learn it in the modern global and competitive business world, it is very important for companies to have economic success. This financial success can be achieved through financial discipline, goal setting and periodic reviews. Companies that have enjoyed financial success have been able to increase employee trust, increase sales, and reduce turnover. These three factors contribute a lot to the stability of the company, which in turn has caused growth, and in fact, the set of these factors defines what financial intelligence is.*

## INTRODUCTION

In today's dynamic business landscape, the ability to understand and utilize financial data is critical not only for financial managers but also for non-financial professionals. Whether steering a small team or overseeing a large enterprise, managers must leverage business intelligence to navigate challenges, drive growth, and ensure sustainable success. Business intelligence for financial and non-financial managers combines data analysis, strategic thinking, and actionable insights to improve decision-making processes. For financial managers, it means mastering tools and techniques to optimize profitability, manage risks, and forecast trends. For non-financial managers, it involves understanding financial concepts, interpreting data effectively, and aligning departmental strategies with broader organizational goals. This section explores how financial intelligence—an essential component of

DOI: 10.4018/979-8-3693-9415-1.ch009

business intelligence—empowers managers to decode complex financial scenarios, make informed decisions, and foster collaboration across diverse functions. By bridging the gap between financial and non-financial roles, organizations can create a unified approach to achieving economic resilience and innovation.

## FAMILIARITY WITH FINANCIAL OR ECONOMIC INTELLIGENCE AND THE NEED TO LEARN IT

In the modern global and competitive business world, it is very important for companies to have economic success. This financial success can be achieved through financial discipline, goal setting and periodic reviews. Companies that have enjoyed financial success have been able to increase employee trust, increase sales, and reduce turnover. These three factors contribute a lot to the stability of the company, which in turn has caused growth, and in fact, the set of these factors defines what financial intelligence is.

### What is Financial Intelligence?

Financial intelligence is a complex and multifaceted concept that cannot be easily defined by a single explanation. It is a subset of business intelligence that involves the ability to understand, interpret, and use financial data to make informed decisions. While some people associate financial intelligence with the ability to make money quickly, it is far more nuanced than that. In its broader sense, financial intelligence encompasses the collection and analysis of financial information—often involving the financial affairs of well-known individuals or businesses—to understand their capabilities, predict their goals, and evaluate financial risks. This process plays a crucial role in various contexts, including law enforcement, where financial intelligence units (FIUs) monitor transactions to prevent crimes like fraud or money laundering.

Financial intelligence can also be seen as a combination of both art and science. The scientific aspect involves technical knowledge, such as the ability to analyze financial statements, assess profitability, manage budgets, and forecast future financial performance. On the artistic side, it requires intuition, creativity, and strategic thinking—knowing how to interpret financial trends and apply them to business decisions in innovative ways.

One important aspect of financial intelligence is its role in empowering individuals and organizations, particularly employees. By providing workers with a basic understanding of financial principles, companies enable them to make sound decisions that align with business goals, helping improve efficiency and profitability. This is particularly important for senior managers, as financial intelligence is a key skill set that allows them to lead organizations effectively. They must be able to analyze financial data, understand market trends, manage risks, and communicate financial information clearly to stakeholders. Ultimately, financial intelligence is a vital tool for anyone involved in making financial decisions. It is not limited to making quick profits but involves a deeper understanding of how financial systems work, how to manage risks, and how to use financial information strategically to achieve long-term success. Whether in business, law enforcement, or personal finance, financial intelligence provides the knowledge and skills necessary to navigate complex financial environments and make informed, effective decisions.

## Financial Intelligence and Its Components

Financial intelligence and success is a set of skills that consists of four competencies, which are: understanding the foundation, understanding the art, understanding the analysis and understanding the goals for complete financial success, all these four competencies must be practiced and implemented. Financial intelligence is a business language that is known and used in all organizations. This is the common denominator on which all organizations succeed.

Understanding the Foundation: To understand what financial intelligence means, an organization must create a solid foundation for its non-financial manager. This foundation requires a basic understanding of profit margins, cash flow statements, and balance sheets. The purpose of financial information is to ensure that when non-financial managers are presented with numbers, they are competent enough to do business with them.

> **Understanding the Art:** Finance and accounting are science and art. These two disciplines try to reduce what cannot always be represented as numbers. This quantification of the concept is based on rules, assumptions, and principles. Non-financial managers should be able to apply this art/science to scenarios and profit from them. By doing this, they will be prepared for any challenging scenario.
> 
> **Understanding Analysis:** Once the basic idea of finance and its usefulness is grasped, this is where the question of financial intelligence comes into play. The numbers presented to non-financial managers can be better understood, the right questions can be asked, and more analysis can be done on that raw data. Having economic intelligence and types of financial intelligence enables managers to determine the return on investment, etc., from various analyses. New understanding helps them make informed and calculated decisions.

**Understanding the Goals and Having a Broad Vision:** It has been observed that the factors that affect the financial status of the organization alone do not tell a complete story about what is happening inside the organization. The financial result or analysis should be understood from the highest level or broader view. A financial result should be analyzed according to the macro environment of the company under it and answer the question of what is financial intelligence. Macro factors affecting financial results are: competitive environment, government regulations, demographic change and transformation.

A judicial model established in the judicial branch of government in which disclosures of suspicious financial activities are received by a country's investigative agencies from its financial sector so that judicial powers can be easily seized. Seizing funds, blocking accounts, conducting interrogations, arresting people, conducting searches, etc. are included in this category of financial intelligence. The law enforcement model implements anti-money laundering measures alongside existing law enforcement systems, supporting the efforts of multiple or sometimes competing jurisdictions to investigate money laundering.

The administrative model is a centralized, independent and administrative authority that receives, and processes information related to the financial sector and will transfer it to judicial or law enforcement authorities for prosecution. It acts as a buffer between the financial and law enforcement communities. The hybrid model serves as a disclosure intermediary and a link to judicial and law enforcement authorities. It combines elements of at least two models of FIU or types of financial intelligence.

They know that they have to be in financial crisis to reduce the excess cost of living and unnecessary circulation of money. If crises can be turned into opportunities, it can be said that you have financial intelligence, and you will easily answer what financial intelligence is. These people are constantly updating their information because they know that the science is advancing and the latest changes in financial knowledge must be caught. People with financial intelligence consider their goals and make a financial goal based on that to increase their income a little every month. In this situation, determining the income standards will be related to the individual's growth. Such people try to increase their income and expenses. People with financial intelligence make the right decision for their budget surplus, while people who are not, focus on their budget deficit. They are patient and don't think of traveling a hundred years in one night. They understand the concept of financial intelligence and know that proper and risky investment requires patience and perseverance. They try to have long-term and short-term financial goals and think about these goals all the time. They consult with first level financial managers and advisors so that they can be successful in managing their money and prevent some bad habits of spending money.

## Solutions to Strengthen and Increase Financial Intelligence

Money, Money, Money! We have been told since childhood that money is important. Even as toddlers learning about colors and numbers, we had enough knowledge to understand that money equals power. But because personal finance isn't always taught enough in schools, a lack of knowledge about what financial intelligence is can affect your financial IQ and economic intelligence. If your goal is prosperity and money, there is more than one way to achieve it. You can increase your income or invest in an individual account. You can pay off high-interest loans, build your savings fund, and save for a specific goal. There are even a few things you can check off your financial list in five minutes or less. Some of the available strategies that you can use to increase your financial intelligence and success include:

Many people looking to learn financial intelligence and success start their journey with a tried-and-true book. Some of the most popular are Rich Dad, Poor Dad by Robert Kiyosaki, The Automatic Millionaire by David Bach, and Total Income by Dave Ramsey, but there are many books that can help you. Think about money in a new way. Pick one or two financial topics that match your goals and study it.

### Assess Your Current Financial Situation

Start by checking your bank statements to see how much you have in savings and how much you owe. The reality may be scary at first, but don't be discouraged! To determine your current net worth, create a list of your assets and their value. Net worth is the difference between your total income and the value of your personal assets, less your debts. By knowing this amount, you can understand how your income affects your net worth and how your money is being spent. You'll see how your debts have changed over time and whether your net worth has increased.

### Track Your Expenses

Knowing how much you cost is only half the battle. It might be a little overwhelming at first, but tracking expenses really helps in the long run. Find out what kind of purchases you make, whether it's for food, entertainment or more. If it seems like one category is too many, try to find a way to reduce your expenses and get to the answer to what financial intelligence is as soon as possible.

### Use Financial Aid to Boost Your Intelligence

Until now, financial intelligence was mostly done automatically through reading financial sources and maintaining a personal budget, but today it is the opposite. If you feel that you need to shake up your life and your pocket, it is worth enrolling in financial classes or seminars that can help you have a better understanding of financial concepts and what financial intelligence is. Having a financial guru guiding you can really boost your financial savvy.

### Marketing is a Way to Increase Economic Intelligence

Marketing or networking definitely plays a big role in increasing your financial literacy and improving your financial intelligence. This will greatly help to grow and maintain a network of people who have financial ability and can gather various financial advice and will increase financial intelligence and success.

### Commit to Healthy Financial Habits

Of course, this will not always be easy! Taking steps towards financial stability is a big commitment and will take more than a day to accomplish. You have to constantly remind yourself not to get caught up in expensive fashions and prefer to save this money for your long-term financial goals and keep in mind the definition of financial intelligence.

## HOW TO BECOME RICH USING FINANCIAL INTELLIGENCE?

If you are one of those people who believe that everyone who has money is rich, you are very wrong!! If you read the biographies of many multi-billionaires in the world, you will realize that their past living standards were low or average, and the reason for their success and wealth is not their father's inheritance. Rather, they had good thinking and talent in making money, which means financial intelligence. In fact, the rich make money by creating and strengthening ways to get money, not by working, which we will discuss further.

*Figure 1. Hand holding lightbulb*

Financial IQ does not have a specific and single definition, but in general, ways of earning money in a short time can be called financial intelligence. In fact, the knowledge, information and abilities of each person in creating wealth, solving economic problems and managing financial crises are called financial intelligence, or in popular terms, his "economic intelligence". Robert Kiyosaki, one of the most prominent self-made rich people whose books are popular in the field of financial intelligence, considers financial intelligence to be a person's behavior with money, which is based on the three concepts of capital, debt and financial flow. The type of business, the amount of income and fixed capital, the amount of money that is withdrawn from the account every month, and most importantly, the path and flow in which these two moves indicate the financial intelligence of a person.

## Types of Financial Intelligence

Financial intelligence has 5 aspects and factors for success, none of which is superior to the other, and by strengthening all of them, a person's financial intelligence increases.

1. Financial intelligence, in earning more money
2. Financial intelligence, in saving money
3. Financial intelligence, in planning and budgeting money
4. Financial intelligence, in the use of money
5. Financial Intelligence, in Advances in Financial Knowledge

## 7 Characteristics of People With High Financial Intelligence

According to a person's performance in each of the types of financial intelligence mentioned above, a person with high financial intelligence is said to have the following characteristics:

1. Has a specific operational idea
2. Investment and savings of at least 10% of income
3. Expense management
4. It has a long-term and short-term plan
5. Reduce debt as much as possible
6. Consultation with specialists and experts
7. Always learning new skills and ways to earn more money

## Strengthening Financial Intelligence

The important point is that financial intelligence is different from financial intelligence. Financial intelligence quotient is a potential ability that becomes actual by strengthening it, which is financial intelligence. Therefore, only a high coefficient is not a sign of intelligence. For example, in two people with the same monthly income, someone with higher financial intelligence has more money left after reducing debts and expenses. Therefore, by training and using methods to strengthen financial intelligence, you can achieve more success in economic matters.

## 5 Simple Solutions to Strengthen and Increase Financial Intelligence

1. **Changing the Way of Thinking:**

Until you change your previous thoughts about money and ways to get it, nothing else will change. Therefore, in the first step, look for more income, not more purchases. Financial intelligence means the art of wise financial thinking, so look at financial issues with a new perspective.

2. **Planning and Targeting:**

Set long-term and short-term goals and have a coherent and specific plan to achieve each one. It is better to divide the goals from small to big and include the details of each one. Success in short-term and small goals will be a good incentive to go the long way of long-term goals.

3. **Time is Money:**

Value every moment of your life and use them optimally. High financial intelligence requires practice and spending a lot of time in order to achieve the desired result, and it takes your laziness and laziness away from your goals.

4. **Controlling Costs and Expenses:**

Start today and keep extra costs as low as possible. Make a shopping list and buy the necessary items accordingly. Pay off small debts and avoid new loans as much as possible. Forget the savings, even if the amount is very small.

5. **Increase Study and Learning:**

Using the experiences and training of successful people plays a significant role in strengthening financial intelligence. Unfortunately, the educational system of schools and even universities in Iran teach more about earning a salary and being an employee than entrepreneurship and making money. But after the expansion of virtual spaces, financial intelligence strengthening courses have grown well, which teach the ways and methods of strengthening financial intelligence in a principled and practical way. Also, reading the books of successful managers and billionaires of the world and getting to know their ways of making money will also help you in strengthening your financial intelligence.

*Figure 2. Diagram*

As mentioned at the beginning of this section, having money is not the only means of being rich, and if a rich person does not know the right ways to spend and increase it, the possibility of losing money and capital is very high. Financial intelligence is a part of the IQ of every person. It is based on his mastery and awareness in solving financial problems and also finding new plans and ideas for earning more. Therefore, it exists in every person's mind that with practice, as well as acquiring knowledge and strengthening proven solutions, he becomes a highly intelligent financial person.

## What are the Effects of Increasing Financial Intelligence on Better Business Management?

Increasing financial intelligence is considered an important category in today's world. Whether you are an ordinary person or someone who is in charge of managing an organization and group, financial intelligence and its improvement can be useful in managing expenses, checking the economic situation, maintaining and improving your capital. In the rest of this section, with more explanations about this issue, we will provide solutions to strengthen financial intelligence.

Increasing financial intelligence in today's world is one of the human needs so that in addition to managing their own expenses, they can interact better with others. Today, the world is in the era of global and competitive business, and for this reason, the importance of financial intelligence is felt in companies and organizations more than in other fields. This type of success can be achieved through financial discipline, goal setting, and periodic reviews.

Financial intelligence is a skill set consisting of five competencies. Including financial intelligence in earning money, saving money, using, and budgeting it, as well as financial intelligence in progress. To be fully successful in this field, all five competencies must be employed and implemented. Investment and finance is a business language that is recognized and used in all organizations. This important factor is the common denominator by which all organizations are judged.

Financial intelligence can help company managers to better understand their economic situation and act accordingly. Non-financial managers should not be confused when presented with a set of numbers. On the other hand, the purpose of financial intelligence is to ensure that when numbers are presented to non-financial managers, they are competent enough to understand them.

In another definition, if we want to express this issue in a more personal way, financial intelligence is the knowledge and ability of people that creates wealth. Improving and increasing financial intelligence helps them to have better economic and management skills in managing financial crises and solving problems in this area (Welsh2, 2021).

## Ways to Strengthen Financial Intelligence

Strengthening financial intelligence is essential for achieving long-term financial stability and success, as it equips individuals with the knowledge and skills necessary to make informed decisions about their finances. Despite the significant benefits, many people overlook the importance of developing their financial intelligence or struggle to implement effective strategies. This can often stem from misconceptions or outdated practices that do not yield positive results. To enhance financial intelligence, there are several key habits and methods that can be adopted:

1. **Focus on Savings and Cost Evaluation:** One of the most fundamental practices to boost financial intelligence is to prioritize savings and conduct a thorough evaluation of expenses. By maintaining a daily, weekly, or monthly budget, individuals can gain insights into their spending habits. Creating a detailed list of expenses not only encourages awareness of financial matters but also helps identify critical expenditures and eliminate unnecessary ones. This practice enables individuals to track important financial trends, optimize their spending, and develop a more strategic approach to managing their money.
2. **Read Books and Resources:** Engaging with literature on financial topics is a powerful way to enhance financial intelligence. Whether through traditional hardcover books or digital formats, immersing oneself in financial literature allows for a deeper understanding of personal finance, investment strategies, and money management principles. There are numerous books available that cover various aspects of financial literacy, offering valuable insights and practical advice. By dedicating time to read and absorb these resources, individuals can expand their financial knowledge and apply what they learn to their own situations.
3. **Utilize Expert Experiences and Discussions:** Another effective method for strengthening financial intelligence is to learn from the experiences and insights of industry experts. This can be accomplished by following programs, podcasts, or webinars where financial managers and successful entrepreneurs share their knowledge. Listening to expert discussions can provide real-world context and practical applications of financial concepts, helping individuals better manage their personal finances and business endeavors. Engaging with this content can also inspire new ideas and strategies for financial growth.
4. **Seek Guidance from a Financial Advisor:** Consulting with a financial advisor is a proactive step that can significantly enhance financial intelligence. Financial advisors are trained professionals with expertise in various aspects of finance, including investment planning, tax strategies, and risk management. By seeking their guidance, individuals can gain tailored advice that aligns with their specific financial goals and circumstances. This specialized support is especially beneficial in more complex financial matters, where professional insights can lead to better decision-making and improved financial outcomes.
5. **Engage in Financial Education Programs:** Participating in workshops, seminars, or online courses focused on financial literacy can further bolster financial intelligence. These programs often provide structured learning environments and cover a wide range of topics, from budgeting and saving to investing and

retirement planning. By actively engaging in financial education, individuals can build a solid foundation of knowledge and enhance their confidence in making financial decisions.
6. **Network with Like-Minded Individuals:** Building a network of individuals who share similar financial goals can also be beneficial. By joining financial clubs or online forums, individuals can exchange ideas, share experiences, and gain insights from others who are on similar journeys. This collaborative approach fosters a supportive environment where members can learn from each other, challenge one another to grow, and celebrate successes.

Enhancing financial intelligence is a multifaceted endeavor that requires dedication and a willingness to learn. By focusing on practical habits like savings and expense evaluation, immersing oneself in relevant literature, leveraging expert insights, seeking professional advice, participating in educational programs, and networking with others, individuals can significantly improve their financial literacy and decision-making skills. Ultimately, these efforts will pave the way for greater financial stability, improved money management, and a more prosperous future.

## Ways to Increase Children's Financial Intelligence

Increasing financial intelligence in children is a crucial investment in their future, enabling them to develop a healthy relationship with money and make informed financial decisions as they grow. By nurturing this skill from a young age, parents can equip their children with the tools necessary for financial success. Here are several effective methods to enhance children's financial intelligence:

1. **Reading Books:** Introducing children to literature that focuses on financial literacy is one of the best ways to lay a strong foundation. Books like *Why Didn't They Teach Me This in School? by Carey Siegel provide valuable insights tailored for younger audiences. Reading together can spark discussions about money management, savings, and the importance of making informed financial choices. Encourage children to explore various financial topics through books, articles, and age-appropriate resources to broaden their understanding.
2. **Investing Education:** Teach children about saving and investing by helping them set aside money for things they desire. This can start with small goals, such as saving for a toy or a game. You can incentivize their efforts by rewarding them for good behavior or contributing to their savings. For example, if they complete chores or achieve a goal, consider giving them a small amount to add to their savings. This not only instills the value of saving but also introduces

them to the concept of delayed gratification, helping them learn to prioritize their financial goals.

3. **Be a Good Role Model:** Children often learn by observing their parents and caregivers. By demonstrating responsible financial habits, such as budgeting, saving, and wise spending, you can set a positive example for your children to follow. Discuss your financial decisions openly, explaining the reasoning behind them, and involve them in family financial discussions when appropriate. This exposure helps children understand real-world applications of financial intelligence and encourages them to adopt similar behaviors.

4. **Household Budgeting:** As children transition into their teenage years, involve them in managing household expenses. Assign them tasks related to budgeting, such as tracking spending, helping with grocery lists, or planning a small family outing within a budget. For instance, you might allow them to manage a portion of the family grocery budget for a week, encouraging them to prioritize needs versus wants. This hands-on experience will foster a sense of responsibility and help them develop essential budgeting skills. Over time, they will gain confidence in handling money and understanding the implications of financial decisions.

5. **Setting Up a Savings Account:** Open a savings account for your child, allowing them to see their money grow over time. Teach them how interest works and how their savings can accumulate with regular deposits. This practical experience reinforces the importance of saving and introduces them to banking concepts. Encourage them to make regular deposits from their allowance or earnings, and celebrate milestones, such as reaching a savings goal.

6. **Games and Activities:** Utilize board games, apps, and online resources designed to teach financial concepts in a fun and engaging way. Games like Monopoly or The Game of Life can introduce children to the basics of budgeting, investing, and financial planning. There are also various educational apps available that simulate real-world financial scenarios, allowing children to make decisions and learn from the outcomes in a risk-free environment.

7. **Discuss Real-Life Financial Scenarios:** Engage children in discussions about real-life financial situations, such as budgeting for a family trip or planning for a major purchase. Encourage them to think critically about choices, trade-offs, and consequences. This practical application of financial concepts will enhance their understanding and help them develop problem-solving skills related to money management.

8. **Encouraging Entrepreneurship:** If your child shows interest in entrepreneurship, support their endeavors by helping them brainstorm business ideas or manage a small project, like a lemonade stand or a car wash. This experience teaches

them about investment, revenue, profit, and the responsibilities that come with running a business. It also nurtures creativity and resourcefulness.

By incorporating these strategies into your child's upbringing, you can help them cultivate financial intelligence that will serve them well throughout their lives. The goal is to create an environment where financial discussions are encouraged, financial literacy is prioritized, and children feel empowered to make informed decisions about their money. Ultimately, instilling these values and skills will prepare them for a financially secure future.

## What are the Characteristics of People Who Have High Financial Intelligence?

1- They learn financial management from experts

People who have high financial intelligence do not consider themselves to be intellectual. They always consult with experts and experienced people in this field.

2- They have stronger, more effective, and more stable communication skills

If you look at the type of relationships and complexities of successful people, you will see that they spend a lot of time and energy on their human networking. Establishing these relationships leads to the formation of a wide and effective network for them and helps them discover different angles of their abilities. They are also more patient, more courageous, have better self-confidence and self-esteem, and have more effective motivation and goal setting.

3- Interact with successful financial managers

In order to be successful in managing your money, you must model the characteristics, habits and daily behaviors of people who have walked this path before you. That's why good managers make friends with successful financial managers. They know very well that through each new relationship, they open a window of awareness and deeper information for their next financial decision.

4- They continuously learn new financial strategies

People with high financial intelligence do not shy away from learning about making money, buying, and selling stocks, investment information and financial issues in general. In fact, take the air from them, not to make money! Most of the time when you see them, they are listening to a program about getting rich, reading books about it, and the center of their talk revolves around money. Making money has become a habit for them.

5- They have an operational plan

People who have high financial intelligence have a comprehensive plan of action to do their financial work and have a daily plan to manage and implement it.

6- They usually save ten percent

People with good financial intelligence, such people regularly keep at least ten percent of their income. Of course, not to put it under the pillow, they are constantly learning ways to invest. Saving 10% at the starting point would be a realistic goal that anyone would be able to achieve. A 10% savings rate won't be enough to secure your financial future, but the first step is always the hardest. Small successes are the beginning of bigger victories.

Two-thirds of Americans don't have enough money in their savings accounts for emergencies. Nearly half of Americans think they need $50,000 to work with a financial advisor. Once you internalize the mindset of saving, achieving a 20% savings rate is very possible. Sure, you'll need to fine-tune your shopping list and find ways to make more money, but the day will come when you'll retire. For some reason, the later you get serious about saving, the tougher your future will be.

## How Reasonable Is The Savings?

You must have a realistic view of your needs. Many times, expensive things that we desire, cannot bring us a long-term happiness. A Chinese proverb says: "A small house is as happy as a big house." By remembering this simple fact, you will be able to save more than you ever imagined. There is no rule that says you can only save 20% of your income.

7- As for debts, their duties are clear

People with a lot of financial intelligence know that being in debt does not have a very good effect in the long run. At the same time, if they have to, they are not afraid of taking a loan or creating debt. In most cases, they clear their debts with the profits they get from smart investments.

8- They have short and long term financial goals

Financial goals are closely related to effective operational plans. The goals of "financially smart" people are divided into two categories, short-term and long-term, and this makes them focus on achieving them throughout the day.

### 9- They have a strategy in spending

Smart people think carefully about any amount they want to spend. Even if they have a lot of money! Successful financial managers are aware of the consequences of their smallest purchases. They know the long-term consequences of accumulating seemingly small purchases. They know that small purchases add up to debt and affect opportunities for profit. People with high financial intelligence have a very good ability to predict the future. This feature helps them to know the consequences of spending their income and make the right decision to spend it or not. If they conclude that spending their money will not benefit them in the long run, they will prioritize their decisions before taking any action.

Robert Kiyosaki divides financial intelligence into 5 areas. In fact, if you have these qualities, you can hope that you will be more successful than others.

### 1- If you can earn more, you have higher financial intelligence

The first depends on the amount of money you earn. If you earn 50 million dollars a year, your financial intelligence is probably higher than someone who earns 20 million. Of course, be careful, we said probably. Because you have to consider the following things as well.

### 2- If you save your money better, you have higher financial intelligence

Your financial intelligence depends on your ability to maintain your income. Once you start earning money, you need to protect it from "financial predators" such as banks and tax collectors.

### 3- If you have high financial intelligence, you should be able to leverage your money

According to Robert Kiyosaki, the return on your money and investments is measured by "how much money can you leverage to increase your wealth?"

### 4- Your financial intelligence is measured by the amount of your financial information

Information means real information, not your way of thinking or relying on information that others give you. It is not very wise to make our financial decisions based on what other people say. Except for those who really have first-hand and reliable information. Knowing the rules as well as patterns and trends is also a very important part of having financial information. Warren Buffett is one of the clear examples of knowing rules, information and patterns. He and his partners do extensive research for their investment decisions. Before they buy shares of a company, they should know everything about it and invest with confidence. Of course, mistakes can happen to anyone. Even the biggest businessmen in the world like Warren Buffett. Good information does not necessarily lead to the right decision, but it increases the probability of the right decision.

Seven ways to strengthen financial intelligence!

If you think you're "financially illiterate," don't worry. Many people think that they do not have any financial intelligence. Many people struggle to prepare for retirement by knowing how to manage personal finances, reduce debt, understand the stock market, and save. Fortunately, there are many resources available today to help improve your knowledge of financial decision-making.

Financial literacy doesn't happen overnight, and it doesn't happen by reading just one book. This happens through education, practical experience and life lessons (Shen,2016). In the following, we will learn how to increase our financial intelligence by introducing practical methods.

1- Start

It's never too late to improve your financial knowledge. Increase your knowledge about investing, estate planning, how credit cards work, loans, saving for the future, Social Security, insurance, retirement, and taxes. Work with one subject at a time. Start with the one you are most interested in learning and build a solid foundation of your financial knowledge.

2- Follow up on financial issues carefully

To strengthen your financial intelligence and make the right decisions, you should keep track of economic newspapers and magazines as much as your time allows. Note down its good points but concentrate well to make the best decision.

3- Search the Internet

There are many online resources to increase your financial literacy. Many news networks also have a financial tab.

4- Take a financial intelligence class with an experienced professor

Although in Iran, this issue is still not well established and experienced people try to reach their deals instead of training, but there are people who have been doing business for years. Find them and train with them. You prefer to stay at home, find a good domestic or foreign online course.

5- Follow the experts

Listen to the radio, TV business programs, and even discussions between entrepreneurs and financially successful people. Sometimes you can get very good tips from them. The secret of financial intelligence is: sharp sense! Be sharp.

6- Start investing. do not be scared

Don't be afraid to make mistakes. Either you succeed or you fail; But if you are going to just sit and read theory, you will never succeed in practice. It is just like a surgical medical student sitting at home and just studying. He must have surgery to learn! Start with less risky investments; But start. A famous saying says: No one has made a mistake who has done nothing.

7- Teach your children basic financial intelligence from now on

Our lack of financial intelligence is mostly because our families did not teach us the basics of investing. From the very beginning, we were taught to save some money in our piggy banks; But did they teach us what to do with the money saved?
Try to introduce them to the topic of wealth and money by using various tools such as financial circulation games, attractive books, and seminars for children. Of course, be careful not to tempt them. Children should not see money as "everything". They just need to know how to make money and save and invest in the right ways.

## What Mistakes Do People With High Financial Intelligence Not Repeat?

People who are financially successful and have high financial intelligence do not make these financial mistakes (Wathanakom, 2020).

### 1- They don't spend too much

One of the characteristics of people with high financial intelligence is that they spend less than what they earn. Even the richest people in the world don't overspend. For example, John Templeton (one of the great billionaires) saved half of his income, even when he was growing and had limited wealth. Don't worry if this amount is much more than what you are saving. You can achieve financial success by saving just 10-15% of your income.

### 2- They usually don't bargain

Highly financially savvy people think a lot about the value of what they are willing to pay for. For example, to invest, they focus on the growth they will see in the future, not the current price. Or when they want to buy something (like shoes) they usually choose high quality. It is true that they pay a lot of money initially, but it will save money in the long run.

### 3- Their financial plans are not static and fixed. It is flexible

Successful people adapt well to sudden events. They manage things with their high financial intelligence. For example, if an illness or marriage happens to them, they have already prepared for it. If you want to increase your financial intelligence, you need to adapt your financial plans to the changes. At least once a year, take a break with yourself to reevaluate your life and financial plans, so you get used to adapting to changes.

### 4- They don't like a fixed income

Most of us end up settling for a 5-10% annual raise. With this amount of increase in income, inflation will soon overtake you. But; Successful people are constantly looking for ways to improve their income and consequently their quality of life.

An increase in income not only increases your options for improving the quality of your life, but also gives you a sense of security and increases your capacity to pay. Successful people do daily tasks to increase their income. They generate passive income.

### 5- Successful people review financial statements periodically

Achieving financial success requires building consistent and gradual habits. One of these habits is the constant and periodic review of financial statements. Successful people spend at least one hour each month reviewing their financial statements such as investments, bank accounts, credit and checks issued. You better do this even if you don't have many financial statements. Naturally, you should spend less time.

6- They don't take dangerous or stupid risks with money!

Warren Buffett, the world's greatest investor, says: "The number one rule is: Never lose money." Of course, every investment has risks; But successful people use two powerful tools to avoid losing money:
The first is specialized insurance and the second is asset allocation. Asset allocation means they don't put all their eggs in one basket. Remember, if you find an opportunity that is much more profitable and optimal than the usual opportunities, be sure to proceed slowly and do some research on it.

7- They do not make strange claims

The world is big and successful people understand this fact deeply. When it comes to money, there is a lot of information about it. That's why people like Warren Buffett keep their limitations in mind and focus on their strengths.
Know exactly how much you know about money and investing. If you are just starting out, read at least a few books on personal finance.

8- They don't listen to experts blindly

We said above that smart people listen to the advice of experts, but not blindly. They take the strengths of the successful and don't repeat their mistakes. These people are constantly looking for the advice of professionals and experts, but they don't give in to their opinions without reason. For example, it makes sense to ask an accountant for help in preparing tax returns; But to evaluate a successful person, when you seek the advice of professionals like accountants or lawyers, ask them questions and ask them to explain their advice to you. Otherwise, it will be difficult to ask experts.

9- Successful people do not prioritize making money over other goals

Achieving financial success is a valid goal. Because the quality of your life increases, and you can help others. You will also have access to technology, medical services, and leisure time; But successful people know that financial success is only one aspect of a successful life. For example, they don't risk their health to earn money. Review your goals and assess whether there is a balance between financial, career, family, and other activities.

## Small Exercises to Strengthen Financial Intelligence

Here are some small exercises that can help you strengthen your financial intelligence:

1. Reduce your food costs

Food is a heavy expense for many of us; But we don't pay attention to it. Reducing the cost of food does not mean reducing the quality of life; But we should not let it get out of our hands. Cut food costs by eating out less and finding cheaper alternatives at home. Buy the things you use the most. Spend your diet on higher value but cheaper foods such as pasta, rice, beans, legumes, etc. An interesting tip: shopping at the beginning of the week makes it more likely to buy expensive things. Shop on weekends!

2. Separate your bank account to get the account

To buy food or groceries from a separate card, to buy clothes from another card and for every type of purchase, have at least 4 credit cards to know exactly what you buy and how much money you spend in each part of life.

3. Reducing transportation costs

If you can, go to work by bike. You exercised, helped the environment, and kept your money in your pocket. Transportation is a big expense for some of us, even if you can't walk or bike, look at public transportation. If you can get to work without a vehicle, you can even sell your car.

4. Have fun, but don't waste!

Save instead of splurging. It's hard at first, but little by little, this will help you create great habits and improve your quality of life. Because then you have enough money to buy the things you want.

5. Stick to your commitments

Commit to how much you will spend in a month. Never spend more than that. Except when there is no other choice.

6. Get advice

Don't be afraid to spend money on education. Spend money if you have to and get valuable advice for your money. Reading this article was the first step to strengthen your financial intelligence; But you want to improve your financial intelligence. So look for great training programs.

## Important Factors in Any Investment

It doesn't matter where you want to invest, whether your capital is 50 million or 5 million, 500 million or 5 billion, you should consider these factors in every investment. In any case, you should have some cash to cover your living expenses for at least 3 months, even if you have no income; In other words, if you don't have even 1 rial in your pocket for the next 3 months, you and your family should be able to cover your expenses. If this is the case, then think about investing.

1. The best use of money and capital

That is, where is your money better spent? If you already have a loan that you are paying a high interest on, and instead of paying the loan installment, you are making a mistake by investing it in a place where the return is lower than the interest on the loan. For example, you got a loan and you pay 20 or 25% interest to the bank every year, do you think it is wise not to pay the installments and instead invest the money somewhere that earns 18% interest per year? Certainly not! Believe it or not, many people make this mistake, but because they have wrong calculations, they don't even realize it. In addition to the best place to invest, the best time is also important. You must protect your capital from falling markets and investment value. If you enter a market where prices are at their peak, there is a high risk that the asset will decline in value. Prices never rise or fall forever, growth and decline in any market stop. Don't let greed and blind decisions make you enter a market at the peak of prices (Walid Mensi, 2019).

2. Liquidity of capital

Is the property you are going to buy good liquidity? If you don't care about liquidity, please think again. Liquidity means how quickly and at what price you can convert your purchased asset or investment into cash or its equivalent. Of course, one should pay attention to the price in terms of liquidity. If you buy a residential unit and sell it 20% below the price, it is obvious that it will be cashed out quickly, so you should consider the right price in cashing. If we want to write the liquidity of markets in Iran in order, it is as follows:

- **Bank Deposit:** You can easily go to the bank and receive your deposit
- **Currency, Gold, and Coins:** If the currency broker, money changer or gold dealer is willing to buy, cash out your assets right away.
- **Stocks and Securities:** If you sell the stock today, it will be credited to your account two business days later. The shares of companies have different liquidity, but on average it can be liquidated quickly.
- **Business Assets (raw materials, equipment, goods, etc.):** It may take a long time to find a suitable buyer for the business assets you already had.
- **Real Estate**: Selling real estate at the right price sometimes takes months.

3. Investment Objectives

This factor together with other factors determines the market in which you invest. Maybe you want your capital to grow quickly, and you don't care about risk because you can easily take losses and rebuild yourself. Or maybe your goal is to grow your capital in the safest way possible and preserving the principal is extremely important. Based on these different goals, different investment decisions can be made:

A low-risk investment Because you'll need the money later, if you're close to retirement, you probably don't want your money to lose value because you're counting on it. For this reason, if you have a financial goal that is approaching, a low-risk investment is wiser. Investments such as buying bonds, buying units of mutual funds.

Investing with moderate risk for better returns Of course, if you can bear more risk and you don't need your money in the near future, investing in stocks of large companies that have high stability and preferably pay good cash dividends is a good option. Risky investing to achieve high returns – If you can afford to risk a large portion of your money to achieve higher returns, then fast growth is a good goal for you. In this situation, you should invest in the stocks of companies that have a good future but are riskier. This option is suitable for when you do not need money for a long time and you can wait until the company in question grows and achieves more profit. Investing with mixed goals is also possible. For example, you may be a fan of high risk and high profit in the long term but spend part of your capital to buy investment funds to reduce risk (Vamvaka, 2020).

4. Your Age

Not everyone has the same investment goal. Maybe one person is thinking of saving enough money for retirement and another person is at the beginning of life and won't need their money for years. Therefore, one of the other factors in investing is how long you can keep the investment; In other words, how long do you have? The longer you can hold your investment; the more profit you can make. If you don't have a lot of time and it would be catastrophic to run out of money, you should stick to low-risk investments.

5. Risk Tolerance

As a general principle, the higher the return expected from an investment, the higher the risk. In addition, some people are not comfortable with the market fluctuations and cannot tolerate the extreme ups and downs of markets like the stock market. In markets like the stock market, there are always losses, but professional investors cover their losses with profits. If you cannot tolerate losses and your heart starts beating fast with every market fluctuation, it is better to look for low risk investments. If you are willing to take some temporary losses to achieve higher returns in the future, then try risky investments.

# REFERENCES

Shen, C.-H., Lin, S.-J., Tang, D.-P., & Hsiao, Y.-J. (2016). The relationship between financial disputes and financial literacy. *Pacific-Basin Finance Journal*, 36, 46–65. DOI: 10.1016/j.pacfin.2015.11.002

Vamvaka, V., Stoforos, C., Palaskas, T., & Botsaris, C. (2020). Attitude toward entrepreneurship perceived behavioral control, and entrepreneurial intention: Dimensionality, structural relationships, and gender differences. *Journal of Innovation and Entrepreneurship*, 9(1), 1–26.

Walid Mensi . (2019) 'Global financial crisis and co-movements between oil prices and sector stock markets in Saudi Arabia: A VaR based wavelet' Borsa Istanbul, Review 19-1, pp. 24 -e38.

Wathanakom, N., Khlaisang, J., & Songkram, N. (2020). The study of the causal relationship between innovativeness and entrepreneurial intention among undergraduate students. *Journal of Innovation and Entrepreneurship*, 9(1), 1–15.

Welsh, D. H. B., Kaciak, E., Mehtap, S., Pellegrini, M. M., Caputo, A., & Ahmed, S. (2021). The door swings in and out: The impact of family support and country stability on success of women entrepreneurs in the Arab world. *International Small Business Journal*, 39(7), 619–642. DOI: 10.1177/0266242620952356

# Chapter 10
# Effective and Key Financial Management Solutions for Entrepreneurs and Business Owners

## ABSTRACT

*These days, business owners are at an unprecedented level of economic anxiety, and this issue threatens the financial stability of companies. Many businesses around the world have been shut down due to social distancing measures, many of which will likely close permanently. Entrepreneurs and start-up business owners who seek to avoid this fate must pay more attention to their financial management, because not paying enough attention to this issue now is like buying a one-way ticket to bankruptcy. Instead of sitting around and waiting for financial salvation to magically appear, try to be cautious and take these steps to protect your company's future (Lusardi,2019).*

## INTRODUCTION

Navigating the financial complexities of entrepreneurship is a cornerstone of business success. In an era where economic uncertainties loom large and market dynamics shift rapidly, mastering financial management becomes not just a skill but a necessity. Entrepreneurs and business owners are constantly confronted with challenges such as fluctuating revenues, increasing operational costs, and evolving consumer behavior. These issues, if unaddressed, can destabilize even the most

DOI: 10.4018/979-8-3693-9415-1.ch010

promising ventures. Effective financial management provides the tools to face these challenges head-on, ensuring sustainability and growth. It encompasses everything from optimizing cash flow and leveraging tax exemptions to embracing technology and making strategic investments. For entrepreneurs, financial acuity is not merely about keeping the books balanced; it is about making informed decisions that drive innovation, adaptability, and resilience. This chapter delves into practical strategies and tools tailored for entrepreneurs and small business owners. From cultivating a robust financial foundation to embracing calculated risks, we explore actionable solutions designed to mitigate risks, enhance profitability, and secure long-term success. By adopting these principles, entrepreneurs can transform their financial management from a daunting obligation into a dynamic driver of business growth.

## PROACTIVE FINANCIAL MANAGEMENT: A LIFELINE FOR BUSINESSES IN TURBULENT TIMES

These days, business owners are at an unprecedented level of economic anxiety, and this issue threatens the financial stability of companies. Many businesses around the world have been shut down due to social distancing measures, many of which will likely close permanently. Entrepreneurs and start-up business owners who seek to avoid this fate must pay more attention to their financial management, because not paying enough attention to this issue now is like buying a one-way ticket to bankruptcy. Instead of sitting around and waiting for financial salvation to magically appear, try to be cautious and take these steps to protect your company's future (Lusardi,2019).

### Take Advantage of Tax Exemptions

Taking advantage of tax exemptions is a strategic move that can significantly benefit entrepreneurs, especially in a business landscape often burdened by high taxation. Entrepreneurs frequently find themselves grappling with substantial tax bills, which can hinder economic growth by limiting their capacity to hire new employees, invest in renovations, or physically expand their operations. Such financial pressures can create a cycle of difficulty, especially in challenging economic conditions where cash flow is critical for survival. By actively seeking out and utilizing available tax exemptions, business owners can mitigate their tax liabilities and free up resources for more productive uses.

For instance, certain tax breaks are specifically designed to encourage the hiring and retention of qualified employees, which can simultaneously reduce a company's overall tax burden. One notable example is the tax incentives provided to small businesses that employ individuals with disabilities. Not only do these exemptions help alleviate financial pressure, but they also promote a more inclusive workplace environment. Creating an accessible workplace for employees with disabilities is not only an ethical responsibility but also a wise economic decision. By installing ramps and implementing other necessary infrastructure, businesses can ensure compliance with accessibility standards while enhancing their reputation as socially responsible employers.

Moreover, fostering an inclusive workforce can lead to diverse perspectives that drive innovation and creativity within the company. In addition to the immediate financial benefits, the long-term advantages of cultivating a diverse talent pool can position a business for sustained growth and success. Therefore, entrepreneurs should remain vigilant about potential tax exemptions and consider how these opportunities can be leveraged not only to alleviate their tax burdens but also to enhance their overall business operations and contribute positively to society. Embracing this approach can empower businesses to thrive even amidst the challenges posed by high taxation and economic uncertainty.

## Embrace Technology Without Spending Extra

Embracing technology has become an essential strategy for business owners who want to remain competitive in today's rapidly evolving market. The common narrative emphasizes the need for digital transformation to ensure long-term sustainability and relevance. However, many entrepreneurs often find themselves overwhelmed by the myriad of digital tools and software services available, leading to uncertainty about where to invest their resources effectively. Not all technological solutions provide a return on investment that justifies their cost; therefore, it is crucial to approach the integration of technology with a strategic mindset that balances necessity and affordability.

To strike this balance, business owners should begin by conducting a thorough assessment of their operational needs and identifying specific areas where technology can enhance efficiency, productivity, or customer engagement. Rather than jumping on every technological trend, entrepreneurs should prioritize tools that align with their business objectives and offer tangible benefits. For instance, adopting cloud-based solutions can streamline data management and collaboration without the burden of significant upfront costs associated with traditional software installations. Moreover, many technology providers offer tiered pricing models or free versions of their services, allowing businesses to access essential features without incurring hefty expenses. Entrepreneurs should take advantage of these options, exploring tools that provide trial periods or limited free access to help them gauge the value they bring before making a financial commitment. This way, they can integrate technology into their operations without compromising profitability.

Additionally, education and training play a vital role in maximizing the potential of technological tools. Business owners should invest in upskilling their teams to ensure they are proficient in using new technologies effectively. This not only enhances productivity but also minimizes the risk of costly mistakes that can arise from improper usage. By fostering a culture of continuous learning and adaptability, businesses can fully leverage technology as a catalyst for growth rather than a financial burden.

In conclusion, while the necessity of integrating technology into business operations is undeniable, it is essential to approach this transition thoughtfully and strategically. By evaluating needs, prioritizing cost-effective solutions, leveraging free resources, and investing in training, entrepreneurs can embrace technology in a manner that enhances their operations and drives success without compromising their financial health. This balanced approach allows businesses to remain agile and competitive, positioning them for sustained growth in an increasingly digital marketplace.

## Build Your Future with Long-Term Investment

Building a secure financial future through long-term investment is a crucial strategy for anyone looking to solidify their financial standing, especially entrepreneurs. While many people are often advised to invest in the stock market as a pathway to wealth, it is important to recognize that not all business owners actively engage in stock trading. The demands of running a business can consume significant time and energy, making it challenging to stay informed about the constant fluctuations and trends of the stock market. However, this does not mean that entrepreneurs should overlook the potential benefits of investing.

Smart entrepreneurs understand the value of diversifying their investment portfolio. By exploring various asset classes—such as real estate, bonds, commodities, and even venture capital—they can mitigate risks and secure more stable returns over time. Diversification is not just about spreading investments across different sectors; it's about strategically identifying opportunities that align with their business goals and market trends. For example, investing in real estate can provide steady rental income and potential appreciation, while bonds can offer more stable, low-risk returns. Furthermore, investment opportunities often arise from a keen understanding of the market and an ability to identify trends before they become mainstream. This foresight can lead to significant profits in the long run. By leveraging their industry knowledge, entrepreneurs can invest in innovative startups, emerging technologies, or sectors poised for growth. These strategic investments not only enhance their financial portfolio but also align with their core business operations, creating synergy between their investments and their entrepreneurial ventures.

In the ever-evolving economic landscape, having a diversified portfolio is essential for weathering financial storms. Economic downturns and market fluctuations can significantly impact a business's revenue and stability. However, a well-structured investment portfolio can act as a buffer, providing alternative income sources and helping entrepreneurs navigate through challenging times. This resilience allows business owners to focus on their primary goals without the constant stress of financial uncertainty. Moreover, cultivating a mindset geared toward long-term investment fosters a more sustainable approach to wealth-building. Rather than seeking quick gains, entrepreneurs who commit to investing with a long-term perspective are more likely to experience compounded growth over time. This patience and strategic planning are essential for achieving financial independence and building a legacy.

While the stock market is often highlighted as a key avenue for investment, entrepreneurs should not confine themselves to this singular approach. By recognizing the importance of a diversified investment portfolio, staying alert to emerging opportunities, and maintaining a long-term vision, business owners can build a robust financial future. Smart investments will not only support their current business endeavors but also create a safety net that allows them to thrive, even in uncertain economic conditions. Ultimately, the key to financial security lies in understanding the intricate relationship between investment and business success, enabling entrepreneurs to take informed risks that propel their ventures forward.

## Make Money From Your Online Presence

Leveraging your online presence to generate revenue is an increasingly vital strategy for entrepreneurs in today's digital age. If you own a website or maintain an active social media profile with a substantial following, there are numerous opportunities to monetize your online visibility. One of the most straightforward methods is through advertising. Many platforms offer affiliate marketing programs where you can earn commissions by promoting products or services relevant to your audience. By strategically placing ads on your website or sharing sponsored content on your social media channels, you can turn your online presence into a source of passive income.

Social media platforms, especially Instagram, have transformed into powerful marketing tools. With their visual-centric approach, they allow businesses to showcase their products and services effectively. By sharing engaging content, such as high-quality images, videos, and stories, you can attract more followers and create a community around your brand. Collaborating with influencers or other businesses can further amplify your reach, driving traffic to your website and increasing sales.

Additionally, consider utilizing social media for direct sales through features like Instagram Shopping or Facebook Marketplace. These tools enable you to list products directly on your profiles, making it easier for potential customers to purchase without leaving the platform. This seamless shopping experience can significantly enhance your sales efforts and foster customer loyalty. Moreover, engaging with your audience is crucial for building a loyal following. Regularly interacting with your followers through comments, direct messages, and live sessions not only helps strengthen relationships but also provides valuable insights into their preferences and needs. This feedback can inform your marketing strategies and product offerings, ultimately leading to increased revenue.

If you overlook the importance of maintaining an active and effective online presence, you risk missing out on valuable financial opportunities. In an era where consumers increasingly turn to the internet for their shopping needs, establishing a strong digital footprint is essential for any entrepreneur. Failing to engage with your audience online can hinder your business growth and limit your ability to adapt to changing market dynamics. Making money from your online presence is not just a possibility; it's a necessity for modern entrepreneurs. By harnessing the power of advertising, social media marketing, and direct sales, you can effectively monetize your digital platforms. Embracing this approach not only enhances your financial management but also positions your business for long-term success in an increasingly competitive marketplace. Investing time and resources into cultivating a vibrant online community will ultimately yield significant returns, allowing you to grow your business and achieve your financial goals.

## THE BEST FINANCIAL PRACTICES OF SUCCESSFUL ENTREPRENEURS

The best financial practices of successful entrepreneurs go beyond merely focusing on the profits generated by their businesses; they emphasize the importance of effectively managing and redistributing those profits. This fundamental principle underscores that a business's longevity and success are rooted in its financial management strategies rather than its revenue alone. Therefore, it is essential for entrepreneurs, regardless of the size of their enterprises, to invest time and resources into establishing robust financial practices that ensure sustainability and growth. By implementing effective financial measures, such as creating comprehensive budgets, maintaining accurate financial records, and setting aside emergency funds, entrepreneurs can better navigate the challenges of the business landscape. Additionally, diversifying income streams, investing in employee development, and leveraging technology for efficiency are crucial steps in building a resilient business model.

Regular monitoring of key financial metrics and seeking professional financial advice can provide valuable insights that drive informed decision-making. Furthermore, practicing smart tax management and nurturing customer relationships can enhance profitability and foster a loyal client base. By embracing these financial practices, entrepreneurs can create a solid foundation for their businesses, ensuring they not only survive but thrive in an increasingly competitive market. Taking proactive steps today will lead to long-term financial health and success, enabling entrepreneurs to achieve their goals and secure a prosperous future for their enterprises.

## Periodic Review of Financial Issues

Periodic review of financial issues is a crucial practice for anyone involved in managing a business, yet it is often overlooked in the hustle and bustle of daily operations. While it may seem like a straightforward task, the demands of running a business can lead to financial oversight becoming a low priority. However, mastering financial matters is essential for success, as it allows entrepreneurs to understand the health of their business and make informed decisions. No matter how experienced you are in building and running a company, fluctuations in turnover are normal, and a decline in revenue can occur unexpectedly. Therefore, regularly reviewing your income and expenses is vital in maintaining control over your financial situation.

Most successful business owners recognize the importance of consistent financial oversight and routinely assess their financial statements. For new business owners, cultivating this habit can prove invaluable. It not only helps in identifying potential problems early on but also empowers you to implement corrective measures before issues escalate into more significant challenges. By regularly examining financial data, such as cash flow, profit margins, and expense patterns, entrepreneurs can make informed decisions that drive growth and sustainability. This proactive approach fosters a deeper understanding of the business's financial dynamics, enabling you to adapt to changing circumstances and seize opportunities for improvement. Ultimately, a periodic review of financial matters is not just a best practice; it is a fundamental aspect of effective business management that can significantly contribute to long-term success.

## Have a Defensive Shield

Having a defensive shield in place is essential for business owners who understand that downturns and declines are inevitable parts of the entrepreneurial journey. A savvy business owner recognizes the importance of preparing for challenging times and takes proactive measures to safeguard their enterprise. One of the most effective strategies for creating this protective barrier is to conduct regular financial reviews, which enable you to assess your current situation and identify areas for improvement.

Establishing a financial cushion, typically in the form of savings or reserves, is a critical component of this defensive strategy. By setting aside funds to cover unexpected losses, you equip your business with the resources needed to navigate through tough times without compromising operations or sacrificing long-term goals. This financial buffer acts as a safety net, allowing you to weather the storm and emerge stronger on the other side. Moreover, maintaining solid relationships with lenders and ensuring a good credit score are vital aspects of your defensive shield. A positive credit history not only enhances your borrowing capacity but also instills confidence in lenders and investors, making it easier to secure financing when needed. Strong relationships with financial partners can provide access to additional resources and support, ensuring that your business has the backing it requires during periods of uncertainty. Ultimately, businesses that prioritize having a defensive shield are better equipped to survive adversity. By implementing strategic financial practices and fostering strong relationships, these businesses can navigate challenging times more effectively and emerge not only intact but also more resilient and prepared for future opportunities. This proactive approach underscores the importance of being prepared, allowing entrepreneurs to focus on long-term growth and sustainability while minimizing the impact of short-term setbacks.

## Calculated Risks

Calculated risks are essential for any business looking to stand out in a competitive landscape. To truly differentiate your brand from others, it's important to step outside your comfort zone and explore opportunities that may not seem immediately safe or conventional. Many globally recognized brands and successful entrepreneurs have reached their status by challenging the limits of what is financially feasible. However, embracing calculated risks does not equate to reckless spending or making outlandish investments; rather, it involves making informed decisions that weigh potential rewards against possible downsides.

To effectively incorporate calculated risks into your business strategy, it's crucial to maintain a balanced approach. Start by ensuring you have a solid emergency fund to cover unexpected setbacks. This financial safety net will give you the confidence to explore new ventures without jeopardizing the stability of your existing operations. Once that foundation is established, consider allocating a portion of your profits toward reinvesting in your company or diversifying into other ventures.

This reinvestment could take various forms, such as exploring new markets, developing innovative products, or adopting cutting-edge technology. By strategically directing resources into areas with high growth potential, you can position your business for long-term success. This approach not only fosters growth but also allows for adaptability in an ever-changing market. Moreover, it's essential to conduct thorough research and analysis before making any significant investment. By evaluating market trends, understanding customer needs, and assessing potential risks, you can make decisions that are not only bold but also grounded in reality. This strategic mindset transforms the concept of risk-taking into an opportunity for growth and innovation, ultimately contributing to your business's competitive edge. Calculated risks are a vital component of entrepreneurial success. By pushing beyond comfort zones while maintaining a prudent financial strategy, you can unlock new avenues for growth and establish a distinct presence in the marketplace. Embracing this philosophy not only enhances your business's resilience but also empowers you to seize opportunities that drive meaningful progress.

**Always be Learning**

As an entrepreneur, never stay still! The moment you stop and think you've created the best product possible, that's the moment you'll lose to the competition. Most successful entrepreneurs are constantly looking to expand their knowledge and find new methods or ideas to implement in their operations (Paiella, 2016).

## GOALS, GOALS, GOALS

Think of your business like driving from point A to point B. If you don't know where you are going, you are likely to get lost. Ask any successful entrepreneur or athlete or anyone you know who is successful and you will likely find that they take the time to set specific and realistic goals for where they are going. They create a road map for success. In all business ventures, take the time to create a financial action plan. Where do you expect your business to be financially in five years? You'll probably be surprised how much easier it is to reach a goal by having realistic but challenging goals. After all, most entrepreneurs and business owners aren't afraid to have a different opinion than others. If you want your business to get where you want it to be, take the time to implement these financial strategies into your operational processes. There is always a way to improve your business. Whether this way is to design goals for the next five years or to use accounting software to review the financial situation.

# Recommendations that Every New Business Should Follow

Launching a product or service and becoming your own boss is an exhilarating journey that many individuals aspire to embark on. However, the road to establishing a successful business is often fraught with challenges and uncertainties. To navigate this complex landscape effectively, it is crucial for aspiring entrepreneurs to have a clear understanding of the market they intend to enter. Conducting comprehensive market research is the first step; this involves analyzing the target audience, evaluating competitors, and identifying industry trends. A deep understanding of customer needs and behaviors allows entrepreneurs to tailor their offerings, while a thorough competitive analysis can reveal gaps in the market that present unique opportunities for differentiation. Furthermore, creating a solid business plan is essential. This plan acts as a roadmap, detailing business objectives, strategies, financial projections, and operational guidelines. A well-crafted business plan not only clarifies the entrepreneur's vision but also serves as a critical tool for securing funding from investors or lenders. Establishing a strong brand identity is equally important; it goes beyond a logo to encompass values, mission, and the overall customer experience. A compelling brand story and consistent messaging can build trust and loyalty, setting the business apart in a crowded marketplace.

Effective financial management is another cornerstone of success. Entrepreneurs should meticulously track income, expenses, and cash flow, utilizing accounting software to simplify the process. Consulting with financial advisors can further enhance budgeting and forecasting strategies, ensuring the business remains financially healthy and prepared for challenges. Networking and mentorship play vital roles as well; connecting with industry peers and seeking guidance from experienced mentors can provide invaluable insights and help avoid common pitfalls. In an ever-evolving business landscape, adaptability is key. Entrepreneurs should remain open to feedback and willing to pivot strategies as needed. Continuous innovation—assessing and improving products, services, and processes—will help businesses stay ahead of trends and competition. Lastly, prioritizing customer experience is paramount; satisfied customers not only return but also spread positive word-of-mouth, which is crucial for growth. By embracing these principles—understanding the market, crafting a business plan, building a strong brand, managing finances wisely, networking, remaining adaptable, and focusing on customer satisfaction—aspiring entrepreneurs can significantly enhance their chances of success in the dynamic world of business.

## Know Your Audience

Understanding your audience is one of the foundational steps in launching a successful business. Before you begin implementing your ideas, it's essential to have a clear vision of who your target audience is and, more importantly, why they need your product or service. To do this effectively, consider a broad range of demographic factors that will help paint a comprehensive picture of your potential customers. Key elements to examine include age, gender, education level, income, and geographic location. For instance, different age groups may have varying preferences and purchasing behaviors; younger consumers might prioritize trends and social media engagement, while older audiences may value reliability and tradition. Similarly, understanding income levels can help you tailor your pricing strategy and marketing messages to fit the financial capabilities of your audience. Geographic location can also play a significant role, as cultural differences and local trends can influence consumer behavior.

The more you can narrow down your target audience to a specific group, the better equipped you will be to engage with them effectively. This segmentation allows you to create tailored marketing strategies and messages that resonate with your audience's unique needs and preferences. Once you have identified this target group, you can determine the most effective channels to reach them and develop communication strategies that align with their interests and values. By investing time in understanding your audience, you can enhance the relevance of your offerings and significantly increase the likelihood of your business's success.

## Know Your Competitors

In addition to understanding your target audience, identifying and analyzing your potential competitors is crucial for developing a successful business strategy. A comprehensive market analysis should include a thorough examination of the competitive landscape, focusing on the key players in your industry, their market share, and the overall saturation of the market. By evaluating your competitors, you gain valuable insights into their strengths, weaknesses, and the strategies they employ to capture their audience.

Analyzing the competitive environment will help you determine the feasibility of your product or service. For instance, if you discover that the market has few significant players, this might indicate a valuable opportunity for entry, making it an ideal time to launch your offering. Conversely, if the market is already saturated with established competitors, you must assess whether your product or service has a distinct point of differentiation. If you cannot identify a unique selling proposition that sets your offering apart, it may be wise to reconsider your approach or refine your business concept. Conducting thorough customer and competitor research not only provides you with a clearer picture of the market landscape but also informs your overall strategy. Understanding where your competitors excel and where they fall short can guide your decision-making, enabling you to capitalize on their weaknesses while reinforcing your strengths. With this knowledge in hand, you can design a compelling marketing program that effectively communicates your unique value proposition or return to the drawing board to rethink your strategy. Ultimately, a deep understanding of both your competitors and your target market will empower you to position your business more effectively and enhance your chances of success.

## What Makes You Different?

As you conduct your research, it's inevitable that you will encounter competitors or similar products targeting your ideal customers. These insights are invaluable for identifying your unique point of differentiation, which is essential for standing out in a crowded market. Understanding what makes your business unique will help you develop a compelling value proposition that resonates with your audience.

Start by asking yourself critical questions: Are you the most cost-effective option available? Do you offer superior quality compared to your competitors? What additional value can you provide that others cannot? Perhaps you have innovative features, exceptional customer service, or a sustainable approach that appeals to environmentally-conscious consumers. Whatever your differentiators may be, it's essential to articulate them clearly and effectively. Focusing on your unique selling point (USP) is crucial for the success of your idea. Your USP should not only highlight what sets your business apart but also emphasize the benefits that your customers will experience. This could mean showcasing the cost savings they'll enjoy, the quality assurance that comes with your products, or the enhanced experience they can expect from your service.

To effectively communicate your differentiators, employ various marketing strategies that resonate with your target audience. Use engaging storytelling, clear messaging, and visual branding to showcase why your business is superior to the competition. By making your unique value proposition clear, you can build trust and loyalty among customers, encouraging them to choose your business over others. Ultimately, demonstrating what makes you different will position your brand as a leader in your market and drive your success in the long run.

## Are You Financially Justified?

One of the most critical elements that can determine the viability of your business idea is its financial foundation, particularly if you are considering going public. Before taking that significant step, you must thoroughly evaluate several key financial aspects. Begin by asking yourself essential questions: What are the expected costs to launch your business? Where will your initial capital come from? What are your ongoing operating expenses? What is the revenue potential of your business? Answering these questions is crucial for understanding the financial landscape of your venture. A detailed financial analysis not only helps you grasp the startup costs involved but also enables you to plan for the long term. You need a clear picture of your business expenses, including fixed and variable costs, to establish a realistic budget. This will help you avoid the common pitfalls associated with inadequate financial planning, such as running out of funds or facing unexpected expenses.

While it may seem daunting at first, conducting a thorough financial analysis is imperative. It provides a roadmap for your business and equips you with the necessary information to make informed decisions. Starting without a comprehensive understanding of your financial situation can lead to disastrous outcomes and increased risk of failure. Many businesses falter within their first few years due to poor planning, inadequate cash flow management, and a lack of awareness of market dynamics. Therefore, as you embark on this exciting journey of entrepreneurship, ensure that you are well-prepared financially. Gather all the crucial information regarding costs, funding sources, and potential revenue streams before moving forward. This proactive approach will not only save you from the grief of business failure but also increase your chances of building a sustainable and profitable enterprise in the years to come. By being financially justified and prepared, you set the foundation for long-term success.

## Five Effective Steps in Small Business Growth

Categorizing the problems and growth patterns of very small businesses and turning them into a systematic method that is useful for entrepreneurs, at first glance, seems very difficult and impossible. Due to the size and capabilities of small businesses, these organizations experience many changes. They are categorized by criteria such as independence in performance, different organizational structures and different management style. Of course, in a very detailed and scrutinizing examination, it is clear that these organizations face the same problems in the stages of growth and development. These common points can be organized into a working framework. This can inform our understanding of the nature, characteristics, and business problems of all types of businesses, from a small laundry with two or three very low-wage employees to a software company with $20 million a year in revenue and growing at 40%. The percentage of progress will increase to a very large extent. For small business owners and managers, such an idea can be very helpful in assessing the challenges ahead. For example, the need to upgrade existing computer systems or to hire and train second-level managers to maintain anticipated growth are among the things that can be mentioned.

These can be very efficient in predicting key requirements in different situations. For example, allocating too much time for startup owners in the early stages and needing to change or eliminate their management role when the companies become larger and more complex. The existence of a pattern provides a background to examine the impact of the presence or absence of regulations and policies proposed by the government in a business. One of the most important points is not paying taxes on dividends, which can be very helpful in creating a profitable, growing, and sustainable business. But this case can't do anything for new businesses that have grown very fast or for companies active in the field of advanced technologies. Finally, the resulting patterns help accountants and consultants to identify problems and provide appropriate solutions for companies with very little capital. The problems and solutions presented for a 6-month-old company with 20 employees are not comparable to the problems and solutions presented for a 30-year-old company with 100 employees. Previously, planning for cash flow was of the greatest importance, but now strategic planning and budgeting to achieve coordination and control in performance are given the highest priority.

## Create a Small Business Framework

Many researchers have tried over the years to create a suitable model for business. Each of them consider the business size as one of the parameters and the life of a company or the growth stage of that company as another parameter. Of course, this point of view has been useful and effective in many cases. This method is unsuitable for very small businesses for three reasons:

*Figure 1. Growth phases*

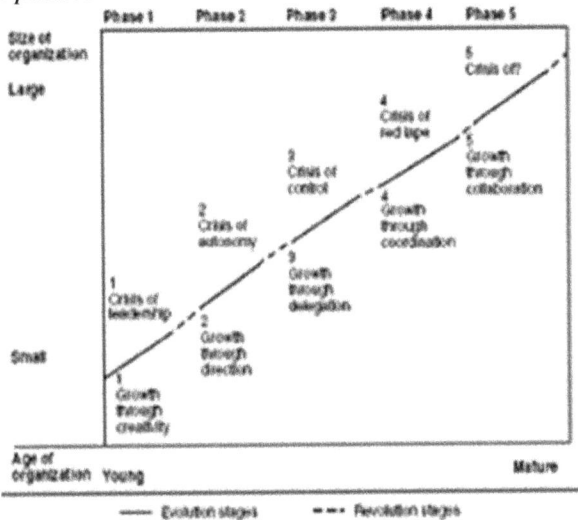

First, this theory is based on the assumption that a company must go through all the stages in order to grow, otherwise it will be destroyed. Second, this model is ineffective in examining and analyzing the most important stages of the formation of companies, which are related to its growth and prosperity stages, and has weaknesses. Thirdly, this framework refers to its annual sales statistics to estimate the size of the company (although some define it by the number of employees). This method ignores other parameters such as added value, number of branches, diversity in the production line, and growth rate in the change of production products or related technology. In order to create a model that can be implemented in small businesses, a collection of experiences, research articles, and empirical observations must be made. The framework resulting from this research can outline the five stages that are needed for the progress of a company. Each of these stages is determined by indicators such as size, organizational structure, extent of government systems, important strategic goals, and the degree of participation of the business owners in the market.

## First Stage: Existential Nature

At this stage, the main problem is to get a customer and deliver the desired product and sign a contract. In between, basic questions are also raised:

Can we get enough customers to become a sustainable business? Deliver the goods to them and provide good service?

Do we have adequate funds to respond to the requests of the start-up part of this work?

The organization of this work is very simple, the owner of this business does all the work and directly supports the sub-departments in the company. This person must have the minimum qualifications for this job. The main strategy of any company is its survival. The owner of a company assumes all important duties and is the sole and greatest supporter in terms of energy and direction for the other employees of that company. Companies in the early stages of their formation, from a restaurant or a retail store to a factory producing highly advanced products, need to stabilize their products and bring them closer to a certain standard. Most of those factories never get the necessary acceptance from the customers' point of view and do not reach the necessary stability in the production of their products. In these fields, business owners stop the business when the necessary capital is exhausted. If they are very lucky, they can sell the business for what its assets are worth. In some cases, business owners cannot meet the amount of energy, capital and time that a business needs, and to get rid of these conditions, they remove themselves from the support cycle of the company, and this causes the destruction of the company. Companies that remain in the business stage are called second-tier companies.

*Figure 2. Growth stages*

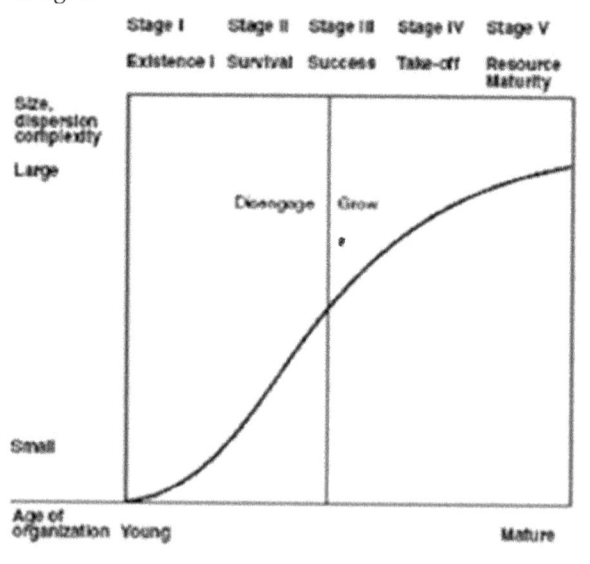

*Figure 3. Characteristics of small business of each stage of development*

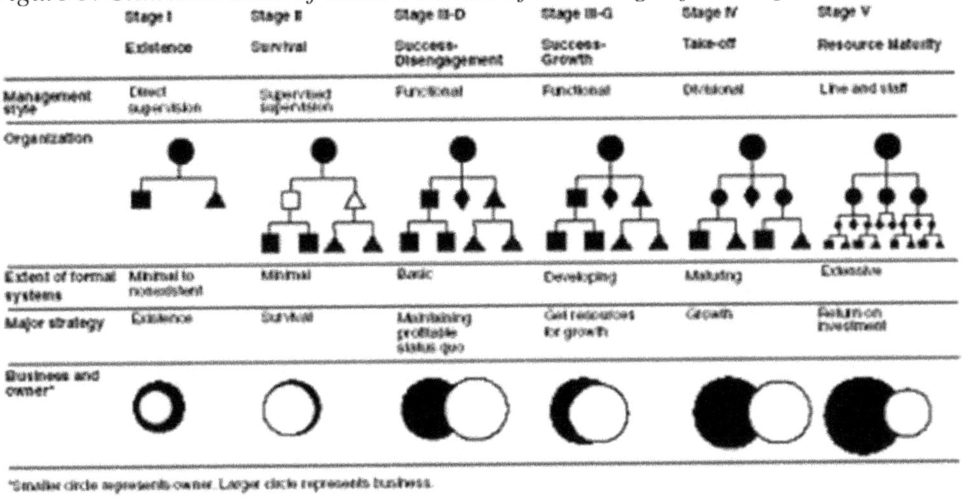

## The Second Stage: Survival

To reach this stage, the business in question must prove that it is a business with an applicable identity. This business must have an acceptable number of customers in its sales market. In addition, this company must have the necessary ability to satisfy its customers so that it can keep them for itself by providing services and products. The main problem in viability comes back to the problem of the relationship between income and cost. The main topics are mentioned below:

- In the case of very small companies, can we solve some problems and help the company survive using the very small budget we have?
- Can we help the expansion and growth of the company on a much larger scale by financing and providing working capital?
- Can we get back into the economic cycle by offering our industry and exclusive market?

Organizing is still very simple. A company may have a very limited number of employees under the management of a sales manager or a general foreman, none of whom make independent decisions. But they follow the orders of the owner of that business well, and this point is considered a bonus for the business owners.

*Figure 4. Evolution of small companies*

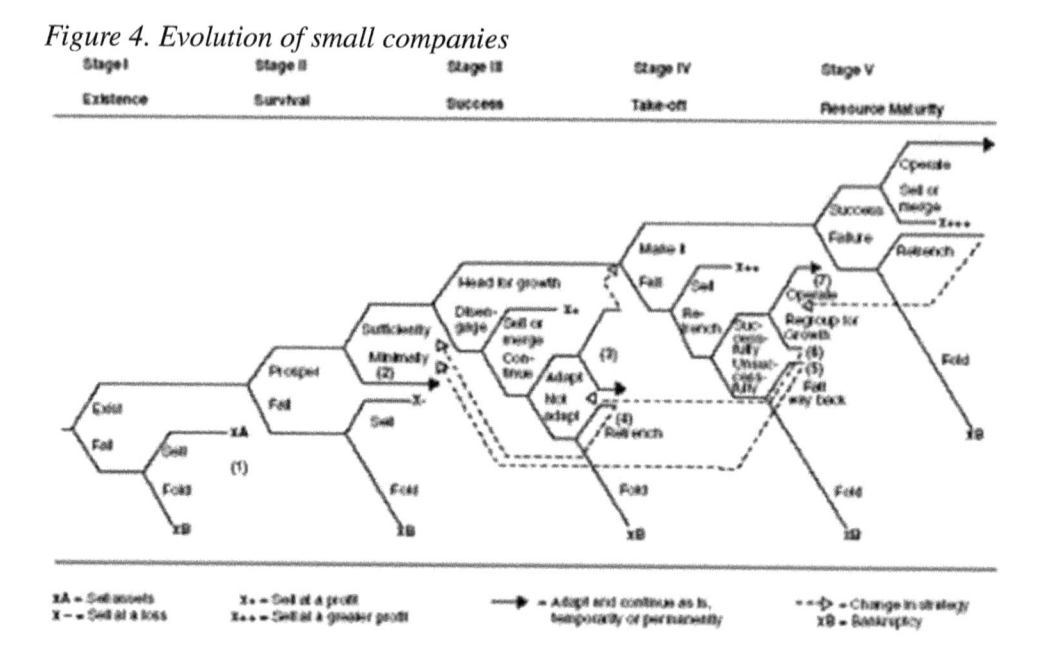

In this case, system dependency is at its lowest level. Planning at its best is cost forecasting. The goal of the company owners is always to maintain and sustain the company, and the company owner is always in touch with his business. In the survival stage, the company may grow well in terms of size and move towards the third stage in terms of profit, or maybe remain in the survival stage for a while, like most companies. to reach the expected return in a certain period of time and with the amount of capital allocated or to exit the business cycle when the owner of that company dissolves the company or retires. Very limited businesses like "mom and pop" fall into this category. These companies usually cannot sell their products as planned. Some of these small businesses have developed enough to be able to sustain themselves and sell their products, sometimes with a very small amount of loss, or they go out of business altogether.

## The Third Stage: Success

The decisions that must be made at this stage depend on two factors: whether the business owners want to take the company's achievements out of it, or whether they will use those achievements to increase the company's sustainability and profitability. Company owners can use those achievements to create infrastructure for the activities of other company stakeholders. Therefore, the important and fundamental point is whether we want to use the company as a platform for growth and development, or whether we want to use it as an infrastructure to help the company's shareholders, who are fully or partially cooperating with the company. We use. Of course, sometimes this separation means starting an independent startup company. Like the activities that are done for government groups, or the actions that happen to achieve personal or any other wishes, which ultimately the goal of all these people is to maintain the business in its current state.

*Sub-Stage 3: D. Success*

In order to pass this stage very successfully, that company must have good economic health and expansion and have a good influence in the market to sell its products to guarantee its economic success. Also, this company should earn moderate and moderate to high profit from the sale of its products. A company with such conditions can easily remain in the current stage and continue its activities. The changes made in the working conditions or sales market of this company can never affect its success and reduce its competitive power. When a company is big enough in terms of organization, it will need pragmatic managers in many aspects. This causes these pragmatic managers to assume specific duties that were previously the responsibility of the company owner. Pragmatic managers must have sufficient competence for this. They do not need special skills and abilities to do this because most of their skills and abilities will be limited by the goals that exist in the company. When there is sufficient budget, the main issue is to prevent waste of money in areas where there is very high income. This is necessary from possible losses to the company's capacities to use them in very difficult times. In addition, the first professional members who exist in that company are elected as the board of directors, usually these people are the office manager and planner of the organization. Core systems in finance, marketing, and manufacturing remain unchanged. Planning based on operating budgets supports the functional board. The owner of a company, or in other words, the management of a company, must have specified a strategy and performance path for his company, which of course must take into account the current conditions and maintain it.

As a business grows and evolves, the company and its owners are largely removed from the business cycle because the company's management is busy in other areas, or the presence of other managers reduces the need for a CEO. Many companies spend too much time below the breakthrough stage. Exclusive sales markets that are available to some people do not allow others to grow. This situation is true for many small and medium-sized businesses, small economic communities, or franchisees of some businesses with a very limited scope.

Other industry owners usually choose this way: if a company can adapt to the changes that have occurred, it can continue on its way, and the owners of that company can sell their business, or make it profitable, or instead, take action to expand your business. For business franchisees, this feature allows them to purchase other existing franchises. If the company can't adapt, like many auto dealers in the late 1970's and early 1980's, it will either end up downsizing or just barely survive.

*Sub-Step 3: Success of J*

In the sub-stage of successful growth, business owners strive to strengthen their business or gather resources to grow and upgrade the company. The owners of the industries accept all the risks and dangers by using the financial resources and using the capacities of the company for its growth and promotion. Due to the existing dangers and risks, the company must maintain its profitability and not lose its financial resources. Provide managers to meet growing business needs. At this stage, the company needs to hire managers who will act according to the future of the company and not based on the current situation. The current system in the company should also be based on the future needs of the company. The operational plan in the company, as mentioned in sub-step 3D, will be in the form of a budget plan. But strategic planning is much broader and requires the cooperation of industry owners. Usually, managers are active in most of the company's departments, but they don't cooperate much when going through the stages. If this process is successful, the company will be promoted from 3rd grade to 4th grade. Step 3 is usually the first step in arriving at a growth strategy. If the 3G stage is unsuccessful for the company, the reasons for its failure to pass from the "3G" to "3D" stage will be determined for the company. If this does not happen, it is necessary to cut costs for the survival of the company before reaching the stage of bankruptcy.

## Step 4: Flight

The biggest problem at this stage is finding ways to have rapid growth and how to finance such a process. The following are the most important questions at this stage:

Representation:

Can business owners have greater managerial impact by delegating responsibility to other team members to grow, rapidly scale, and address the company's evolving complex businesses? In addition, will entrusting the affairs of having control over the performance of employees and monitoring the defects and problems that have arisen, or will it be a kind of abdication of responsibility, as in many cases?

Liquidity:

Will the benefits of business growth and promotion be enough to satisfy managers and shareholders? (In most cases, we have to make the high debt-to-rights ratio bearable and satisfactory for the shareholders). Another point is that the financial circulation should not cause a waste of capital due to lack of proper control, or cause business owners discomfort with wrong investment advice. At this stage, the organization has become decentralized, or it has been divided into departments. Usually, this division occurs both in the sales department and in the production department. Top managers must have high competence to manage the growing and complex business environment. When the work system is accompanied by proper growth, the transparency of affairs increases, and business expands easily. Two functional and strategic planning are running simultaneously and each of them has its own managers. The business owners and the business itself are logically separated. Of course, the company is still under the influence and domination of its owners and the control of the shareholders.

This state is one of the most important periods of a company during its life. If company owners increase the number of challenges facing a growing company, that company can become a large company, both financially and managerially. Otherwise, usually these businesses are sold or remain at a fixed amount of profit, and these results are obtained if the manager of that group is fully aware of the limitations and conditions of his business. In most cases, those who take a business to the success stage usually fail at stage 4. Because they try to progress quickly and usually face financial problems (usually the company owners are victims of absolute power syndrome) or maybe they can't very effectively and efficiently hand over existing responsibilities to others, and this causes power syndrome. becomes absolute. Of course, it is possible for the company to go through the rapid growth phase without management. In most cases, the entrepreneurs who were the founders of the company and made it a success, are replaced by themselves or by investors and shareholders. If the company cannot reach its highest position, it may be able to continue its activities as a successful and prominent company or it may return to stage 3. If the amount of problems that arise is very high, the company may return to the survival stage or even face complete destruction. (Extremely high tax rates and unfair economic conditions made the latter two very common options in the 1980s.)

## Step 5: Maturity of Resources

The most important challenge for any company in entering different stages is firstly stabilizing the position and controlling the costs due to rapid growth and secondly maintaining the advantages of the company's limited volume. These advantages include flexibility in response and having an entrepreneurial spirit. A company should increase its management speed and power so that it can eliminate existing destructive events, which are formed as a result of the growth and expansion of the company. Using budgets, strategic planning, goal management, and standard costing systems, disruptive events can help a company become more specialized. Destructive agents can do this without destroying the spirit of entrepreneurship and reducing the quality of a company's products. A company in stage 5 has both the manpower and the financial base necessary to participate in strategic planning and very detailed performance plans. By decentralizing management, hiring the right employees, and with experience, this can be done easily. The systems used are very extensive and well developed. Business owners and the business itself, both financially and functionally, are two completely separate parameters. Currently, the company has reached a place where it has a very good position in terms of its scope, financial status, and management talent. If the company can maintain its entrepreneurial spirit, it will become a very powerful unit in the market, and if this does not happen, the company will enter the sixth stage: consolidation and formation.

The sixth stage, which is called idea stabilization, can be recognized by the reduction of innovative ideas and unwillingness to accept risk. This issue is a very common phenomenon in very large companies. Companies whose size, purchasing power, and financial resources make them sustainable, unless new conditions prevail in the market. Of course, for such businesses, the presence of competitors with a very high growth rate usually causes initial changes in the market.

Basic management parameters

There are many factors, the importance of which changes with the growth and expansion of the business and become important in the ultimate success and failure of a company. We have found eight of these cases during our research. Four of these cases are related to the company and the remaining four are related to the owners of the company. The four items related to the company are:

1. Financial resources include the company's liquidity and borrowing power.
2. Personnel resources, which depend on the number, quality, and knowledge of people, especially at the managerial and employee levels.
3. System resources are determined by considering the complexity of data, planning and control system.
4. Business resources include relationship with customers, market share, relationship with sponsors, production and distribution process, technology, and reputation. All these cases will be effective in determining the position of the company in the industry and market.

The four items that are relevant to the owners of the company are:

1. The personal goals of the company owners and their decisions regarding their business
2. The functional abilities of the company owners in doing very important things such as business, innovation and invention, production, management, and distribution of products.
3. The managerial ability of the company owners and their willingness to entrust the responsibilities and manage the activities of others.
4. The strategic abilities of company owners to maintain the current situation and coordinate the company's strengths and weaknesses with personal goals

When a business goes from one stage to another, the importance of the parameters in it changes. According to the conducted research, the importance of factors in companies always changes and shifts in three levels of importance:

The first level, the critical variables that are very important to achieve success and should have the highest priority. The second level, the factors that are very important for the success of a company and should be paid attention to. The third level, the factors that have the least importance in high-level management. If we want to categorize each of the eight mentioned factors according to their importance and in each of the company's progress levels, we will see fundamental changes due to the variety of managerial demands.

*Figure 5. Management factors and the stages*

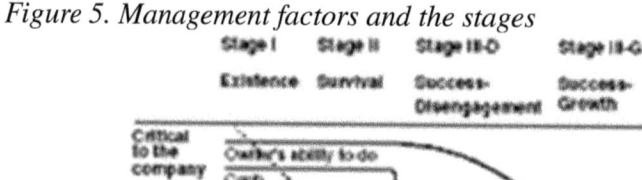

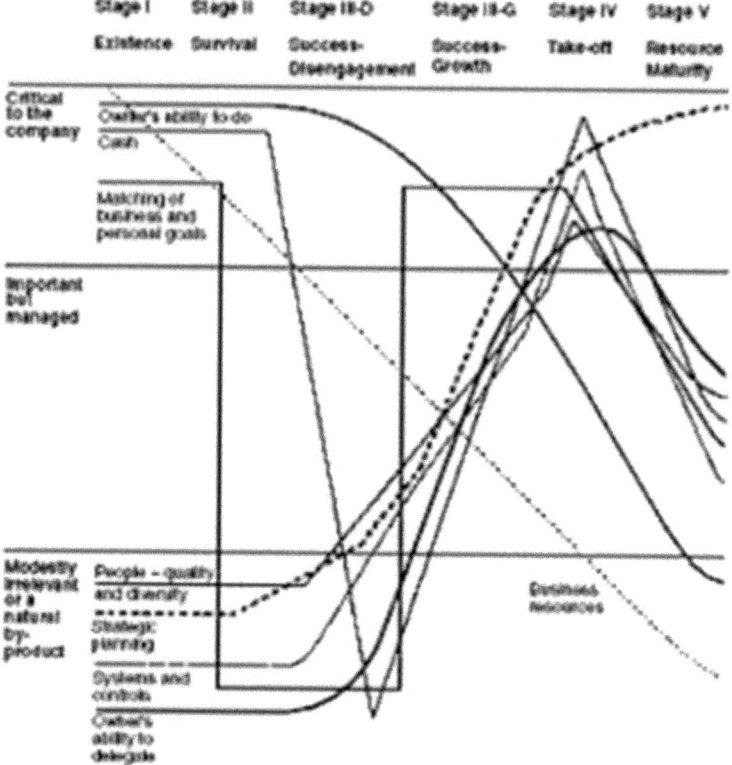

## Variable Demands

The changing nature of management challenges becomes apparent when one examines Figure 5. In the early stages, the ability of the company owners to get things done breathes new life into the business. Small businesses are founded on the talent of their managers and founders: the ability to sell, produce, innovate or any other skill can be the start of a successful company. These skills are the most important, when there are no qualified people to entrust matters, the ability of the owner of a company to entrust matters to others will be of the least importance. With the expansion of the company, other people also enter the sales, production or engineering department and support the activities performed at the beginning of the work, and even their skills replace the skills of the founder of the company. This reduces the importance of agency factor in the company. At the same time, the owner of the company should spend less time working in the company and spend more time managing it. He must increase the amount of work done by others, which entails delegating things to others. The inability of some managers to entrust matters to others is the reason for the destruction of many businesses in the "3rd" and "4th" sub-stages.

Company owners should take into account the changes that occur in people's personalities so that they can make appropriate decisions about growth and development strategies. Such decisions include management needs and their evaluation. Similarly, an entrepreneur thinking and creating a company, or a new business must anticipate all the needs that exist in areas such as the amount of sales, production or engineering and are effective from the beginning of the work. He must do this along with managing financial resources and business matters. Such needs require high energy and commitment and must be addressed and controlled. The importance of liquidity changes as the business changes. This resource is of particular importance at the beginning of the work, and it will be much easier to control it in the success stage, and it will gain special importance with the re-expansion of the business and become the most important priority. If growth occurs in stage 4 or 5, liquidity becomes important again. Companies in stage 3 should pay special attention to financial issues. These companies will always face risk to move to stage 4. The issue of employees, planning and the existing system in the company will gradually become more important and will expand with the promotion of the company from the early growth stage (stage 3) to the rapid growth stage (stage 4). The necessary resources to enter these steps should be determined in advance so that they are ready when you need them. The existence of our coordination between people, desires and goals of the company is of the greatest importance at every stage. Because managers and company owners have to coordinate between very heavy costs and the need for a lot of energy, all of which are part of the basic needs of a new business. These needs and demands for some people are much more than their capacity and ability. Although in the survival phase, reaching an agreement and the ability to survive is of the greatest importance. The existence of coordination among the goals in the second stage is not very important(Jiang et al,2019).

The second stage for our alignment between goals occurs in the achievement stage. Does a manager tend to devote all his time and capital to the promotion and advancement of the company, or does he prefer to use all that he has earned and spend it outside the company? In most cases, managers tend to have both. But the rapid promotion and advancement of the company along with the huge expenses for travel, the company will face many risks. Making a very sensible decision and determining the course of action requires consideration of the needs of the people and the business in question. This work should be done by using different strategies and by evaluating the management abilities of the company owner in facing the challenges. Finally, the main capital of any company is the characteristics or parameters by which that company has achieved success. These can include company stock, customer relationships, or fixed sales resources. The foundation of the technology is very important in the early stages. In later stages, the loss of a large pool of customers, sponsors, and technology resources will be easily compensated. Therefore, the relative importance of these items decreases at this stage. Changing the role of existing factors clearly indicates the need for flexibility of the company owner. At some levels worrying and overthinking about money is very important and at other levels it is less important. The delay in tax payment is almost more important in most cases, especially in stage 1 and 2. But this issue can make financial data very difficult and complicated and will take a lot of time from the management department in the stages of success and growth. Doing things instead of delegating work to others requires very flexible management. Adhering to old strategies and methods causes a company's illness, and when the company enters the growth stage, it can even be destructive for that company.

## Avoid Future Problems

Even a cursory glance at Table 5 reveals the demands of a growing company. Almost all existing factors challenge the performance abilities of company owners. This stage is the time to do work and creates high capacities for people. Looking at this chart, company owners who want such growth in their company should answer the following questions:

> Do I have the necessary skills and people to manage a growing company?
> Do I currently or in the near future have systems in place to replace the existing system so that it can meet the needs of a larger company with different capabilities?
> Do I have the desire and ability to entrust decision-making to my managers?
> Do I have enough money and credit to borrow in an emergency? Can I risk everything to have more and faster growth and promotion?

Capable entrepreneurs are aware of the fact that establishing and starting a successful business requires doing very important and quality work. Having a marketable idea, spending a lot of energy, predicting the amount of acceptable money in circulation (having a significant amount of cash) are among the things that should be considered. These items are the least important in step 5. When management skills are very good and have proper development and expansion, appropriate information systems and budget controllers are of high priority. Perhaps for this reason, some very experienced people from very large and prestigious companies cannot become successful entrepreneurs or managers of small companies. They do not have the necessary abilities to entrust matters to others.

## Applying the Model

This schematic can be used to evaluate all types of trades in different situations, even those that seem exceptional at first glance. Consider franchises, these companies begin their existence under very different conditions than startups. Franchises usually enjoy the following benefits:

- A marketing plan developed as a result of primary research.
- Very complex information and control system
- Performance guidelines that are standardized and well developed.
- Promotion and other support such as brand recognition
- These franchises usually require much more capital than startups.

If the franchisees do a "sound market" analysis and have a stable and unique product, the new investment can quickly go through the stages of existence and survival. Where most venture capitalists reach the early stages of success. The cost of franchisees to achieve the mentioned advantages is as follows:

- Limited growth due to limited territory
- Too much dependence on the franchise selling company to have a healthy economy
- Having the capacity and possibility of failure in the future, when entering the third stage, without having enough experiences in stages one and two.

One of the ways to promote franchises is to acquire multiple units or areas of activity. Managing many of these cases, of course, requires a whole new set of skills, and it's at this point that the lack of business survival can spell company ruin.

Another exception that may happen are startups active in the field of advanced technologies. These cases or in better words these companies are very specific companies. Like computer software businesses, genetic engineering companies, laser development companies that are more attractive to investors. Entrepreneurs who start their activities in the mentioned fields usually establish these companies with the aim of quickly promoting these companies and presenting their products to the public or handing them over completely to other companies. Such a vision and strategy require permanent financing from outside the group, from the very beginning. The providers of these costs are usually risk-taking investors who may have prepared the functional planning of steps 3 and 4 along with a group of investors who monitor the capital available in the company. Collected resources allow companies to easily pass the first stage and remain in the second stage until the product production stage and then reach the third stage. At this stage, the planned strategy for progress is sometimes beyond the management capabilities of a person or a group of people. Sometimes the owners of that company or the investors who are outside the company impose orders or management changes on the company at some stages. In such a situation, the company reaches stage 4 very quickly. Depending on the competence of the people who are responsible for production, marketing and business development, these things can make a company very successful or make it fail. The problems that involve franchises and companies active in the field of advanced technologies arise from the mismatch in the ability and skills of managers and the demands that create drastic changes for the company. With so many examples of franchises and top tech companies out there, we've noticed that there are a lot of other companies in the development stages. With a more detailed investigation, it was found that each of them is placed in a specific stage due to a specific factor, and due to another factor, they are placed in another stage. For example, a company has a large amount of funds from the controlled growth stage (sub-stage 3G) and is ready to accelerate its expansion. At the same time, the owner of the company wants to have all the people of the company under his supervision. In the other case, a manager plans to manage a city (substep 3D). But he is not satisfied with the very slow growth in the company (sub-step 3G).

Although it is usually rare that a factor is several steps ahead or behind a company, the inconsistency between the factors in the company and the position of that company can cause serious problems for entrepreneurs. In fact, one of the most important challenges in small companies is that the problems facing a company and the skills needed to run it change as the company grows and develops. Therefore, company owners should manage and predict the factors that are important for the company at different stages. The growth stage of a company determines the management factors that should be considered. These programs determine which factors the company will face in the future. Knowing a company's growth stage and future plans helps managers, consultants, and investors make very informed decisions. Since every company is unique in all areas, they all face similar problems and they all will face huge changes. For this reason, being the owner of a company at the same time will be very exciting, as well as experiencing a great challenge (Torres,2017).

## Cyber Business Finance and Financial Management

Business finance (Finance) examines and manages financial resources and business income, expenses, profits, and losses. This term includes all activities related to taxation, accounting, budgeting, banking, and business investment. The main goal of financial management is more productivity of financial resources and increasing profit and business value. To properly manage business finances, you must accurately monitor revenues, expenses, capital, and budgets. For example, you should spend financial resources on things that help your business grow and develop, such as hiring staff, equipment, or workspace.

Also, to manage costs, you should carefully examine the costs of producing your product or service so that you can consider optimizing costs and increasing profits. For this purpose, you can use different methods such as determining the right price, reducing direct and indirect costs, and increasing productivity. Finally, you need to have a proper accounting system in place to monitor spending trends. Therefore, you should always review and monitor your expenses and make necessary changes and improvements if needed. To monitor your business finances, as a first step, you should carefully consider the following:

- What are the financial resources used for? (Employment of personnel, equipment, work space, etc.)
- How much does it cost to produce or supply your product?
- What is the process of monitoring your business expenses?

By knowing the above and using the tips that will be mentioned below, you can properly manage your business finances.

**Business Financial Planning**

To get a healthy and active body, we need to leave bad habits and do sports and elderly activities. But for the sustainability of physical health, we must plan and follow the principles of health. Also, in order to obtain a sustainable financial health for the business, we must have proper planning and follow the principles of financial management. To earn money, maintain and grow the business, one should use a correct planning and spend financial resources on important and necessary things.

In general, like physical health that needs planning and compliance with health principles, business finances also need planning and compliance with financial management principles. By following these principles and using a regular schedule, you can ensure a stable financial health. In order to achieve a complete and effective planning for business financial management, many things must be considered. The most important things to consider are:

- The amount of income and profit from the business, which is very important for planning and setting financial goals.
- Cash and non-cash balance that can be used to pay expenses and financial obligations.
- Costs and expenses that are very important to determine the level of profitability and significant profit of the business.

- Financial obligations that must be considered in order to be aware of the financial status of the business and make the necessary plans to pay them.

On the other hand, for effective financial management of the business, you should always be aware of the process of monitoring the expenses and income of the business and make changes if necessary. Also, it should be kept in mind that in order to have an effective planning, one should use appropriate tools such as financial management software. By following these and having an effective plan, you can ensure that you get a sustainable business financial management.

## Financial Planning Steps

Financial planning is an important management process that must be used in six main stages to have a stable and effective business financial management. These steps are:

- To determine your current financial situation, you can create a basis for your financial planning by making a list of your current assets and liabilities.
- To determine financial goals, you can analyze your needs and desires and separate them from each other. This will help you set your financial goals more accurately and effectively.
- Identifying available options can help you make better decisions. By knowing more about your options, you can make more confident financial decisions.
- Evaluating available options can help you better understand the implications and requirements of each option and make better decisions.
- Creating an action plan can help you to achieve your financial goals in an organized and regular manner.
- Revising your financial plan is a dynamic process and should be reviewed and modified on a regular basis. This will help you to update your financial plan according to new conditions and required changes.

## Business Cash Flow Tracking

Cash flow actually refers to the amount of cash or similar cash balances that enter and leave the business. Liquid assets include cash, checks received and paid, electronic banking, credit cards, etc.

Considering the importance of cash flow in business financial management, many financial experts consider it as one of the most important criteria for evaluating business performance. Cash flow can be one of the factors that determine the success or failure of a business.

If the cash flow is positive, it means that the business is attracting more liquid assets so that it can pay its investors and debtors, as well as invest in the development of its business. But if the cash flow is negative, it means a reduction in the cash assets of the business, which may be out of reach, and as a result, the business cannot pay its debtors and investors.

In other words, cash flow can be considered as a basic criterion in business financial management. To improve cash flow, measurable goals should be defined according to cash flow and appropriate strategies should be adopted to achieve these goals. Also, you need to record expenses and expenses on time so that you can ensure that you are in control of your budget and avoid wasting your cash assets.

## Example

Suppose you have an online business that offers your products to customers through an online store. To know the financial status of your business and to avoid possible problems, you need to carefully check your cash flow.

Suppose that in the first month, your income was 10 million dollars, and considering the costs of producing products, advertising costs, and employee wages, your total expenses were 8 million dollars. Therefore, your positive cash flow this month is $2 million.

Now in the second month, your income has increased to 15 million dollars, but due to the increase in expenses and the need for more investment, your total expenses have increased to 14 million dollars. As a result, your cash flow this month is $1 million negative.

If you do not pay attention to the accuracy of your cash flow, you may face potential problems. For example, you may not be able to pay your debts on time and as a result, you may inadvertently increase your business debts and expenses. For this reason, improving the cash flow can help you to be aware of the financial situation of your business in time and invest for the growth and development of your business.

## Fluctuations in Income

The world of entrepreneurship always creates challenges for entrepreneurs due to its instability and dynamism. In this world, entrepreneurs face various obstacles such as intense competition, dynamic changes in the market, innovation, and continuous growth of businesses. For this reason, having a steady and stable cash flow is very important for entrepreneurs.

Although entrepreneurs spend most of their time on their business, it is better to be careful and focus enough in recording their cash flow. Accurate recording of business income and expenses helps entrepreneurs to better predict their income and expenses and make appropriate planning and decisions based on it. Obtaining accurate information about cash flow helps entrepreneurs improve their business financial management and avoid financial problems.

Cash flow, as one of the most important financial concepts in businesses, shows how much money the business earns and how much it spends. Investigating this issue helps entrepreneurs better predict their financial problems and implement appropriate plans to control costs and increase their business income and profits. Improving cash flow can help entrepreneurs improve the growth and development of their business and, as a result, be more successful in the entrepreneurial world.

## Example

Suppose an entrepreneur is selling his products but does not record his cash flow properly. In this case, he may unconsciously need bank loans to expand his business. If he does not record his cash flow correctly, he may not be able to pay the bank installments and therefore be denied a bank loan. For this reason, accurate recording of cash flow helps entrepreneurs plan more accurately to attract financial resources and manage them and avoid financial problems.

## Number of Transactions

The first law of financial management states that you should never spend more than your income, and this is the basic rule in managing business finances. To comply with this law, one must be aware of one's expenses and control them. Major expenses such as monthly rent and utility bills are relatively easy to track, but minor expenses should also be considered.

The best way to do this is to record the expenses in the business expenses worksheet, every day you should set aside time to record the expenses and update the worksheet. By doing this, it is possible to avoid forgetting the previous and insignificant expenses and to update the amount of the remaining budget. As a result, you can have the best cost control and make the most accurate financial decisions for your business.

## Getting to Know the Types of Expenses

Costs, as one of the most important factors in determining business profitability and competitiveness, have always been considered in business planning and management. In general, costs are divided into two categories: fixed and variable. Fixed costs have a fixed amount at each level of production or business activity and are independent of the volume of production or activity. But variable costs change with the increase or decrease in production volume and business activity.

Also, semi-variable or quasi-variable costs are also divided into two parts: fixed cost and variable cost, and they are known as fixed cost in part of the production or business activity range, and in another part, they are known as variable cost.

Proper categorization of costs and focusing on reducing unnecessary costs and improving business efficiency can help improve business profitability and competitiveness. For this reason, cost management is very important as one of the most important topics in business management.

## Business Financial Management

Business financial management is one of the most basic and important parts of any business. In this case, it can be summarized as follows:

Financial Planning:
- For financial planning, you must first determine the financial goal of the business.
- Planning for income and expenses should be developed based on the business plan.
- Financial planning should be developed for long-term periods so that you can make the best decisions for your business growth.

Financial Organization:
- Categorize all business expenses and divide them into different categories.
- For each cost category, a budget should be set so that costs can be carefully controlled.
- You should review financial plans periodically and make necessary changes if needed.

Cash Management:
- You should always manage your cash balance carefully.
- You should look for ways to attract new liquidity.
- You should carefully calculate the costs related to liquidity such as bank fees.

Cost Control:
- You should always look for ways to reduce your expenses.
- You must carefully control your expenses.
- You should consider the pros and cons of each option when deciding on new expenses.

Debt Management:

- You should manage your debts carefully.
- You should pay attention to the time of debt payment.
- You should try to pay your debts on time.

Capital Management:
- You must manage your capital in the best possible way.
- You should look for ways to make smart investments.
- You should invest your capital for long-term periods.

Financial Reporting:
- You should periodically prepare your financial report and be informed about the financial status of your business.
- You must accurately report your income, expenses, and net profit.
- Any changes in the financial position of the business must be carefully reported in your financial report.

In general, in order to optimally manage business finances, you must, most importantly, have accurate and correct planning and organization. Also, you should be looking to cut costs and attract new liquidity so that you can continue to grow your business in the best way possible. By applying these techniques as well as staying up-to-date with market changes and financial regulations, you can make the best decisions to grow your business (Sukavejworakit,2018).

# REFERENCES

Jiang, L., Levine, R., & Lin, C. (2019). Competition and bank liquidity creation. *Journal of Financial and Quantitative Analysis*, ●●●, 1–50.

Lusardi, A. (2019). Financial literacy and the need for financial education: Evidence and implications. *Swiss Journal of Economics and Statistics*, 155(1), 1. DOI: 10.1186/s41937-019-0027-5

Paiella, M. (2016). Financial literacy and subjective expectations questions: A validation exercise. *Research in Economics*, 70(2), 360–374. DOI: 10.1016/j.rie.2015.11.004

Torres, F. C., Méndez, J. C. E., Barreto, K. S., Chavarría, A. P., Machuca, K. J., & Guerrero, J. A. O. (2017). Exploring entrepreneurial intentions in Latin American university students. *The Japanese Psychological Research*, 10(2), 46–59. PMID: 32612764

Sukavejworakit, K., Promsiri, T., & Virasa, T. (2018). Oetel: An Innovative Teaching Model for Entrepreneurship Education. *Journal of Entrepreneurship Education*, 21(2), 1–11.

# Chapter 11
# Entrepreneurship and Financial Management

## ABSTRACT

*What is entrepreneurship? Who is an entrepreneur? The economic conditions of countries are such that the need to create and develop businesses is felt more and more day by day. In this situation, governments should invest in "entrepreneurship" and improve the process of creating income and employment by training entrepreneurs. But the important issue is what is entrepreneurship? In this article, we are going to describe the creative work. In simple words, "entrepreneurship" is the process of establishing a business (company) based on a new thought and idea. Now, in the global arena, creative and innovative people as entrepreneurs have become the source of great changes in the field of production and services. Even large global companies turn to entrepreneurs to solve their problems. The wheels of economic development move with the development of entrepreneurship. America owes its economy to these people.*

## INTRODUCTION

In an era marked by rapid technological advancements and dynamic global markets, entrepreneurship has emerged as a cornerstone of economic progress and innovation. Governments, businesses, and educational institutions alike recognize its pivotal role in creating jobs, driving economic growth, and fostering creativity. However, the path of entrepreneurship is not merely about starting a business; it is a disciplined journey of innovation, strategic risk-taking, and financial stewardship. Entrepreneurs, often hailed as agents of change, challenge the status quo by introducing groundbreaking products, services, or processes. Their endeavors fuel competitive markets and contribute to societal progress, but success in this realm demands more than just vision and creativity. Effective financial management plays

DOI: 10.4018/979-8-3693-9415-1.ch011

an equally critical role, enabling entrepreneurs to allocate resources wisely, navigate risks, and achieve long-term sustainability. This chapter delves into the intricate relationship between entrepreneurship and financial management, exploring the essence of entrepreneurial thinking, the challenges entrepreneurs face, and the tools they use to build and manage thriving ventures. From understanding the traits of successful entrepreneurs to examining the principles of entrepreneurial financial planning, we aim to provide a comprehensive foundation for aspiring business leaders to embark on their journey toward innovation and economic contribution.

## WHAT IS ENTREPRENEURSHIP? WHO IS AN ENTREPRENEUR?

In today's rapidly changing economic landscape, the necessity for creating and developing new businesses is becoming increasingly apparent. This need has prompted governments worldwide to recognize the importance of fostering "entrepreneurship" as a means to stimulate income generation and job creation. Consequently, there is a growing emphasis on training aspiring entrepreneurs to navigate the complexities of business development. But what exactly is entrepreneurship, and who qualifies as an entrepreneur?

At its core, "entrepreneurship" refers to the process of establishing a business or company based on innovative ideas and unique concepts. It is more than just the act of starting a business; it embodies the spirit of creativity and problem-solving that drives individuals to bring new products or services to market. In the global context, entrepreneurs are seen as catalysts for significant shifts in the production and services sectors. Their creative and innovative approaches often lead to breakthroughs that can revolutionize entire industries. Even large multinational corporations frequently seek the insights and solutions provided by these entrepreneurial thinkers to tackle complex challenges. The economic development of nations is inextricably linked to the advancement of entrepreneurship. In fact, the success of the American economy, renowned for its innovation and competitiveness, can be largely attributed to the efforts of entrepreneurs who have transformed their visions into reality. By taking risks and pursuing their ideas, these individuals contribute not only to their own success but also to the overall economic growth of their communities and countries.

Historically, the drive for change has been a hallmark of human civilization. Throughout time, certain individuals have distinguished themselves by defying conventional norms and pursuing their own paths, leading to profound changes in society. Today's advanced societies owe much of their progress to those who had the vision to transform their dreams into tangible outcomes, the independence to explore uncharted territories, and the courage to challenge established practices.

These agents of change are often characterized by what is now referred to as "creative work." Entrepreneurship encompasses both theoretical and practical dimensions, making it essential to develop effective educational programs aimed at nurturing entrepreneurial talent. Since an individual's character and spirit are primarily shaped during adolescence and youth, implementing targeted educational initiatives can cultivate the entrepreneurial mindset and skills necessary for success in these formative years. By fostering a spirit of innovation, resilience, and problem-solving, we can empower the next generation of entrepreneurs to make a meaningful impact in their communities and beyond. Entrepreneurship is about more than just starting a business; it is about harnessing creativity, driving change, and contributing to the socio-economic fabric of society. As we continue to invest in entrepreneurship education and support aspiring entrepreneurs, we lay the groundwork for a more dynamic and prosperous future for all.

## Definition of Entrepreneur: What Does Entrepreneur Mean?

The word entrepreneur is derived from the word Entrepreneur (meaning to commit), which originally came from French to other languages. The English used three terms with the names of adventurer, undertaker, and employer about the workaholic. According to them, the definition of an entrepreneur means someone who undertakes to organize, manage, and bear the risks of an economic activity.

But who are called entrepreneurs? In answer to this question, we must say that an entrepreneur is someone who has a special innovation. This innovation can be in providing a new product, providing a new service, designing a new process, or innovation in customer satisfaction, etc.

Entrepreneurs actually look at change as a defining category, they change values and transform their nature. They use their risk-taking power to realize this idea. They make the right decision and therefore anyone who makes the right decision is considered as an entrepreneur. An entrepreneur always knows some tips about financial management and tries to improve his knowledge in this field by studying accounting.

According to "Shoomiter", the entrepreneur is the driving force and engine of economic development. He considers the characteristic of an entrepreneur to be innovation. Also, "Jeffrey Timmons" believes that in the definition of entrepreneurship, he is a person who creates a valuable insight from nothing. Now that you know what an entrepreneur means, you should know about the factors influencing entrepreneurship (Grohmann,2018)!

## Key Factors of Entrepreneurship

There are six key factors in entrepreneurship, which are:

- Knowing the goal
- Having a horizon
- Using mental creativity
- Being sociable and sociable
- Courage, initiative, hope and risk-taking
- Be realistic about the difference between creativity and opportunity

## What are the Advantages and Benefits in the Entrepreneurial Process?

- Entrepreneurship is the factor of persuasion and encouragement of investment.
- Entrepreneurship stimulates and encourages the sense of competition.
- Entrepreneurship is the agent of change and innovation.
- Entrepreneurship creates employment.
- Entrepreneurship improves the quality of life.
- Entrepreneurship leads to proper distribution of income.

According to the mentioned interests, nowadays, in all the investments in the world, they try to identify and attract industrial thinking minds, because today's world is the world of science and technology, and the main value of production lies in the human brain.

Does work and entrepreneurship mean separation from the current business?

Those who think about work and entrepreneurship and independent business can be divided into two categories:

- Those who are currently working.
- Those who are not currently present and employed in a particular business or organization.

Compared to the second group, the first group also faces an important challenge: what should I do with my current business? Remember that entrepreneurship does not necessarily mean quitting your current job.

There are two other options regarding entrepreneurial conditions, which you should not neglect:

The first option: intra-organizational entrepreneurship

If your managers and coworkers at your current job are smart enough, they may be able to create an environment where you can become an intrapreneur.

An intrapreneur is someone who does not leave his current structure and business for value creation and innovation, and of course, he is given more power and authority to implement his ideas.

Second option: Part-time entrepreneurship

Your current job environment may not allow you to create an organization. In the sense that either the managers and those around you do not have such a capacity, or that the field you are considering has nothing to do with your current workplace.

In this case, an option can be part-time entrepreneurship. In other words, devote your time outside of your official working hours to starting a new business.

Of course, this way of working has its own buts and ifs. For example, the new work may require more time and resources, and a financial software is also needed to manage accounts and books, and also that part-time entrepreneurship cannot be continued for a long time, and anyway, at some point, you have to stop earning. And leave your current job.

## Types of Entrepreneurial Approaches

Two main approaches are usually used in the field of entrepreneurship research, which are:

Content approach or characteristic features (characteristics)
- Process or behavioral approach

## Content Approach

The purpose of using the content approach is to distinguish entrepreneurs from non-entrepreneurs and determine their characteristics. Based on this, the personality characteristics of an entrepreneur are: the need to seek success, willingness to accept risk, having an internal control center, having a creative spirit and tolerance of ambiguity.

## Process Approach

The purpose of using this approach is to focus on identifying the activities of entrepreneurs and expressing the nature of the entrepreneur. In the scope of the study of this approach, the investigation of all the influencing factors in the establishment of a new company, such as environment, person, process and organization, is considered. For example, things like access to capital, the presence of experienced entrepreneurs, the existence of a skilled workforce (technically), the extent of access to suppliers, customers or new markets are examined. People are also examined in terms of having entrepreneurial characteristics. Now that you are familiar with the various approaches to entrepreneurship, you should know about the beliefs and misconceptions about entrepreneurship.

## What are Misconceptions in Entrepreneurship?

Successful Entrepreneurship Only Needs a Big Idea: The big idea is only part of success in entrepreneurship. Understanding the needs of the different stages of the entrepreneurial process, using an organized method in order to expand and manage the entrepreneurial business, and being able to handle management challenges are the key elements for success.

Entrepreneurship is easy: You might think that the process of entrepreneurship is easy because you follow your passions and are passionate about success. It requires commitment, determination, and hard work. Entrepreneurs experience difficulties and continue despite difficulties!! Entrepreneurship is a risky bet: entrepreneurship is calculated risk. Successful entrepreneurship means avoiding unestimated risks or minimizing risks. Entrepreneurship is found only in small businesses: Entrepreneurship is found in any size of organization. Small and entrepreneurial businesses are the same: there are, of course, differences between an entrepreneurial business and a small business.

In the definition of entrepreneurship, small businesses are not necessarily entrepreneurial, creativity and looking for opportunities are necessary for entrepreneurship. Small businesses can grow and become entrepreneurial businesses. Of course, there are different opinions about the number of employees. For example, in another definition, a company with less than 500 personnel is considered a small business (Torres,2017).

## What is the Difference Between Entrepreneur and Mere Management?

The distinction between an entrepreneur and mere management lies fundamentally in their approaches to decision-making and their overarching goals. Entrepreneurs often operate using heuristic procedures, relying on intuition, creativity, and experiential knowledge to make decisions. This allows them to navigate complex situations filled with ambiguity and uncertainty, where conventional methods may fall short. In contrast, managers typically ground their decisions in statistical information, credit assessments, and numerical budgets, emphasizing a more analytical and data-driven approach to foster growth. While management focuses on maintaining operational efficiency and achieving specific targets based on factual data, the entrepreneur's mindset is shaped by deep-seated beliefs and personal experiences that guide their vision for the future.

Entrepreneurs are known for their capacity to make mental leaps and embrace innovative ideas, frequently deviating from linear managerial thinking. This ability to think outside the box enables them to identify new opportunities and potential markets that may be overlooked by more conventional management practices. However, the reliance on empirical data in management can sometimes restrict organizations from seizing transformative opportunities, as adhering strictly to reality may render risk-taking and experimentation costly or impractical. Therefore, effective entrepreneurship management is often a synthesis of both entrepreneurial intuition and managerial rigor, allowing for a more dynamic organizational approach that fosters creativity while ensuring sustainable growth.

When examining the types of entrepreneurships, they can be broadly categorized into two main types: individual (independent) entrepreneurship and organizational entrepreneurship. Individual entrepreneurs typically embark on their ventures independently, driven by personal aspirations, innovative ideas, and the desire for autonomy. In contrast, organizational entrepreneurship involves established entities fostering a culture of innovation and risk-taking within their structures, encouraging employees to think creatively and act like entrepreneurs. Each type has distinct characteristics and goals, but both contribute to the overall landscape of entrepreneurship and economic development. By understanding these differences, we can appreciate the varying roles that entrepreneurs and managers play in driving business success and innovation in today's competitive environment.

## What is an Entrepreneurial Job?

Organizational entrepreneurship is also based on innovation. An independent entrepreneur seeks to take the product market by his own power, but an organizational entrepreneur must overcome organizational issues in addition to the market. In the entrepreneurial organization, resources are more easily allocated to implement ideas. In the entrepreneurial organization, quality is institutionalized in all dimensions.

There is self-selection in this organization and entrepreneurs do not wait for orders from above, supervisors also provide them with resources and time. For example, in General Motors, employees are allowed to spend 15% of their time on selected projects. In fact, they start the work themselves, but the work is not delegated, and the person remains in the project team from the beginning to the end. In such an organization, the decision-maker makes decisions because when there are many organizational layers, the decision-making speed decreases.

Organizational entrepreneurship is a process in which innovative products or processes emerge through the creation of an entrepreneurial culture in an organization. Organizational entrepreneurship relies on the resources and support of the organization. Innovation can be in the field of new products, organizational processes, and management methods. In an entrepreneurial organization, everyone is an entrepreneur and the entrepreneur manager is at the top.

An organizational entrepreneur is someone who discovers and exploits new products, activities, and technology under the support of an organization.

## Types of Entrepreneurs

- Emerging (located at the beginning of a business)
- Beginner (no previous business experience)
- Veteran (has experience in business)
- Sequential or chain (constantly changing business)
- Collection (maintains the main business and starts other (additional) businesses)

An entrepreneur in any situation and stage should know about the proper management of expenses and corporate taxes.

## Entrepreneurial Culture in Entrepreneurial Business

Entrepreneurship thrives in a culture that fosters innovation, creativity, and a willingness to take risks. However, in many societies, there is often a limited desire and capacity for entrepreneurial pursuits, compounded by a general resistance to change—a common phenomenon in organizational behavior. Recognizing the critical role entrepreneurship plays in modern economies, especially in the growth of small and medium-sized enterprises, governments are increasingly prioritizing educational programs to nurture this entrepreneurial spirit. The United States stands out as a successful model in this regard, having cultivated an environment where entrepreneurship is not only encouraged but celebrated.

In contrast, some countries exhibit a prevailing mentality of "employee and boss-supervisors," where traditional hierarchies stifle creativity and risk-taking. This mindset can hinder the development of an entrepreneurial culture, which should instead be viewed as a collective set of beliefs, rituals, ideas, customs, and values that shape a society's approach to business. Culture operates on both societal and group levels, facilitating communication and interaction among individuals. It represents an intellectual framework that influences behavior and decision-making. In essence, culture can be described as a "way of life," and it is inherently dynamic, evolving in response to various influences, including economic conditions and societal shifts. The relationship between culture and entrepreneurship is multifaceted. On one hand, entrepreneurship significantly contributes to cultural development by creating job opportunities, generating wealth, and enhancing economic conditions. This process lays the groundwork for improving the cultural fabric of society. As basic needs are met, individuals can aspire to fulfill higher-order needs, as outlined in Maslow's Hierarchy of Needs. This progression leads to personal and collective prosperity, encouraging individuals to pursue aspirations that contribute to the overall cultural advancement of society.

Moreover, innovation—a hallmark of entrepreneurship—drives the creation of diverse products and services, broadening the range of choices available to consumers and ultimately simplifying their lives. As overall well-being and comfort levels rise, individuals find themselves with more leisure time to engage in cultural activities, thereby enriching the cultural landscape of society in the long run. Conversely, fostering an entrepreneurial culture necessitates the adoption of unique methods grounded in specific values that prioritize creativity, risk-taking, and collaboration.

Cultivating an entrepreneurial culture is essential for stimulating economic growth and fostering societal development. By recognizing the interplay between culture and entrepreneurship, societies can create environments that not only support innovative endeavors but also enhance the overall quality of life for their citizens. This symbiotic relationship ensures that as entrepreneurship flourishes, it simultaneously enriches the cultural tapestry of society, paving the way for a more dynamic and prosperous future.

## What Does Entrepreneurial Organizational Culture Mean?

Entrepreneurial organizational culture refers to the set of shared beliefs, values, and behavioral norms among members of an organization that foster an innovative and risk-taking environment. This culture significantly influences how employees approach their work, make decisions, and interact with one another. In essence, organizational culture is an understanding of the underlying principles that guide the organization's operations and behaviors. Employees develop this understanding based on their observations, experiences, and interactions within the organization.

While individuals may hold different job roles and responsibilities, a cohesive entrepreneurial culture provides them with a common framework that shapes their perceptions and attitudes toward the organization. This shared culture often emphasizes characteristics such as creativity, collaboration, and a willingness to take calculated risks, enabling the organization to adapt to changes and seize new opportunities.

In an entrepreneurial culture, members are encouraged to think outside the box, propose innovative solutions, and challenge the status quo. This environment not only empowers employees to take initiative but also fosters a sense of ownership and accountability for their work. As individuals feel supported in their creative endeavors, they are more likely to contribute positively to the organization's goals and objectives. Furthermore, the way culture is articulated within the organization influences its overall performance and success. Organizations with strong entrepreneurial cultures often experience increased employee engagement, improved problem-solving capabilities, and heightened resilience in the face of challenges. By promoting an atmosphere where experimentation and learning from failures are valued, these organizations position themselves to thrive in dynamic and competitive markets. entrepreneurial organizational culture serves as a foundational element that shapes the identity and functioning of the organization. It is essential for driving innovation, fostering collaboration, and achieving sustainable growth, making it a critical aspect of any successful entrepreneurial endeavor.

## Forms of Organizational Culture

- Innovation and risk-taking: the extent to which employees are encouraged to innovate and take risks.
- Attention to detail: The extent to which employees are expected to perform their tasks carefully through scrutiny and attention to detail.
- Output orientation: the amount that results and outputs are more important than the methods and processes used.
- People orientation: how much organizational decisions consider the impact on the people of the organization.
- Team orientation: the extent to which work is done by groups instead of individuals.
- Pioneering: the extent to which people in the organization are pioneers and have a sense of competition rather than being easygoing.
- Stability: the extent to which organizational decisions and actions emphasize maintaining the status quo and resisting changes. For example, an organization can place a lot of importance on stability, but less on teamwork. How much an organization places importance on each of these creates a composite picture of the organization's culture.

## Problems and Obstacles of Entrepreneurial Conditions in the Organization

- The nature of discontinuity in large organizations: the existence of communication problems between employees and management. Due to the multiple layers of decision-making, ideas can get lost in any part of the organization.
- Short-term benefits: In large organizations, short-term benefits are the measure of success (to prevent stock value from falling).
- Absence of entrepreneurial culture: entrepreneurs prefer a risky life, but the organization does not encourage them.

## Personality Characteristics of Entrepreneurial Managers

Entrepreneurial managers possess a unique set of personality characteristics that distinguish them from their peers in traditional management roles. While definitions of an entrepreneur may vary, there is a consensus on several key traits that are often associated with successful entrepreneurial managers. One of the most prominent characteristics is "high motivation". Entrepreneurial managers are typically driven by an intrinsic desire to achieve their goals and to make a meaningful impact in their chosen field. This motivation fuels their perseverance, allowing them to engage with their ventures for extended periods, often overcoming obstacles that would deter others. Coupled with this motivation is a "high level of self-confidence". Entrepreneurial managers believe in their abilities and ideas, which enables them to take bold steps and make critical decisions, even in uncertain conditions.

In addition, these individuals display a "high energy level" and a "strong degree of initiative". Their enthusiasm for their projects and ventures often inspires others around them and contributes to a vibrant workplace atmosphere. They are proactive in seeking out opportunities and are not afraid to take the lead in driving their vision forward. This ability to "set clear goals" is another hallmark of entrepreneurial managers; they know what they want to achieve and can develop actionable plans to reach those objectives. When it comes to risk-taking, entrepreneurial managers are often "balanced and calculated". They understand the importance of taking risks to innovate and grow, yet they are also adept at evaluating potential downsides, allowing them to navigate challenges effectively. This is complemented by their "eagerness to solve problems", as they thrive in environments where they can identify issues and develop creative solutions.

Furthermore, these managers exhibit traits such as "high insistence and follow-up", which reflects their determination to see projects through to completion. They possess a "desire for self-leadership", allowing them to manage their time and resources effectively while cultivating a sense of independence in their work. This independence often comes with a "relative need for autonomy", as entrepreneurial managers prefer to operate in environments that allow them to express their creativity and ideas freely.

Additionally, their "desire for financial success and recognition" can be strong motivators, driving them to work diligently to achieve their objectives. However, they typically experience "little self-doubt" and are often characterized by a "minimal level of worry". This mental fortitude enables them to take calculated risks without being paralyzed by fear of failure.

Finally, entrepreneurial managers often "go above and beyond" the typical demands of their roles, demonstrating a commitment to doing more work than required and often exceeding the contributions of their peers. This relentless pursuit of excellence and a strong work ethic further contribute to their success in navigating the complex landscape of entrepreneurship.

In summary, the personality characteristics of entrepreneurial managers encompass a combination of high motivation, self-confidence, initiative, goal orientation, balanced risk-taking, problem-solving abilities, persistence, and a desire for independence. These traits not only define their approach to management but also significantly contribute to the overall success of their entrepreneurial ventures.

## The Role of the Family in the Development of Work and Entrepreneurship

Entrepreneurship is an acquired process and the family plays an essential role in the formation of this process. The family can inject dynamism and mobility into the depth of existence of the people under its influence, so that the individual and the society interact in a harmonious environment and innovative social formats are formed. The role of the family as a center of innovation and creativity in people is undeniable. The realization of this depends on the amount of attention parents pay to their children from birth to the formation of their personality. When parents appear in the field of trying business, the results have a positive effect on children and make them focus on continuing their parents' profession or a new job.

For such a person, access to economic resources is considered valuable. This kind of perception of the surrounding world transforms one's mind to create a new idea and economic independence. A teenager or young person presents his idea in the family. It can benefit from parents' experiences and possibly their financial and social support. The level of education, the type of occupation of the parents, the structure of the family, the relationship between parents and children, the income of the family and the level of comfort facilities have an effect on the formation of work culture in the family. The rich are advised to let their children taste hardships, face difficulties, feel failure and leave a small amount of their capital to them. In rich families, there have been children who have taken this procedure themselves. Many successful people in business and entrepreneurship have emerged from the deprived class of society (Tshikovhi,2015).

## Experiences of the Entrepreneurship Process of Several Countries

The first country to promote entrepreneurship culture from high school level was Japan. The first institute was opened in Tokyo in 1956. In 1958, the Japan Education Organization launched and implemented a plan to spread the culture and importance of entrepreneurship under the title of Japan's selfless economic soldiers. Based on this plan, people from high school level studied the issue of entrepreneurship and were taught how to work while studying and seek to earn profit and how to free their country from industrial dependence. Gradually, the problem and definition of entrepreneurship in Japan was extended to the level of universities. There are now more than 250 large entrepreneurship institutes in Japan.

Between 1970 and 1992, more than 96 percent of the industrial innovation that made Japan's position in the world economy a superior one was done by entrepreneurs. Of course, it goes without saying that the support of the government has played an important role in this field. In England, the government pays subsidies to universities for training and entrepreneurship. In the Netherlands, SME personnel were given vocational training, so that in 1998, 32% of SMEs were involved in vocational training. Also in Italy, 855 business courses are offered to 10,000 participants at more than 20 universities.

## What is Entrepreneurship and Who is an Entrepreneur?

Entrepreneurship is a dynamic process of creating and managing a new venture that seeks to bring innovative ideas to life. It involves identifying opportunities, taking calculated risks, and mobilizing resources to transform ideas into viable businesses. Entrepreneurs are the driving force behind this process; they are individuals who not only recognize gaps in the market but also have the vision and determination to fill those gaps. They possess a unique mindset characterized by creativity, resilience, and a willingness to challenge the status quo.

Entrepreneurial managers play a crucial role in this landscape. Unlike traditional managers who may wait for changes to occur, entrepreneurial managers actively seek to initiate transformation and innovation within their organizations. They do not simply react to external circumstances; instead, they take proactive measures to reshape their environment. This involves breaking free from entrenched behaviors, challenging outdated attitudes, and instilling a culture of change and adaptability among their team members. By doing so, they create a dynamic work environment where innovation flourishes and new ideas are welcomed.

The primary goal of entrepreneurial managers is to align their innovations with the interests and objectives of their organizations. They achieve this by introducing advancements in production technology, finding alternative raw materials, and implementing more effective strategies. Their approach often leads to the creation of unique products or services that stand out in the market, making them rare and valuable. Moreover, entrepreneurial managers embrace environmental changes rather than resisting them. They understand that the business landscape is constantly evolving, and they are adept at riding the waves of these changes to achieve their goals. This proactive stance not only enhances their ability to innovate but also positions their organizations as leaders in their respective industries. They envision a world that is ideal and internationally prominent, and they think and act in ways that make that vision a reality. Entrepreneurship is a transformative process fueled by innovative thinkers who are willing to take risks and challenge norms. Entrepreneurs, particularly entrepreneurial managers, are pivotal in creating change and driving growth within organizations. Their proactive mindset and commitment to innovation not only benefit their companies but also contribute to the broader economy by fostering competition, creating jobs, and enhancing overall prosperity.

## Entrepreneurial Management

Entrepreneurs who are born with management skills are very rare and have special abilities. A large part of the entrepreneurs who have achieved great success in the world today are people who have learned these skills! Yes, fortunately, entrepreneurial management skills can be learned and applied by those who do not have innate management talent. To express this through the definition of management, we can say that entrepreneurial management is a science that empowers an entrepreneur to guide others effectively to achieve the organization's goals. In the following, you will learn more about entrepreneurial management and its principles.

Entrepreneurs usually have certain characteristics such as innovation and passion that help them to create a new business. But for a new business venture with a more precise direction, it is necessary that they learn entrepreneurial management! Understanding the management structure can help these people to take steps towards the development of their business. But what is entrepreneurial management?

Peter Drucker defines entrepreneurial management as the method of applying entrepreneurial knowledge and using it to increase the effectiveness of investment in new business as well as small and medium businesses. Robert Price from the Global Institute of Entrepreneurship also considers entrepreneurial management as a method of using entrepreneurial knowledge to increase the effectiveness of start-up businesses. In general, entrepreneurial management is a method that gives a firmer management structure to the inherent innovation of entrepreneurship.

Many entrepreneurs probably have ideas for their business and launch it, but do not know how to effectively control and manage them. The task of entrepreneurial management is to guide a business in the path of growth without limiting the entrepreneur's creativity and enthusiasm. In simpler terms, it can be said that "entrepreneurial knowledge" is limited to the concepts, skills and mindset that business owners must use to start and grow their business.

But "entrepreneurial management" is concerned with critical management issues for these entrepreneurs. That is, entrepreneurial management solves critical management issues continuously and centrally. In fact, entrepreneurial management helps an entrepreneur to answer the following questions:

- What is this business about? (Mission and values statement)
- Where should he go? (Goals)
- How will it get there? (development and growth)
- What does he need to get there? (forces and resources)
- Which structure is better? (organizational abilities)
- How much capital and time does it require? (financing strategy)
- How will it determine the final destination? (Prospect of success)

The difference between entrepreneurial management and corporate management
Unlike managers, entrepreneurs are directly involved in the complex relationship between financial management and business strategy. They also have to make decisions that may involve personal risks. Entrepreneurial management teaches these people how to manage such roles and risks. This issue can express the significant difference between entrepreneurial management and other management practices. Robert Herrich and Michael Peters, authors of the book Entrepreneurship, say that managing a business is fundamentally different from corporate management in the following five areas:

- Strategic orientation
- Being committed to the upcoming opportunities
- Commitment to resources
- Resource control
- Management structure

# The Importance of Entrepreneurial Management

*Figure 1. Analyzing graph*

Entrepreneurship is one of the important concepts in business management. An entrepreneur is someone who starts an economic activity or business. But not all entrepreneurs have enough knowledge and skills to start a successful business! So, what to do? This is where entrepreneurial management comes in handy. Entrepreneurial management is a type of management that can give people about to establish a startup or any other type of business activity, a deep understanding of the needs and necessities of work (Usman,2019). Having an entrepreneurial management plan is important; Because it pursues the following goals:

## Setting Clear Goals

An entrepreneurial management plan will help you determine the goals you want to achieve through your business. This includes short-term goals, such as producing and launching the first product or service, and long-term goals, such as achieving a certain amount of sales within a specified time. Having clear goals helps people involved in a business to stay motivated and work towards a common goal. In addition, entrepreneurial management helps you to know what tasks and activities you need to do to achieve these goals.

## Coordinate Actions

When you coordinate all your actions, it becomes easier to achieve your goals. Entrepreneurial management helps you identify and determine the actions to be taken and who should do them. Mapping of these actions also helps to identify leftover and forgotten tasks and actions before starting and to ensure that each task is assigned to at least one person for execution.

## Improved Resource Management

New businesses usually face limited resources of budget, staff and time. As a result, they try to get more resources by growing their customer base. Therefore, it is important for an entrepreneurial manager to ensure that available resources are used effectively. You can determine where to spend your resources through entrepreneurial management. This ensures that all available resources are used and that exploitation is done in the best possible way.

## Establish Performance Standards

Through an entrepreneur management program, you can specify the expected results and the time to reach them. You can also use these as your performance standards and judge whether your business is on track or not. For example, if your goal is to ship a product over a six-month schedule, you can evaluate your progress halfway through the three months to ensure that half of the process has been completed. If not, you can change the methods to make it easier to achieve the goal.

## Risk Balance

An entrepreneurial management plan specifies how the entrepreneur balances personal risk with his role in the company. Learning how to balance personal risk helps entrepreneurs better prepare for the unexpected. For example, risk balance can determine how much money an entrepreneur can safely invest.

## Principles of Entrepreneurial Management

*Figure 2. Stacking coins*

Entrepreneurial management has several principles that aim to give entrepreneurs more control over the course and success of their business. The following are considered the principles of entrepreneurial management:

## Mission Statement and Values

A mission statement is an explanation of why an entrepreneurial company exists. The goal is to be able to define why you started the business and what you hope to achieve. This statement describes the values you want your business to achieve. For example, a developer of a photography mobile app might point to creativity and ease of access as their mission statement. Common values for entrepreneurs are:

- Innovation
- Variety
- Curiosity
- Sustainability
- Courage
- Enthusiasm

## Specific Goals

Entrepreneurial management involves setting specific goals for a new venture. Setting specific goals may help the entrepreneur manage his innovation to achieve a specific outcome. For example, a mobile app developer might set a goal of ten thousand downloads by the end of the year. In this situation, instead of developing additional features for the program, the entrepreneur focuses on marketing it. These goals are in line with the company's mission statement and why, and they can be long-term or short-term.

## Growth and Development Strategy

Entrepreneurial management determines how the organization's goals will be achieved through growth strategy. They consider the resources needed and the best way to exploit them. It is important for entrepreneurs to spend enough time planning their growth strategy and efficient use of resources. Common growth strategies for new businesses include market penetration, product expansion, and diversification. Standards like ISO 56000 allow organizations to reach a common understanding of innovative concepts and improve themselves in today's changing world.

## Organizational Structure

The structure of an organization determines how processes flow throughout the organization. For example, you as the head of a business may entrust the creation of a new advertising plan to your marketing manager. This causes different tasks to be assigned to the people who work in the marketing department of your company. The structure basically defines the hierarchy of your business. It is important for entrepreneurs to consider the best structure for their business to implement an efficient portfolio. By creating an orderly and effective organizational structure, everyone knows who they report to and this helps the overall decision-making process (Ha, 2018).

## The Right People

Hiring the right people is an important step for entrepreneurs to create an efficient and effective team. As the business grows, they may decide to delegate some tasks and look for the right people to handle them. First employees are also important resources to help the business achieve its initial goals. When choosing a team, an entrepreneur usually looks for people who have the right skills and knowledge and who can work easily in the company environment. It is necessary that the employees are aligned with the specific goals of the organization and have the ability to maintain interaction with each other.

## Financial Strategy

Entrepreneurs determine how they want to spend the various resources of their business. Creating a strong financial strategy can help the entrepreneur to have a better understanding of his financial situation when preparing business plans. In entrepreneurial management, the entrepreneur determines all his financial resources. They also predetermine and explain the details of their various operations and when these payments need to be made. That is, a person knows when and at which stage of his business growth process he needs to inject money and allocate how much financial resources.

## The Prospect of Success

Having a vision of success is very important for an entrepreneurial business. In fact, this vision is the future that you have planned for your business. This vision goes beyond the defined goals of the organization and provides the context for the realization of smaller goals.

## The Role of Entrepreneurial Management in Dealing With Risk

Calculated risks are part of any business investment. For this reason, understanding the structure of risk and uncertainty is very important and vital in the management of any business. The events of the last few years around the world have shown that in today's business world, risk is a reality. Every investment must have the necessary management systems and processes not only to identify the risks associated with business activity, but also to measure, monitor and control them effectively.

Identification and ability to deal with potential risks are very key in investing. These cases demonstrate the entrepreneur's leadership and management skills and increase one's credibility with investors and strategic partners. At the same time, it increases his self-confidence and quickly opens communication channels. The strategy for coping with risk and uncertainty includes three key components:

- Business plan (the general line of work that will be your guide even in the most difficult situations)
- Knowledge of entrepreneurship (knowing the problems and risks ahead)
- Entrepreneurial management (the ability to guide and control the created problems)

Increasing awareness and trying to follow the mentioned strategies and concepts will turn people into experts in the field of risk. In fact, entrepreneurial management makes entrepreneurs become experts who know risks, are aware of how to manage them, and do not feel afraid and worried in high-risk environments. Creating an effective strategy to deal with risk and uncertainty is what separates these entrepreneurs from the losers.

## Risks Facing Entrepreneurial Management

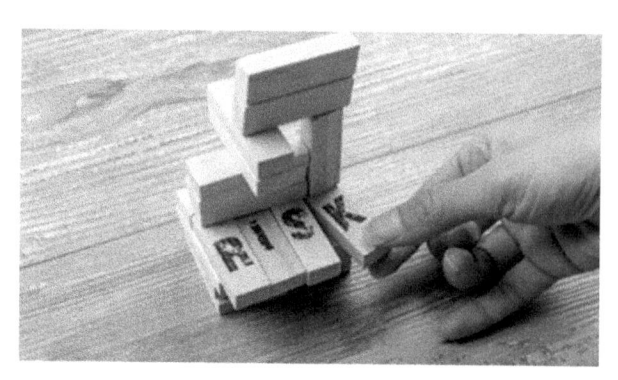

*Figure 3. Risk*

Risk taking is essential for capitalism. Without risk, the organizational system cannot function freely. Although not all risks and challenges are predictable, once identified they can be managed by core entrepreneurs, executives and board members working together. We all believe in some way that entrepreneurship is a risky business; But the facts are surprising. Estimates from the SBA database show that of the approximately 850,000 new businesses started each year, about 60 percent fail in the first six years and more than 70 percent fail in the first eight years. In the following, we mention the risks that are specific to entrepreneurial capitalism. Entrepreneurial management knows how to manage these specific risks.

## Economic Risk

Economic risk depends on how the business world is today, and the entrepreneur is looking for the answer to the question, what are the opportunities for this investment? Economic risk depends on geopolitical threats, economic cycles, interest rates and government regulations.

## People's Risk

This risk is about the investment team. How are people gathered together? Have they worked together before? Can they grow up together or will each play their own game?

## Market Risk

What is the dynamics of this part of the industry? Is there enough room for business growth? What are the risks of the presence of other competitors in the market?

## Technical Risk

Does the product work properly? At what speed will the technologies that will be released to the market in the future affect the process of this product becoming worthless or less valuable?

## Strategic Risk

It involves linking risk with strategic units and finding the right operational strategy with a sustainable business model and answers the question of whether there is a sustainable competitive advantage.

### Financial Risk

Can this investment or activity be financed now? What are the guarantees for subsequent financing periods? What about when the business starts to grow, and we need to inject money?

### Personal Risk

Entrepreneurs must make a lot of sacrifices in the way of business development, and sometimes family, friends, vacations, etc. are their second priority. Can original entrepreneurs really commit?

## CONCLUSION

Entrepreneurship is known as an effective and important field in business. Because an entrepreneur, in addition to creating a business for himself, also has a direct role in creating employment and generating income for others. For an entrepreneur, failure means loss of credit, capital, property, and sometimes even the collapse of family relationships. For this reason, entrepreneurial management has a very vital role and helps entrepreneurs to use management skills in their business. If you are looking for more information about the types of management and issues in this field, you can use the articles on our website. Contact our consultants and experts for more information.

### Investment for Entrepreneurship

In the realm of entrepreneurship, attracting the right investors is a pivotal concern for every entrepreneur. The infusion of capital not only helps to launch a new business but also plays a crucial role in its growth and sustainability. Effective investment strategies can significantly enhance the value of an entrepreneur's capital, turning innovative ideas into successful ventures.

At its core, investment refers to the allocation of resources, usually money, into assets with the expectation of generating returns over time. This could involve investing in stocks, bonds, real estate, or other financial instruments. Each type of investment comes with its own unique set of risks, benefits, and considerations, making it essential for entrepreneurs to understand their options thoroughly. For entrepreneurs, smart investment decisions can create a foundation for financial stability and growth. It is imperative to conduct thorough research and educate oneself about the various investment avenues available. This knowledge enables entrepreneurs to make informed choices that align with their financial situation, long-term goals, and risk tolerance.

Moreover, a strategic approach to investment involves evaluating the potential risks associated with different opportunities. Higher returns often come with higher risks, and understanding this trade-off is crucial for any entrepreneur looking to secure funding. By identifying investments that match their comfort level with risk, entrepreneurs can make decisions that will foster growth without jeopardizing their financial stability.

Investors are not merely sources of capital; they can also bring invaluable expertise, networks, and resources to the table. Building relationships with potential investors can lead to strategic partnerships that enhance the entrepreneurial venture. Therefore, entrepreneurs should not only seek financial backing but also look for investors who share their vision and can contribute to the growth of the business. Investment is a critical aspect of entrepreneurship, requiring a thoughtful and informed approach. By understanding the landscape of investment opportunities, assessing risks, and forming strategic relationships with investors, entrepreneurs can position their businesses for success and ensure sustainable growth in an ever-evolving market. Ultimately, wise investment decisions can provide the necessary fuel for innovative ideas to flourish and transform into thriving enterprises.

## Understanding the Benefits of Investment for Entrepreneurship

The concept of investing in entrepreneurship is often overlooked by aspiring business owners. Investing in entrepreneurship is a process in which individuals or organizations provide financial resources to support the growth and development of a business project. Investing in entrepreneurship can be in the form of capital, resources, or marketing assistance. Investing in entrepreneurship can be a great way to ensure financial returns while also supporting the growth of an innovative business. By understanding the basics of investing in entrepreneurship, entrepreneurs can use their resources to maximize their potential for success. Entrepreneurs often invest in their private businesses (Utami,2017).

## Effective Communication with Investors

Building strong relationships with investors is a fundamental aspect of entrepreneurial success, and it hinges on effective communication. Entrepreneurs must recognize the significance of these relationships and actively engage in clear, transparent dialogues that keep investors informed while managing their expectations. By fostering trust through consistent and meaningful communication, entrepreneurs can navigate conflicts and challenges, leading to a more productive partnership. Here are several strategies for enhancing communication with investors:

1. **Communicate Clearly and Concisely:** Investors typically operate on tight schedules, making it essential for entrepreneurs to convey important information in a straightforward manner. Avoid jargon and overly complex language; instead, focus on delivering key messages clearly and concisely. Summarizing critical points can help ensure that investors grasp the essential elements of your business proposition quickly.
2. **Utilize Visuals:** Visual aids, such as charts, graphs, and presentations, can significantly enhance understanding and retention of information. By presenting data visually, entrepreneurs can illustrate trends, financial projections, and key performance indicators more effectively. This approach not only captures investors' attention but also makes complex information more accessible.
3. **Practice Effective Listening:** Communication is a two-way street, and effective listening is just as important as articulating your thoughts. When interacting with investors, take the time to listen attentively to their questions and concerns. Acknowledging their input and responding thoughtfully fosters a sense of respect and partnership, demonstrating that you value their perspectives.
4. **Anticipate Potential Investor Questions:** Investors are likely to have a variety of questions regarding your business model, market strategies, and financial forecasts. Prepare for these inquiries by thinking critically about the information you provide and identifying potential areas of concern. Having clear, concise answers ready can instill confidence in your investors and reassure them about their investment decisions.
5. **Be Upfront and Honest:** Transparency is crucial in building trust with investors. Clearly articulate your business objectives, as well as the challenges you anticipate facing. Investors appreciate honesty regarding both the risks and opportunities associated with your venture. This approach not only sets realistic expectations but also demonstrates your commitment to ethical practices.
6. **Follow Up:** Maintaining ongoing communication is vital. After initial meetings or presentations, be sure to follow up with investors to address any lingering questions or concerns. This proactive approach reinforces your dedication to effective communication and strengthens the relationship. It shows that you are engaged and committed to keeping investors informed about developments within your business.
7. **Tailor Communication Styles:** Different investors may have varied preferences for how they receive information. Some may prefer detailed reports, while others might favor brief summaries or visual presentations. Pay attention to individual

investor preferences and adapt your communication style accordingly to foster better engagement.
8. **Use Technology:** Leverage digital tools and platforms to streamline communication with investors. Regular updates through emails, newsletters, or dedicated investor portals can keep them informed about milestones, achievements, and any changes in strategy. This ongoing engagement helps maintain interest and enthusiasm for your venture.
9. **Encourage Feedback:** Creating an environment where investors feel comfortable providing feedback is essential. Actively seek their input on your business strategies and be open to constructive criticism. This dialogue can provide valuable insights that enhance your business operations while reinforcing the collaborative nature of the relationship.

By incorporating these strategies into your communication practices, you can build robust and productive relationships with investors that contribute significantly to the success of your business. Effective communication is not merely a skill but a strategic investment that pays dividends in fostering trust, securing funding, and achieving long-term entrepreneurial goals. Taking the time to develop and refine these communication skills will yield substantial benefits in the competitive landscape of entrepreneurship.

## Managing Expectations and Setting Goals With Investors

Managing expectations and setting coordinated goals with investors is one of the most important aspects of building strong relationships in the business world. Here's how to do it effectively:

**Articulate Your Vision:** Investors want to know what your entrepreneurial business goals are. Be clear about your vision for the future and explain how their investment will help you achieve your goals.
**Entrepreneurs Should Set Realistic Expectations:** It is important to set realistic expectations of investors. Entrepreneurs should be honest about what they can do and not make promises they can't keep.
**Setting Specific Goals:** Setting specific goals can help entrepreneurs and investors move in the right direction. Make sure your goals are realistic and achievable and involve investors in the process of setting and achieving them.
**Be Receptive to Feedback:** Investors can provide valuable feedback that can help entrepreneurs improve their business. Be open to suggestions from investors and willing to make changes based on their feedback.

**Review Progress Regularly:** It is important to regularly review progress against goals to ensure they are on track. It also gives entrepreneurs the opportunity to modify their processes as needed.

**Entrepreneurs Need to be Transparent:** Be transparent about your progress and any challenges you may face. Investors want to know what's going on with the business they've invested in. Being honest helps build trust. By managing expectations and setting goals with investors, entrepreneurs can create a clear roadmap for the future, build trust, and ensure the success of their business. Regular communication and a willingness to adapt with feedback and the correct course will be key to maintaining strong relationships with investors (Vamvaka,2020).

## Maintaining long-Term Relationships Between Entrepreneurs and Investors

Maintaining long-term relationships with investors is critical to the success and growth of your business. In the following, we will discuss some important points for maintaining long-term relationships:

Entrepreneurs should inform investors about their work. Regular communication is one of the tips to improve the level of strong relationships with investors. Entrepreneurs should inform investors about the progress of their business.

Entrepreneurs should consider the important opinions of investors. They should involve investors in decision-making processes and seek their opinions on important decisions. This helps entrepreneurs become more invested in the success of the business and fosters a positive and productive relationship.

Entrepreneurs must meet the expectations of investors. Entrepreneurs make sure they meet the expectations they set with their investors. If they promise to deliver certain results, be sure to follow through and keep investors informed of their progress.

Celebrate your successes with your investors and tell them how their investment helped make these achievements a reality. These people are required to address any concerns for investors. If investors have concerns or feedback, they must address them quickly and professionally. Be transparent about any problems and show that they are taking steps to solve them.

Entrepreneurs must plan carefully for the future and formulate activities in a model that involves their investors in this process. Set goals, discuss business growth plans, and work together to increase your business's chances of long-term success. In fact, by maintaining strong and positive relationships with investors, they can ensure the success and growth of their business. Regular communication, transparency, and a commitment to meeting expectations and addressing concerns will be key to maintaining long-term relationships with investors (Wathanakom,2020).

## Attracting Investors for the Project

The role of transparency in the relationship between entrepreneurs and investors

Transparency is one of the important points of creating and maintaining strong relationships with investors. For the reasons that we will discuss in the following section:

Transparency in entrepreneurs' relationships with investors creates trust among them. When entrepreneurs fully explain their goals, finances, and plans, investors trust them more and feel confident in their investment.

The transparency of having entrepreneurs with investors increases accountability and ensures that entrepreneurs are responsible for their actions and the right decisions. This helps build trust and reinforces the importance of making informed decisions.

Transparency also improves communication between entrepreneurs and investors. When entrepreneurs share with investors what they are doing, they can give investors a clear picture of the business and its progress, making it easier to discuss and address any concerns.

When there is transparency between entrepreneurs and investors, they help facilitate decision-making by providing investors with the information they need to make their investment decisions.

When investors are informed about the progress and operations of their invested businesses through entrepreneurs, they are more likely to be actively involved and involved. This can help build stronger relationships and increase investment success.

Transparency between employees and investors also supports long-term development by creating a foundation of trust, accountability and informed decision-making that can help businesses succeed in the long term. In short, transparency is essential to building strong relationships with investors. Entrepreneurs being honest about their goals can build trust, increase accountability, improve communication, facilitate informed decision-making, encourage active participation, and support long-term growth.

# REFERENCES

Grohmann, A. (2018). Financial literacy and financial behavior: Evidence from the emerging Asian middle class. *Pacific-Basin Finance Journal*, 48, 129–143. DOI: 10.1016/j.pacfin.2018.01.007

Ha, K.-M. (2018). Changing the emergency response culture: Case of Korea. *International Journal of Emergency Services*, 7(1), 60–70. DOI: 10.1108/IJES-12-2016-0026

Tshikovhi, N., & Shambare, R. (2015). Entrepreneurial knowledge, personal attitudes, and entrepreneurship intentions among South African Enactus students. *Problems and Perspectives in Management*, 13(1), 152–158.

Torres, F. C., Méndez, J. C. E., Barreto, K. S., Chavarría, A. P., Machuca, K. J., & Guerrero, J. A. O. (2017). Exploring entrepreneurial intentions in Latin American university students. *The Japanese Psychological Research*, 10(2), 46–59. PMID: 32612764

Utami, C. W. (2017). Attitude, Subjective Norms, Perceived Behavior, Entrepreneurship Education and Self-efficacy toward Entrepreneurial Intention University Student in Indonesia. *European Research Studies Journal*, 20(2), 475–495.

Usman, B., & Yennita. (2019). Understanding the entrepreneurial intention among international students in Turkey. *Journal of Global Entrepreneurship Research*, 9(10), 1–21.

Vamvaka, V., Stoforos, C., Palaskas, T., & Botsaris, C. (2020). Attitude toward entrepreneurship perceived behavioral control, and entrepreneurial intention: Dimensionality, structural relationships, and gender differences. *Journal of Innovation and Entrepreneurship*, 9(1), 1–26.

Wathanakom, N., Khlaisang, J., & Songkram, N. (2020). The study of the causal relationship between innovativeness and entrepreneurial intention among undergraduate students. *Journal of Innovation and Entrepreneurship*, 9(1), 1–15.

# Chapter 12
# Conclusion

## ABSTRACT

*Entrepreneurship in today's world - infrastructure, necessity and importance In today's evolving world, success belongs to those societies and organizations that establish a meaningful relationship between scarce resources and the managerial and entrepreneurial capabilities of their human resources. In other words, the society and the organization can move forward and with momentum in the path of development, by creating the necessary bases for equipping its human resources with the knowledge and skills of productive entrepreneurship, so that by using this valuable ability, other resources of the society and the organization to create value and achieve growth and development, manage and direct.*

## INTRODUCTION

In today's evolving world, success belongs to those societies and organizations that establish a meaningful relationship between scarce resources and the managerial and entrepreneurial capabilities of their human resources. In other words, the society and the organization can move forward and with momentum in the path of development, by creating the necessary bases for equipping its human resources with the knowledge and skills of productive entrepreneurship, so that by using this valuable ability, other resources of the society and the organization to create value and achieve growth and development, manage and direct.

Today, work and activity has taken a new form and is moving towards self-employment. Entrepreneurship and entrepreneurs play a key role in the economic development and progress of different societies. The experiences of countries like Japan, South Korea, Malaysia, and India have been full of remarkable activities of entrepreneurs who today are proud of the development of their country. It should be noted that entrepreneurs do not only create new job opportunities, but also engage in creative destruction with the necessary structure, thinking, mobility and culture

DOI: 10.4018/979-8-3693-9415-1.ch012

in order to raise the lofty building of prosperity and progress from the heart of the old ruins.

Considering the role and importance of entrepreneurship and the brilliant history of entrepreneurs in the development of many countries and considering the many economic problems that our country is facing and requires help from all sides, promoting and spreading the concept of entrepreneurship, creating a platform for a culture that supports entrepreneurship and Most importantly, training people (especially educated people) as organizational entrepreneurs is of vital importance and necessity for all societies, especially for developing societies.

Today's economic, industrial, social, and cultural conditions of the country are such that it demands new and different models and solutions to solve problems and bottlenecks. The composition of the country's young population, the need to create job opportunities, and the fluctuation of oil prices are three major factors that make the country's policy makers and decision makers think of another easy source of income other than oil, and without a doubt, that source is innovation, creativity, and innovation. There is nothing else.

Now in the global arena, creative, innovative, and innovative people as entrepreneurs have become the source of great developments in the fields of industry, production and services, and they are also referred to as national heroes. The wheels of economic development always move with the development of entrepreneurship. In the importance of entrepreneurship, it is enough that only 500 entrepreneurship institutes have started working in one of the third world countries (1960-1980) and even many big companies of the world have turned to entrepreneurs to solve their problems.

In the current difficult situation, the necessity of it is felt more than ever in the society, is to deal with this basic category, that is, entrepreneurship. Because of course, due to their distinguished and outstanding characteristics, entrepreneurs are able to provide the necessary resources for growth and development in the fields of production and human resources, create employment and new business, and expand the range of products and services with industrial innovation.

Today, human power is considered as an unlimited resource and the center of any kind of development. Meanwhile, entrepreneurs have a more effective role in the process of economic development. Research has shown that there is a positive correlation between economic growth and the number of entrepreneurs in a country. Because a country with a large number of entrepreneurs has stronger commercial and economic incentives (Welsh, 2021).

The education and training of organizational entrepreneurs requires an executive education methodology for close cooperation between industry and university to face the severe social pressures resulting from the rapid growth of technology and the lack of specialized human resources in today's world. In this method, which is called entrepreneurship, people are trained in such a way that they can create work themselves. The observations resulting from the application of this methodology have been reflected on a case-by-case basis in the form of social mission, goals, specific destination, and its related activities.

Entrepreneurship is a new word that cannot be understood from its meaning. This word is used instead of the word ENTERPRENEURSHIP, which originally comes from the French word ENTERPRENDER, which means undertaking. According to the definition of Webster's dictionary, an entrepreneur is someone who undertakes to organize, manage, and assume the risk of an economic activity. Some scientists, such as Schumpeter, have considered the entrepreneur to be the most important factor in economic development. He believes that an entrepreneur is a thoughtful and innovative manager who creates golden opportunities along with creativity, risk-taking, intelligence, thought, and breadth of vision. He is able to transform with innovations and make a loss-making company profitable.

The course of development of economic activists or entrepreneurs shows that entrepreneurship is crystallized in economic theories and recognized as the main factor of wealth creation or creator of economic value and has been in the focus of discussion of various economic schools since the 15th century. But the history of the concept of entrepreneurship in today's knowledge goes back to two hundred years ago. The first person who raised this issue is a person named Cantillon. This word has been subjected to new definitions and its translation in Iran means the same person who goes under the burden of commitment. Today, many companies have realized the need for organizational entrepreneurship (Grohmann, 2018).

According to the above, it can be said that, in fact, a complete, comprehensive definition of the term entrepreneurship that is accepted by all experts has not yet been provided, but in the meantime, the theory and definitions of the famous Austrian economist Joseph Schumpeter) of entrepreneurship and the role of entrepreneurs in the development process is agreed and referred by most researchers in this field. According to him, the entrepreneur is the main driving force in economic development and the engine of development, and his role is to innovate or create new combinations of materials. Schumpeter considered the main characteristic of an entrepreneur to be "innovation" and defined the work of an entrepreneur as "creative destruction". He points out in the book "Theory of Dynamic Economy" that dynamic balance is created through innovation and entrepreneurship, and these are the characteristics of a healthy economy.

## Experience of Entrepreneurship in the World

At the beginning of the 16th century, those who were on a military mission were called entrepreneurs, and after that, the same term was used with limitations for other risks as well. From around 1700 onwards, the word "entrepreneur" has been used a lot for government contractors who were involved in civil works.

Entrepreneurship and entrepreneurs were first noticed by economists and all economic schools have described entrepreneurship in their theories since the 16th century. By presenting his theory of economic development in 1934, which coincided with the Great Depression, Joseph Schumpeter drew attention to his opinion about the central role of entrepreneurs in creating profits, and for this reason, he has been called the "Father of Entrepreneurship".

According to him, "the entrepreneur is the main driving force in economic development" and the role of entrepreneurship is "innovation or creating new combinations of materials". Also, entrepreneurship has been considered by psychologists and sociologists by understanding the role of entrepreneurs in the economy and in order to identify their characteristics and behavioral patterns by examining and researching them.

Sociologists have considered entrepreneurship as a social phenomenon and have investigated the mutual relationship between entrepreneurs and other parts and groups of society.

Management scientists have explained entrepreneurial management and the creation of an entrepreneurial atmosphere and environment in organizations.

## The Historical Course of the Concept of Entrepreneurship

In general, and taking into account the points mentioned above, the historical course of the concept of entrepreneurship can be divided into five periods:

The first period (15th and 16th centuries AD): In this period, the owners of large projects were entrusted with the executive responsibility of these projects, such as the construction of churches, castles, military facilities, etc., by the local governments. The entrepreneur was referred to risk acceptance is not included in the definitions of this period.

The second period (17th century AD): This period coincided with the beginning of the industrial revolution in Europe and then risk-taking was added to entrepreneurship. Entrepreneurs in this period include people such as merchants, artisans, and other private owners.

The third period (18th and 19th centuries AD): In this period, an entrepreneur is a person who takes risks and secures the capital he needs through loans. There is a distinction between the entrepreneur the capital provider (investor) and the business manager in the definitions of this period. has it.

The fourth period (middle decades of the 20th century): In this period, the concept of innovation, including the creation of a new product, the creation of a new distribution system, or the creation of a new organizational structure, has been added to the definitions of entrepreneurship as a main component.

The fifth period, the contemporary period (from the late 1970s until now): In this period, at the same time as the wave of creating small businesses and economic growth, as well as the identification of the role of entrepreneurship as an accelerator of this mechanism, much attention was drawn to this concept, and the approach of several in addition to this, it was done. Until this period, most of the attention of economists was focused on entrepreneurship, but in this period, psychologists, sociologists scientists, and management science researchers have also paid attention to different aspects of entrepreneurship and entrepreneurs.

Until the 1980s, three broad waves pushed the subject of entrepreneurship forward:

- **The first wave:** the general explosion of study and research in the form of publishing books on the lives of entrepreneurs and the history of their companies, how to create a personal business, and quick ways to get rich. This wave starts from the mid-1950s.
- **The second wave:** This wave, which started in the 1960s, includes the provision of entrepreneurship education courses in the fields of engineering and commerce, which have now been extended to other fields as well.
- **The third wave**: This wave includes the increasing interest of governments in research in the field of entrepreneurship and small businesses, encouraging the growth of small companies and conducting research on industrial innovations, which began in the late 1970s.

Unfortunately, the word entrepreneurship, which is a translation of the word Entrepreneurship, has caused that the meaning of creating work or creating employment is taken from this word. While entrepreneurship has a broader and more valuable concept than job creation. This incorrect understanding of this concept, as well as the inflation of unemployed human resources in the society (especially among university graduates), has caused many policies that have been adopted for its development, as well as in the circulars and speeches of officials in this regard, only the aspect of job creation for it in be considered While entrepreneurship has other positive and important consequences such as: the fertilization of creativity, encouragement to innovation and its development, increasing self-confidence, creating and developing technology, generating wealth in society and increasing public welfare, and if only the aspect of job creation is considered If it happens, we will not benefit from its other consequences.

## Entrepreneurial Roots

No teacher is more powerful and penetrating than a good example. Studies in this field show that more than half of the beginners had parents who had a profession. The author summarizes it as follows: people who start a company are most likely from families where their parents or close relatives were engaged in the same profession. Older people were examples or models for their children and probably did not care if they were successful in their work or not. However, for the children who grew up in such families, the act of starting a new career seemed possible and something they were able to do.

### The Impact of Experience

Experience and technical knowledge play an essential role in creating a successful company. Management skills and competencies are necessary to establish a company. Many studies show that 90% or more founders start their companies in the same market and industries they have been active in.

### Acquired Characteristics and Individual Role Needs

Another set of important factors that founders can usefully consider as part of the start-up process is their own talent, discretion, and characteristics. The studies of the last few years about entrepreneurs who have learned in practice and the characteristics of working people throughout their employment period.

Unfortunately, the measurement tools have not yet advanced enough to allow us to do such research, based on which these factors can be clearly determined with reliable accuracy and clarity.

## The Role of Entrepreneurs in Development

Entrepreneurs play a crucial role in driving development and economic growth, serving as catalysts for innovation and change within their communities and nations. Recognizing their significance, many governments in both developed and developing countries are actively working to foster an environment that encourages entrepreneurial characteristics among individuals. This effort involves providing maximum support through facilities, resources, and the practical application of research achievements, alongside promoting entrepreneurial education and activities.

Entrepreneurs are adept at identifying opportunities and capitalizing on emerging situations, positioning themselves as the true pioneers of change in both economic and social contexts. They understand that success and sustainability in the face of evolving market conditions require agility, initiative, and creativity. Moreover, entrepreneurship embodies essential qualities such as risk-taking, innovation, and proactive action. As outlined in various economic theories and substantiated by the experiences of growing economies, entrepreneurs are often seen as the driving force behind economic development and growth, significantly contributing to job creation and enhancing the overall quality of life. Despite this, the concept of entrepreneurship has not received the attention it deserves in some regions, including our own. Recent development programs have often overlooked the importance of cultivating an entrepreneurial spirit, resulting in a general unfamiliarity with entrepreneurial principles among many individuals within society. This lack of awareness and emphasis has led to inadequate planning and structural foundations for fostering entrepreneurship within the economic, social, and educational systems, particularly in universities.

The absence of a robust framework for promoting entrepreneurship means that potential entrepreneurs may lack the necessary support, mentorship, and resources to transform their ideas into viable businesses. It is imperative for policymakers, educators, and community leaders to recognize the transformative potential of entrepreneurship and take decisive steps to integrate entrepreneurial training and resources into educational curricula and public initiatives. By doing so, they can empower individuals to harness their creativity and initiative, ultimately leading to sustainable economic growth, job creation, and improved societal well-being. Emphasizing entrepreneurship as a key driver of development will not only elevate individual potential but also enhance the overall resilience and competitiveness of the economy.

## Entrepreneurship Strengthens Competition in Business

Entrepreneurship plays a pivotal role in enhancing competition within the business landscape. The introduction of new entrepreneurial ventures or the revitalization of existing businesses—such as transferring ownership of an economic unit to a new proprietor—significantly contributes to increased productivity across various sectors.

This surge in entrepreneurial activity intensifies competition, compelling existing businesses to either boost their efficiency or innovate to stay relevant in the market.

As new businesses enter the fray, they bring fresh ideas, unique products, and innovative services, which ultimately challenge established companies to rethink their strategies. This heightened competitive pressure acts as a catalyst for efficiency improvements and technological advancements. Organizations are prompted to streamline operations, reduce costs, and enhance their offerings to attract and retain customers. Consequently, the overall productivity of job units, whether they are involved in manufacturing, service delivery, or other economic activities, experiences a significant boost.

The implications of this competitive environment extend beyond businesses themselves; they significantly benefit consumers as well. A marketplace characterized by vigorous competition leads to a broader range of choices for consumers, allowing them to select products and services that best meet their needs and preferences. Furthermore, as businesses strive to outdo each other, they often lower their prices to attract customers, resulting in improved affordability for consumers. This dynamic fosters a culture of high utilization, where consumers can enjoy the advantages of high-quality offerings at competitive prices. Entrepreneurship not only stimulates individual business performance but also elevates the competitiveness of the economy as a whole. By fostering an environment where innovation and efficiency thrive, entrepreneurship drives economic growth, enhances consumer welfare, and ultimately contributes to a more vibrant and dynamic marketplace. As new ventures emerge and existing ones adapt, the landscape of business becomes increasingly robust, ensuring that competition remains a fundamental force in driving progress and prosperity.

## Entrepreneurship Releases Accumulated Individual Abilities

Entrepreneurship serves as a powerful catalyst for individuals seeking to unlock their accumulated abilities and talents beyond the conventional boundaries of traditional employment. While a job often provides a steady income, it does not encompass the full spectrum of desires that individuals may have. Factors such as security, independence, variety in tasks, and the pursuit of personal interests play significant roles in shaping one's professional journey. As entrepreneurship gains momentum, it allows individuals to not only improve their financial situation but also to fulfill deeper, intrinsic needs related to independence and self-reliance.

Research conducted among households in England highlights that many individuals are drawn to entrepreneurship to satisfy a blend of spiritual and material needs. The desire for freedom, a sense of autonomy, and a vibrant life are compelling motivators that often accompany financial aspirations like wealth and status. For some individuals, particularly those who have found it challenging to secure their ideal jobs, entrepreneurship can emerge as a viable solution to their economic needs. It opens doors to better job opportunities that align with their passions and skills, enabling them to carve out a fulfilling professional identity. Moreover, job satisfaction rates reflect the significant psychological benefits of entrepreneurship. Studies show that entrepreneurs report much higher levels of job satisfaction compared to traditional employees. For instance, approximately 33% of individuals engaged in freelance work without employees express satisfaction in their jobs, while this figure rises to 45% for freelancers who do have employees. In stark contrast, only about 27% of traditional employees report feeling satisfied in their roles. This disparity underscores how entrepreneurship not only enhances income potential but also provides a sense of ownership and fulfillment that is often lacking in conventional employment settings.

In essence, entrepreneurship empowers individuals to tap into their latent abilities and pursue paths that resonate with their values and aspirations. It facilitates the alignment of professional endeavors with personal goals, enabling individuals to achieve a greater sense of purpose in their work. As more people embrace entrepreneurship, they contribute to a dynamic economy that fosters innovation and diverse opportunities, ultimately enriching both their lives and the communities they serve.

## Organizational Entrepreneurship

In addition to people who want to become entrepreneurs and investors who want to support them, many people are interested in what is known as intra-organizational entrepreneurship or entrepreneurship within the context of a large joint-stock company. Since the early 1980s, with the importance of entrepreneurship and companies' emphasis on innovation for survival and competition with entrepreneurs who appeared more and more in the market scene, entrepreneurial activities were directed inside companies.

Along with the penetration of administrative and bureaucratic processes in the corporate culture, in the 1960s and 1970s, entrepreneurship in large organizations increasingly attracted the attention of senior managers of companies so that they too could engage in the process of inventing, innovating and commercializing their new products and services. With the beginning of the 1980s, and the sudden progress of industries in the field of global competition, the importance of entrepreneurial thinking and processes in large companies was emphasized more than in the past, and researchers focused their attention on how to induce entrepreneurship in the administrative structure of large companies (Darabi, 2017). Of course, it is necessary to explain that risky activities in independent and individual entrepreneurship means organizing a new organization or establishing a company, and risky activity in the concept of corporate entrepreneurship means developing a new activity within the framework of the company.

A very simple principle led to the emergence of intra-organizational entrepreneurs. The mentioned principle is as follows: there is a blessing in the existence of a human being that forces him to be creative, that is, he creates something that did not exist before or did not do any good. It is concluded that companies can by encouraging employees and persuading them to behave like "internal entrepreneurs of the organization, make them innovate in order to increase profits, and then these people are given the freedom to act without conflicting with laws and regulations. Pagir (bureaucracy) to implement their plans.

## Organizational Entrepreneurship Framework

The emergence of the concept of entrepreneurship, particularly organizational entrepreneurship, underscores its critical role in fostering the development of both organizations and society. Organizational entrepreneurship is recognized as a powerful engine driving innovation and growth, making the training and cultivation of organizational entrepreneurs essential to achieving significant progress. To effectively ignite this engine, it is crucial not only to start it but also to ensure its sustained operation. This requires providing the necessary "fuel"—resources, support, and a conducive environment—that enables organizational entrepreneurs to thrive.

At the heart of this framework is the recognition that awareness and motivation are the first steps in the entrepreneurial journey. By equipping individuals with relevant training and knowledge, organizations can spark the entrepreneurial mindset needed for innovation. It is essential for aspiring organizational entrepreneurs to understand the importance of their roles and the potential impact they can have on their organizations and communities. This awareness can be fostered through targeted educational programs, workshops, and mentorship opportunities that highlight the significance of entrepreneurial thinking and action. Moreover, continuous support from management is vital for nurturing organizational entrepreneurship. Leaders must create an environment that encourages risk-taking, experimentation, and creative problem-solving. This can be achieved by implementing policies that reward innovative ideas and facilitate open communication among team members. Additionally, establishing structural and cultural factors conducive to entrepreneurship—such as flexible organizational hierarchies and a culture that values collaboration and diversity—can further enhance the entrepreneurial spirit within the organization.

Creating strategic entrepreneurial thinking within the organization is also crucial. This involves aligning organizational goals with entrepreneurial initiatives and fostering a culture that prioritizes innovation as a key driver of success. Organizations should actively seek to embed entrepreneurship into their strategic planning processes, ensuring that entrepreneurial activities are integrated into the overall business strategy. The organizational entrepreneurship framework emphasizes the need for a multi-faceted approach to cultivate organizational entrepreneurs. By providing the necessary training, management support, and structural and cultural conditions, organizations can ignite the entrepreneurial spirit and sustain it for long-term success. Through these efforts, organizational entrepreneurs can become instrumental in driving development, fostering innovation, and contributing to the broader economic and social landscape.

## Organizational Entrepreneurship Training

In general, according to a comprehensive definition, education means information and intellectual growth that is obtained through formal and informal education and study. Education is based on learning and every organization tries to help the performance of people in their jobs. The educational program is the organization of these experiences in a way that adapts and improves the required attitudes or skills. Therefore, training is an effort made by organizations to change people's behavior through the learning process and to increase their effectiveness. Training is all efforts and efforts that are carried out in order to improve the level of knowledge and awareness, technical, professional and job skills, as well as create favorable behavior in the employees of an organization and make them ready to perform their job duties and responsibilities. The purpose of training employees is not to transfer information and reservations. The goal is not to store the results obtained in the minds of employees. Because these achievements are available in books and libraries. The right education is to equip a person to constantly search for new solutions. The attitude that comes along with the acquisition of knowledge is far more important than the knowledge itself. The first center in the world to hold a special intra-organizational entrepreneurship course is the Institute of Entrepreneurship Development in India. Among the major goals of this course, the following can be mentioned:

1) To inform the participants about the latent talents of entrepreneurship and guide them towards innovation.
2) Developing and creating an entrepreneurial atmosphere within the organization.
3) Creating confidence in the participants of the course that the insight and insight created will lead to further growth and development.
4) Helping to develop an entrepreneurial leadership style in the organization.
5) Motivating people to become success leaders in the organization.

Educational items in this course include enabling and creating an entrepreneurial environment for innovation, promoting and understanding opportunities, transformational leadership, developing entrepreneurial motivations and abilities, presenting creative ideas, and strategic planning to provide new products and services. The participants in this course are public sector managers and managers-owners of industrial companies (manufacturing and service), who are tested for psychological characteristics at the beginning of the course.

Among the entrepreneurship training programs is the SIYB program, which was provided by the International Labor Organization and implemented in more than 60 developing countries. The SIYB educational program is an educational and consulting program designed to educate and nurture entrepreneurs in small units (both industrial, service and commercial). SIYB training program includes various training packages. SYB and IYB packages are the most important packages of this educational program. The SYB program is a training program for those who have an idea to start a practical business. And the IYB program teaches management principles and concepts and company management methods to the owners and managers of small production and service units who intend to grow and develop their company. During a decade of implementation of the SIYB program by the International Labor Organization in the countries of the world, more than one hundred thousand entrepreneurs were trained, and research shows that the participants were satisfied with the program and found it useful, and the programs were not irrelevant in their opinion. and research shows that IYB trainings have a new impact on the employment rate and profitability of enterprises.

## Cultivating Organizational Entrepreneurs

Education of any kind is useful when it shows its results in practice. When it can be claimed that learning has happened in a person and the person has learned something from the training provided to him, we can see a significant change in his behavior and practical actions. This issue is also true for the organization, so that when learning happens in the organization, there is a noticeable change in the performance of the organization, and it goes without saying that the organization is a collection of human people, and its learning and knowledge is also a collection of the learnings of the employees of that organization. Therefore, in order to provide any type of training, both at the individual level and at the organizational level, you should think about the practical effect of that training from the beginning and think of arrangements that will create the context of behavioral changes in the individual and functional changes in the organization.

In an article he published in 1978, the originator of the term organizational entrepreneurship, Pinkatt, explained the principles of establishing and cultivating organizational entrepreneurship as follows:

To become an organizational entrepreneur, a person must accept the risk of an activity that is valuable to him and in this way, he should not be afraid of material and spiritual costs such as a 20% reduction in salary. Rewards resulting from the success of an entrepreneurial project should be shared between the company and the entrepreneur in a fair way, and for this purpose, a trusted committee should be formed to purchase and evaluate the completed project. The organizational entrepreneur should have enough opportunity to create capital (within the organization). In addition to cash rewards, the successful corporate entrepreneur gains full control over a certain amount of R&D funding and his hands are free to invest the resources he has made available to him on behalf of the company. The company should allow employees to become entrepreneurs. Successful organizational entrepreneurs should not be limited by the internal discipline of the company. An entrepreneur who does not have capital must look for risk investors within the organization to start a new business. Venture capitalists are people who invest in new and innovative projects of entrepreneurial employees. If a new product or service is provided by an organizational entrepreneur, that product should not be delivered or sold to other parts of the company in a commercial and profitable manner. The new business can be organized as a new division within or even as a new company owned by the parent company. The boundless energies of entrepreneurial employees may cause problems for the central management, but they should know that the advantages of organizational entrepreneurs are more than the harms, and managers can understand that welcoming the challenges has begun.

A selected group of company employees attend the entrepreneur school, especially in the organizational entrepreneurship department.

A consulting group in the field of creating and establishing quasi-entrepreneurial systems within the organization should be selected and hired.

The consulting company, together with the company managers, establish rules such as how other company departments (such as production and sales) participate in the losses and losses of the production of a new product or process in the places where the entrepreneurs are supposed to operate (Westhead,2016).

The consulting company, along with the company's managers, act as members of the initial group of domestic investors, and their goal is to select entrepreneurial projects that the company intends to invest in. Consulting companies provide advice to organizational entrepreneurs on how to manage projects and improve ideas.

The consulting company, with the cooperation of managers, identifies and tracks potential entrepreneurs, as well as the type of their relationships and interactions within the organization.

## Structural Dimensions of Organizational Entrepreneurship

- **Complexity:** If the organization has complexity on the horizontal level (number of jobs and tasks) or on the vertical level (number of management positions) and its organizational communication becomes more legal and formal, the possibility of group interaction in the organization is greatly reduced and this takes the organization away from its entrepreneurial goals. The research conducted in this regard also confirms the negative relationship between the complexity of the structure and organizational entrepreneurship.
- **Formality:** In the situation where the organization has high formality, people do not have freedom of action. The work does not have acceptable and tolerable flexibility and the occurrence of different behaviors from the employees is denied. In this situation, because learning will not play a role in advancing the program and improving performance, employees will also lose the desire to learn. While in the entrepreneurial organization, learning, flexibility and risk acceptance are considered central principles from the organization. In other words, the organization can be considered an entrepreneur in a situation where, while accepting the risk, it leaves the decision-making power and competent judgments to its members and allows them to use their individual creativity in doing things. This becomes possible when the amount of instructions, directives and operational standards is reduced as much as possible and employees are given the opportunity to show their abilities. With this definition, the relationship between organizational entrepreneurship and formality will be an inverse relationship.
- **Concentration:** In entrepreneurial organizations where decision-making powers must be delegated to units and individuals so that they can design and implement the right move at the right time, the concept of concentration fades and due to the creativity, talent and intellectual and executive power of specialists and The experts of such organizations will find a clear effect of lack of concentration. This is while other content dimensions of the organization, especially size and technology, also have a significant impact on the level of concentration. So that the bigger the size of the organization or the more the organization benefits from the presence of experienced professionals and has a communication network suitable for modern technology, the issue of delegation of authority and decentralization becomes more meaningful. If the

employees are professionally qualified, the risks related to delegation will be reduced and the field of decentralization will be provided.

- **Organizational Culture:** Organizational culture represents a set of values, beliefs and norms in which the organization has common features with its employees. One of the characteristics of entrepreneurial organizations is to have a culture of flexibility or entrepreneurship (meaning that) through flexibility and strategically to the external environment is taken into consideration and efforts are made to meet the needs of customers. In this culture, norms and beliefs are confirmed by means of which one can identify and interpret the signs in the environment and show a suitable reaction based on that, or adopt a suitable behavior. Such an organization must react quickly to new plans and be able to restructure and adopt a new set of behaviors to do a new job (Wibowo, 2016).

"Organizations that have inflexible culture and structure, in order to create cooperation and unity in times of crisis, will suffer chaos, while organizations that foresee the possibility of establishing relationships, especially informal and flexible relationships in their structure, have positive factors and They are effective for encouraging and developing creativity and innovation in their organization.

## Facilitating Factors in the Growth of Entrepreneurship

### Management Support

The values and philosophy of management and the level of senior management support for risk-taking and innovative people are very important in entrepreneurial organizations, and basically, management support is one of the most important factors among the five main factors of organizational entrepreneurship - that is, encouragement and reward, organizational structure, risk-taking, access to resources., and it is the support of the management, many researches have been done about this factor and the following characteristics in the senior management of the organization show the support of the management for entrepreneurship.

- Personal characteristics of the CEO
- Financial support to start and move new projects
- Using new ideas of employees
- Compatibility of values and philosophy of management or entrepreneurship
- Belief in joint management
- Tolerance of deviation from the rules
- Appreciation of risk takers

- Decision-making power of senior management
- Accepting responsibility for entrepreneurial activities
- Accepting risk as a positive trait
- Diversity in financial support
- Appreciation of people with ideas
- Senior management innovation experience
- Supporting small pilot projects

## Strategic Thinking

One of the very important measures that has a significant role in developing educational concepts at both individual and organizational levels and provides the necessary platform for the implementation of those concepts in the form of behavioral and functional changes is the creation of strategic thinking in the organization. Strategic thinking at both individual and organizational levels with its comprehensiveness and special foresight that it creates causes a better understanding of the organization and its environment and leads to frequent creativity. On the other hand, it provides the context for more communication and interaction between managers and employees and makes use of the ingenuity and creativity of employees in the organization (Yamina,2019).

Organizational entrepreneurship leads to the improvement of organizational performance, and it can be said that it will have a synergistic effect on the long-term development of the society in various economic, social, and cultural dimensions, hence the education and training in different organizations of our country. It is thirsty for development; it finds a double necessity.

## How to Manage Scientific and Research Parks and Growth Centers

Science and technology parks are an infrastructure to support small companies and businesses based on knowledge-based entrepreneurship. The duty of these parks is financial, moral and legal support, providing necessary equipment and facilities, consulting and providing work space for innovative small and medium companies. The main point of view is to provide communication intermediaries between university and industry.

Among the advantages of the town are the consolidation of knowledge-based companies, better service to them, and the use of scientific and research capacities of universities.

Forming a joint consortium between the scientific and research town and universities in order to use their abilities as much as possible. Special attention of the governorates to the elements of innovation and technology in the discussion of entrepreneurship and pursuing the creation of science and technology corridor are other priorities. Financial support for knowledge-based companies and economic enterprises through facilitating the payment of special facilities in the banking system is also considered an important step in the development and promotion of the goals of science and research parks and growth centers.

## Digital Entrepreneurship

Digital entrepreneurship is considered one of the most important infrastructures for productive employment in the third millennium, and the industrialized countries of the world, including the Group of Eight countries, have valuable organizational behaviors in this field. Digital entrepreneurship is an opportunity to use creative forces with the lowest cost and maximum effectiveness in business.

Today, digital entrepreneurship is reflected in the business methods of Bill Gates, the leader of Microsoft. The method that made the young "Gates" along with his colleague, within two decades, the richest man on the planet. Competitive advantage and excellent production potential in the field of IT are the main components of business prosperity in this field.

Digital entrepreneurship is now being examined and basic training in the country's higher education centers, and it is hoped that the fields of its actual occurrence in the country's business will increase day by day.

Google is another successful company in the field of digital entrepreneurship. A company with 2,000 employees and a turnover of several billion dollars, has more than 300 million contacts per month only through www.google.com.

Statistics are still not available to what extent, people who seek to create businesses in the digital world in the country, benefit from the minimum required in production, business and management and the art of communication. Of course, the statistics published in the beginning of 2018 by the technical and professional organization of the country show that more than 85% of the job applicants in the country do not have the minimum scientific and practical requirements for job creation and even employment in an organization. to be It is clear that the weakness of competent and knowledgeable human resources in the entrepreneurship of digital organizations is a strategic and extremely sensitive issue. Therefore, the government and universities should have a program for nurturing and educating people in this field. Certainly, the levels of education and training of those who intend to be in the field of process: leadership, management of units, use of job opportunities and other issues are different from each other. Providing these educational opportunities at different levels is an important need that should be paid attention to(Yildirim, 2020).

In a country like America, there are many centers for training people to create and manage and expand business processes in digital organizations, which provides the platform for the success of digital organizations.

The effort that has now emerged in the country to develop the penetration rate of IT in the society and to provide platforms for defining new courses at the master's level for the development of such things as marketing, entrepreneurial management, e-commerce and the like, is a good and young approach that is now taking shape. If we want organizations like Google, we must provide the necessary infrastructure from all aspects, and in this way, all factors, including the government, industry, universities, and all people interested in participating in this field, must pay serious attention.

## The Role of Information and Communication Technology (ICT) in Entrepreneurship

The term "new economy" has gradually become popular and draws a new perspective that is associated with the development of information technology. In such an economy, information and communication technology expands and becomes increasingly important. During the past centuries, human society has accepted the significant effects of technological changes. ICT satisfies communication and information needs that help create knowledge and create new possibilities for information exchange. ICT has the potential to increase the human ability to create new knowledge.

Frank Webster in the book Theory of Information Society states that the first definition of information that comes to mind is the semantic definition. Meaningful information has a subject and its content is knowledge or instruction about something or someone. But "Kenneth Arrow" believes that the meaning of information in a nutshell is to reduce uncertainty. Information enables the user to gain knowledge about something and use that knowledge to communicate, learn, think, make decisions, and innovate when needed.

## Theory of Social Networks in Relation to Entrepreneurship

According to the theory of social networks, entrepreneurship is a process that is located in a variable network of social relationships, and this social relationship can limit or facilitate the entrepreneur with resources and opportunities. The development of information and communication technology has created a huge network with a global scale (Internet). In developed countries, the Internet is one of the most important tools for entrepreneurs. These people increase their capabilities through this network and take advantage of its benefits.

Entrepreneurship, the engine of information and communication technology development

It is with entrepreneurship that the needs are recognized and by meeting the needs, progress is achieved. Industrialized countries are advanced because they have made progress in information technology, and through it they have taken over the world economy and become a military power, and they are directing the world's culture towards their desires. Information entrepreneurship can be done at different levels of hardware, software, information and communication. At each of these levels, there are many opportunities for entrepreneurship that require the support of the investment center and entrepreneurial efforts, and interestingly, entrepreneurship in the field of information is much easier and more practical than entrepreneurship in other fields. For example, in the field of nuclear power plant, there are fewer ideas due to limited application. In addition, extremely high investment and a low percentage of feasibility is an obstacle to any entrepreneurial activity, while in the field of information and communication technology, many ideas are created and the amount of investment required to bring the ideas to fruition. not so much

## The Role of the Government in Information Technology Entrepreneurship

It was observed that information and communication technology has brought many changes in all social activities including entrepreneurship and has been considered as the most important tool of modern entrepreneurship. Also, entrepreneurship in information technology has a wide scope for activity. Entrepreneurship is a requirement of technology development and technology development is the basis of entrepreneurship. Based on this, the importance of the role of entrepreneurship and the role of the government is determined. The government should develop the platform for entrepreneurship in the field of information technology, which is communication and information networks, and provide easy access to this network for everyone, while creating and expanding the culture of using the network and the necessary rules and regulations. Compile and implement.

The phenomenon of brain drain, which is especially common in new technology, is the result of weak entrepreneurship in developing countries. Many of the educated forces of these countries have only come and been trained to be practical and should be managed by others, and on the other hand, people who have an entrepreneurial personality do not find a platform for entrepreneurship in these countries. Entrepreneurs can create jobs in the field of technology for domestic specialists and prevent brain drain due to the job satisfaction they create, in addition to all the benefits of entrepreneurship.

## Successful Experiences of Other Countries

One of the solutions that have been discussed so far in countries like our country due to population and unemployment crisis and the inefficiency of production factors is the creation of small economic enterprises, such as Australia, China, Japan and other countries, because small enterprises can make a significant contribution to creating employment:

1) Public participation of people in creating these enterprises due to the need for limited financial and non-financial resources.
2) The productivity of these enterprises relatively and concretely reaches the people or the middle classes of the society.
3) Due to the increase of unemployed people, especially women and those who are glorified on the one hand, and the inability of the government to create jobs for all people, these companies can take steps to create jobs for people and so-called non-wage employment.
4) One of the merits of creating small economic enterprises is that these enterprises can firstly: identify the potential and secondly: according to the existing potential (manpower, capital resources and regional management) produce the product or service specific to the region. to estimate the needs of the region and employ the unemployed.
5) Perhaps one of the fairest methods of income distribution is the creation of small economic enterprises. In fact, based on the Lorenz curve, the coefficient of such income distribution will be more equal, and this is a scientific work all over the world.
6) The government has the duty to create the necessary platform for employment and take responsibility by creating mother and specialized industries, taking into account the cost-effectiveness, and also creating electricity, water and gas communication routes. Therefore, if the government deals with these matters and leaves the issue of production of goods and services to the people, which was and is one of the necessary solutions for the creation and expansion of small economic enterprises.

# The Importance of Financial Literacy as a Factor in the Success of Entrepreneurs

Lack of financial literacy skills is observed worldwide. This is an important issue that should be taken seriously and efforts should be made to improve it. Startups are at risk of failure due to poor financial management, which is mainly caused by the lack of financial literacy of their entrepreneurs. As mentioned above, entrepreneurs can find countless benefits to being financially literate, only a few of which are discussed in the article above:

- Financial literacy allows you to budget properly.

To achieve the business goals, you set at the beginning of the year, you need to stay on budget.

- Financial literacy enables credit management.

Financial literacy enables entrepreneurs to manage business credits in a better way to spend them in a way that is useful for the business itself.

- Financial literacy allows decision making based on analysis.

An entrepreneur who can make sound financial analysis in addition to understanding business financial reports can make reliable decisions that are supported by proper reasoning.

- Financial literacy helps business growth

Most startups lose their way due to failure to manage their finances. Therefore, with the increase in financial literacy of entrepreneurs, the possibility of business growth increases.

- Financial literacy gives you control over your business

Having financial skills and literacy gives you the ability to control your business. Normally, if you are good with finances, you will be in a better position to make decisions about them.

Financial literacy for entrepreneurs, meaning mastery of numbers and financial concepts, is one of the fundamental pillars for success in the business world. Mastering numbers allows you to make smarter financial decisions, budget properly, and generally make the most of your finances. Here are some important reasons to master numbers in financial literacy for entrepreneurs:

- **Assessing the Financial Situation:** By mastering the numbers, you can properly assess the financial situation of your business. This includes knowing your business's income, expenses, capital, liabilities, and assets. With this information, you can make decisions such as resource allocation, investment, debt management, and proper budgeting.
- **Financial Planning:** Mastering numbers will help you plan better. By setting financial goals and planning carefully to achieve them, you can use your resources optimally and face financial problems.
- **Financial Data Analysis:** Mastery of numbers allows you to analyze financial data and identify financial patterns and trends. This analysis can include financial ratios, sales trends, profitability, and growth rate. By carefully analyzing this data, you can make decisions that will improve the performance and profitability of your business.
- **Risk Management:** Having a mastery of numbers will help you better manage financial risks. By knowing exactly the amount of financial risks associated with your business, you can adopt appropriate strategies to reduce and control them. This includes the use of financial tools such as insurance, capital strategies, adjusting the amount of cash holdings, and creating plans to deal with financial crises.
- **Attracting Capital:** Mastering numbers and being financially literate can help you attract capital for your business. Investors and investment funds in the industry tend to work with businesses that have the ability to manage finances and have a strategic vision. By demonstrating your mastery of numbers and the ability to provide strong financial reports, you can get the capital you need.
- **Make Smart Financial Decisions:** Mastering numbers and financial concepts allows you to make smarter financial decisions. With a deeper understanding of financial numbers and indicators, you can make decisions about capital structure, resource allocation, investments, pricing of products and services, and cost management (Darabi,2017).

# REFERENCES

Grohmann, A. (2018). Financial literacy and financial behavior: Evidence from the emerging Asian middle class. *Pacific-Basin Finance Journal*, 48, 129–143. DOI: 10.1016/j.pacfin.2018.01.007

Darabi, Roya. (2017). The Relationship between Financial Crisis and Capital Structure. *Quarterly Journal of Financial and Economic Policies*, (17), 72–51.

Welsh, D. H. B., Kaciak, E., Mehtap, S., Pellegrini, M. M., Caputo, A., & Ahmed, S. (2021). The door swings in and out: The impact of family support and country stability on success of women entrepreneurs in the Arab world. *International Small Business Journal*, 39(7), 619–642. DOI: 10.1177/0266242620952356

Westhead, P., & Solesvik, M. Z. (2016). Entrepreneurship education and entrepreneurial intention: Do female students benefit? *International Small Business Journal*, 34(8), 979–1003. DOI: 10.1177/0266242615612534

Wibowo, B. (2016). Relationship between Entrepreneurial Intention Among Undergraduates Student and Entrepreneurship. *Asia-Pacific Management and Business Application*, 5(1), 30–50.

Yamina, G., & Mohammed, B. S. (2019). Factors Affecting Students' Entrepreneurial Intentions in Algeria: Application of Shapero and Sokol Model. *American Journal of Economics*, 9(6), 273–281.

Yıldırım, G., Tarınç, A., & Kılınç, C. C. (2020). Women entrepreneurship in tourism: The case of Turkey. *Journal of Tourism and Gastronomy Studies*, 8(4), 2462–2477. DOI: 10.21325/jotags.2020.721

# Compilation of References

Ai, H., Croce, M., & Li, K. (2018). News shocks and the production-based term structure of equity returns. *Review of Financial Studies*, 31(7), 2323–2467.

AL-Barakani, A., Bin, L., Zhang, X., Saeed, M., Qahtan, A. S. A., & Hamood Ghallab, H. M. (2022). Spatial analysis of financial development's effect on the ecological footprint of belt and road initiative countries: Mitigation options through renewable energy consumption and institutional quality. *Journal of Cleaner Production*, 366, 132696. DOI: 10.1016/j.jclepro.2022.132696

Anderson, D. (2016). *Organization development: The process of leading organizational change. Translated by SeyedNaghavi MA, Masoud Sinaki S, Kosar Z &Khosravi SH*. Koohsar Publication. [Book in Persian]

Andreou, P. C., Karasamani, I., Louca, C., & Ehrlich, D. (2017). The impact of managerial ability on crisis-period corporate investment. *Journal of Business Research*, 79, 107–122. DOI: 10.1016/j.jbusres.2017.05.022

Arner, D. W., Buckley, R. P., Zetzsche, D. A., & Veidt, R. (2020). Sustainability, FinTech and financial inclusion. *European Business Organization Law Review*, 21(1), 7–35. DOI: 10.1007/s40804-020-00183-y

Babiak, M. (2023). Generalized disappointment aversion and the variance term structure. *SSRN*, 1–48. DOI: 10.2139/ssrn.4197174

Banga, J. (2019). The green bond market: A potential source of climate finance for developing countries. *Journal of Sustainable Finance & Investment*, 9(1), 17–32. DOI: 10.1080/20430795.2018.1498617

Battiston, S., Dafermos, Y., & Monasterolo, I. (2021). *Climate Risks and Financial Stability* (Vol. 54). Elsevier.

Boratyńska, K. (2016). FsQCA in corporate bankruptcy research. An innovative approach in food industry. *Journal of Business Research*, 69(11), 5529–5533. DOI: 10.1016/j.jbusres.2016.04.166

Chiaramontea, L, & Casu, B. (2017). Capital and liquidity ratios and financial distress. Evidence from the European banking industry. *The British Accounting Review*.

Christensen, H. B., Nikolaev, V., & Wittenberg-Moerman, R. (2016). Accounting information in financial contracting: The incomplete contract theory perspective. *Journal of Accounting Research*, 54(2), 397–435. DOI: 10.1111/1475-679X.12108

Cohn, J. B., Liu, Z., & Wardlaw, M. I. (2022). Count (and count-like) data in finance. *Journal of Financial Economics*, 146(2), 529–551. DOI: 10.1016/j.jfineco.2022.08.004

Coombs, W. T., & Laufer, D. (2018). Global Crisis Management- Current Research and Future Directions. *Journal of International Management*, 24(3), 199–203. DOI: 10.1016/j.intman.2017.12.003

Darabi, Roya. (2017). The Relationship between Financial Crisis and Capital Structure. *Quarterly Journal of Financial and Economic Policies*, (17), 72–51.

Dekamini, Fatemeh, Javanmard, Habibollah, & Ehsanifar, Mohammad. (2023). Identifying the factors of the financial crisis and presenting a model in the hotel industry in the critical conditions of COVID-19 (5 and 4-star hotels in Iran). *The Quarterly Journal of Transformative Human Resources*, 2(6).

Demerjian, P. R., & Owens, E. L. (2016). Measuring the probability of financial covenant violation in private debt contracts. *Journal of Accounting and Economics*, 61(2-3), 433–447. DOI: 10.1016/j.jacceco.2015.11.001

Ellul, A., & Panayides, M. (2018). Do financial analysts restrain insiders' informational advantage? *Journal of Financial and Quantitative Analysis*, 53(1), 203–241. DOI: 10.1017/S0022109017000990

Fallah, M. F., Pourmansouri, R., & Ahmadpour, B. (2024). Presenting a new deep learning-based method with the incorporation of error effects to predict certain cryptocurrencies.[-. *International Review of Financial Analysis*, 103466, 103466. Advance online publication. https://climbtheladder.com/sales-planning-manager/. DOI: 10.1016/j.irfa.2024.103466

Grohmann, A. (2018). Financial literacy and financial behavior: Evidence from the emerging Asian middle class. *Pacific-Basin Finance Journal*, 48, 129–143. DOI: 10.1016/j.pacfin.2018.01.007

Ha, K.-M. (2018). Changing the emergency response culture: Case of Korea. *International Journal of Emergency Services*, 7(1), 60–70. DOI: 10.1108/IJES-12-2016-0026

Heath, D., Ringgenberg, M. C., Samadi, M., & Werner, I. M. (2023). Reusing natural experiments. *The Journal of Finance*, 78(4), 2329–2364. DOI: 10.1111/jofi.13250

Jiang, L., Levine, R., & Lin, C. (2019). Competition and bank liquidity creation. *Journal of Financial and Quantitative Analysis*, •••, 1–50.

Li, K., & Xu, C. (2023). Asset pricing with a financial sector. *Financial Management*, 52(1), 67–95. DOI: 10.1111/fima.12407

Lusardi, A. (2019). Financial literacy and the need for financial education: Evidence and implications. *Swiss Journal of Economics and Statistics*, 155(1), 1. DOI: 10.1186/s41937-019-0027-5

Nejad, Ali, & Mehdi, Tarfi, Setareh. (2017). The Impact of Management Ability on Financing Policy. *Accounting Knowledge Quarterly*, 8(2), 180–159.

Paiella, M. (2016). Financial literacy and subjective expectations questions: A validation exercise. *Research in Economics*, 70(2), 360–374. DOI: 10.1016/j.rie.2015.11.004

Peyravan, L. (2020). Financial reporting quality and dual-holding of debt and equity. *The Accounting Review*, 95(5), 351–371. DOI: 10.2308/accr-52661

Pourmansouri, R., Fallah, M. F., Birau, R., Dekamini, F., & Nioata, R. M. (2024). *Exploring Governance, Ownership, and Auditor Impact on Company Risk: A Comparative Analysis Before and After COVID-19 pandemic. Multidisciplinary Science Journal.* Accepted Articles.

Pourmansouri, R., Fallahshams, M. F., & Afshani, R. G. G. (2024). Designing a Financial Stress Index Based on the GHARCH-DCC Approach and Machine Learning Models. *Journal of the Knowledge Economy*, •••, 1–30. DOI: 10.1007/s13132-024-02075-9

Pourmansouri, R., Mehdiabadi, A., Shahabi, V., Spulbar, C., & Birau, R. (2022). An investigation of the link between major shareholders' behavior and corporate governance performance before and after the COVID-19 pandemic: A case study of the companies listed on the Iranian stock market. *Journal of Risk and Financial Management*, 15(5), 208. DOI: 10.3390/jrfm15050208

Shen, C.-H., Lin, S.-J., Tang, D.-P., & Hsiao, Y.-J. (2016). The relationship between financial disputes and financial literacy. *Pacific-Basin Finance Journal*, 36, 46–65. DOI: 10.1016/j.pacfin.2015.11.002

Sukavejworakit, K., Promsiri, T., & Virasa, T. (2018). Oetel: An Innovative Teaching Model for Entrepreneurship Education. *Journal of Entrepreneurship Education*, 21(2), 1–11.

Sun, H., Ni, W., Teh, P. L., & Lo, C. (2020). The Systematic Impact of Personal Characteristics on Entrepreneurial Intentions of Engineering Students. *Frontiers in Psychology*, 11, 1–15. PMID: 32581939

Torres, F. C., Méndez, J. C. E., Barreto, K. S., Chavarría, A. P., Machuca, K. J., & Guerrero, J. A. O. (2017). Exploring entrepreneurial intentions in Latin American university students. *The Japanese Psychological Research*, 10(2), 46–59. PMID: 32612764

Tshikovhi, N., & Shambare, R. (2015). Entrepreneurial knowledge, personal attitudes, and entrepreneurship intentions among South African Enactus students. *Problems and Perspectives in Management*, 13(1), 152–158.

Usman, B., & Yennita. (2019). Understanding the entrepreneurial intention among international students in Turkey. *Journal of Global Entrepreneurship Research*, 9(10), 1–21.

Utami, C. W. (2017). Attitude, Subjective Norms, Perceived Behavior, Entrepreneurship Education and Self-efficacy toward Entrepreneurial Intention University Student in Indonesia. *European Research Studies Journal*, 20(2), 475–495.

Vamvaka, V., Stoforos, C., Palaskas, T., & Botsaris, C. (2020). Attitude toward entrepreneurship perceived behavioral control, and entrepreneurial intention: Dimensionality, structural relationships, and gender differences. *Journal of Innovation and Entrepreneurship*, 9(1), 1–26.

Walid Mensi . (2019) 'Global financial crisis and co-movements between oil prices and sector stock markets in Saudi Arabia: A VaR based wavelet' Borsa Istanbul, Review 19-1, pp. 24 -e38.

Wathanakom, N., Khlaisang, J., & Songkram, N. (2020). The study of the causal relationship between innovativeness and entrepreneurial intention among undergraduate students. *Journal of Innovation and Entrepreneurship*, 9(1), 1–15.

Welsh, D. H. B., Kaciak, E., Mehtap, S., Pellegrini, M. M., Caputo, A., & Ahmed, S. (2021). The door swings in and out: The impact of family support and country stability on success of women entrepreneurs in the Arab world. *International Small Business Journal*, 39(7), 619–642. DOI: 10.1177/0266242620952356

Westhead, P., & Solesvik, M. Z. (2016). Entrepreneurship education and entrepreneurial intention: Do female students benefit? *International Small Business Journal*, 34(8), 979–1003. DOI: 10.1177/0266242615612534

Wibowo, B. (2016). Relationship between Entrepreneurial Intention Among Undergraduates Student and Entrepreneurship. *Asia-Pacific Management and Business Application*, 5(1), 30–50.

Yamina, G., & Mohammed, B. S. (2019). Factors Affecting Students' Entrepreneurial Intentions in Algeria: Application of Shapero and Sokol Model. *American Journal of Economics*, 9(6), 273–281.

Yıldırım, G., Tarınç, A., & Kılınç, C. C. (2020). Women entrepreneurship in tourism: The case of Turkey. *Journal of Tourism and Gastronomy Studies*, 8(4), 2462–2477. DOI: 10.21325/jotags.2020.721

Zarefard, M., & Beri, S. E. C. (2018). Entrepreneurs' Managerial Competencies and Innovative Start-Up Intentions in University Students: Focus on Mediating Factors. *International Journal of Entrepreneurship*, 2(2), 2–22.

# About the Authors

**Fatemeh Dekamini** holds a doctorate in industrial management(financial)/ author and national-international researcher in the field of management, tourism and hospitality/member of the editorial board and reviewer of international journals/ university lecturer and top researcher/member of the Iran Managers Group/member of the Merchant Mariners Association of Iran.

**Abbas Dastanpour Hossein Abadi**, born on November 22, 1986, is an expert in auditing, financial services, and management consulting with 16 years of experience. He specializes in designing accounting and financial processes with an organizational approach. Abbas has authored three articles, co-authored two, and is in the process of publishing two books, showcasing his dedication to advancing knowledge in his field. Residing in Tehran, he is known for his strategic insight and impactful contributions.

**Amin Entezari** holds a master's degree in Business Management from the University of Tehran and is currently pursuing a Ph.D. in Business Management at Allameh Tabataba'i University. He also has significant experience as a marketing manager in the industry. His research interests encompass the fields of business management, marketing, and strategy.

**Ramona Birau** is a Lecturer on the Faculty of Economic Science at the Constantin Brancusi University of Targu Jiu, Romania. She is Doctoral Supervisor in Finance at University of Craiova, Faculty of Economics and Business Administration, Doctoral School of Economic Sciences since 2021. She has published more than 300 research papers in journals and conferences and has authored/co-authored several books. Her current research interests include financial markets, economics, cybernetics and statistics, quantitative finance, financial econometrics, economics, management, behavioral psychology, human resources, economic sociology, management. Apart from that she is also a member of the Romanian Body of Chartered and Certified Accountants (CECCAR) since 2012.

**Rezvan Pourmansouri,** holding a Master's degree in Financial Management from Islamic Azad University, Iran, boasts several years of experience in teaching and research in econometrics and finance. With numerous research articles published in esteemed scientific journals, she has also served as a financial consultant for diverse companies. Her primary expertise encompasses time series analysis, volatility models, and the application of machine learning in finance.

# Index

## A

action  1, 8, 86, 107, 131, 135, 150, 183, 184, 203, 213, 219, 224, 265, 268, 272

## B

balance  1, 2, 7, 23, 24, 25, 27, 29, 30, 35, 36, 40, 42, 44, 47, 52, 54, 57, 61, 63, 68, 69, 70, 71, 72, 74, 85, 86, 92, 93, 99, 131, 137, 171, 189, 197, 223, 227, 247, 261

business  2, 3, 4, 5, 6, 7, 8, 9, 10, 12, 14, 15, 16, 17, 18, 22, 25, 26, 31, 32, 33, 34, 43, 44, 46, 50, 51, 55, 56, 58, 61, 63, 67, 69, 72, 74, 75, 83, 84, 89, 91, 92, 93, 94, 95, 99, 101, 102, 104, 105, 106, 107, 108, 109, 116, 118, 136, 138, 139, 143, 148, 149, 151, 152, 154, 158, 159, 160, 162, 163, 164, 165, 166, 169, 170, 171, 175, 178, 179, 181, 182, 186, 191, 193, 195, 196, 197, 198, 199, 200, 201, 202, 203, 204, 205, 206, 207, 208, 209, 210, 211, 212, 213, 214, 215, 216, 217, 218, 219, 220, 221, 222, 223, 224, 225, 226, 227, 228, 231, 232, 233, 234, 235, 236, 237, 238, 242, 243, 244, 245, 246, 247, 248, 249, 250, 251, 252, 253, 254, 255, 256, 257, 260, 263, 265, 266, 269, 270, 271, 275, 276, 279, 280, 281

## E

economic  1, 2, 3, 4, 5, 9, 10, 11, 12, 13, 14, 15, 18, 21, 22, 23, 24, 25, 26, 30, 31, 33, 36, 37, 38, 39, 40, 41, 46, 48, 56, 57, 59, 62, 64, 72, 73, 75, 76, 83, 84, 86, 93, 97, 98, 115, 116, 117, 119, 121, 122, 123, 124, 128, 132, 134, 135, 141, 142, 143, 144, 145, 148, 151, 152, 159, 160, 164, 165, 169, 170, 171, 173, 174, 175, 176, 178, 185, 195, 196, 197, 199, 211, 213, 215, 231, 232, 233, 237, 239, 242, 243, 246, 251, 259, 260, 261, 262, 263, 264, 265, 266, 267, 269, 274, 275, 278, 281

Entrepreneurial  1, 2, 3, 4, 10, 89, 113, 158, 167, 193, 199, 201, 203, 215, 216, 226, 229, 232, 233, 234, 235, 236, 237, 238, 239, 240, 241, 242, 243, 244, 245, 246, 247, 248, 249, 250, 251, 252, 253, 255, 258, 259, 262, 264, 265, 266, 267, 268, 269, 270, 271, 272, 273, 274, 276, 277, 281

entrepreneurs  2, 3, 4, 5, 6, 7, 10, 19, 117, 152, 179, 186, 193, 195, 196, 197, 198, 199, 200, 201, 202, 203, 204, 207, 215, 220, 221, 222, 225, 226, 231, 232, 233, 235, 236, 237, 238, 241, 243, 244, 245, 246, 247, 248, 249, 250, 251, 252, 253, 254, 255, 256, 257, 259, 260, 261, 262, 263, 264, 265, 267, 268, 269, 270, 271, 272, 277, 279, 280, 281

entrepreneurship  1, 2, 3, 4, 5, 10, 113, 158, 177, 181, 193, 195, 207, 216, 225, 229, 231, 232, 233, 234, 235, 236, 237, 238, 239, 242, 243, 244, 245, 246, 250, 251, 252, 253, 255, 258, 259, 260, 261, 262, 263, 265, 266, 267, 268, 269, 270, 271, 272, 273, 274, 275, 276, 277, 278, 281

## F

financial  1, 2, 5, 6, 7, 8, 9, 10, 11, 12, 13, 14, 15, 16, 17, 18, 19, 20, 21, 22, 23, 24, 25, 26, 27, 28, 29, 30, 31, 32, 33, 34, 35, 36, 37, 38, 39, 40, 41, 42, 43, 44, 45, 47, 48, 49, 50, 51, 52, 53, 54, 55, 56, 57, 58, 59, 60, 61, 62, 63, 64, 65, 66, 67, 68, 69, 70, 71, 72, 73, 74, 75, 76, 77, 78, 79, 80, 81, 83, 84, 85, 86, 87, 88, 89, 90, 91, 92, 93, 94, 95, 96, 97, 98, 99, 100, 101, 113, 115, 116, 117, 118, 119, 120, 121, 122, 124, 125, 126, 127, 128, 129, 130,

131, 132, 133, 134, 139, 141, 142, 143, 144, 145, 146, 147, 148, 149, 150, 151, 152, 153, 154, 155, 156, 157, 158, 159, 160, 161, 162, 167, 169, 170, 171, 172, 173, 174, 175, 176, 177, 178, 179, 180, 181, 182, 183, 184, 185, 186, 187, 188, 189, 190, 191, 193, 195, 196, 197, 198, 199, 200, 201, 202, 203, 204, 205, 207, 214, 215, 216, 219, 220, 222, 223, 224, 225, 226, 227, 228, 229, 231, 232, 233, 235, 242, 245, 249, 252, 253, 254, 258, 266, 273, 274, 275, 278, 279, 280, 281

# I

improve  1, 2, 7, 8, 9, 21, 22, 23, 43, 50, 62, 63, 73, 94, 102, 110, 111, 131, 134, 135, 137, 141, 142, 147, 148, 149, 156, 169, 170, 180, 185, 187, 189, 190, 203, 225, 226, 227, 231, 233, 248, 255, 256, 257, 266, 269, 271, 279, 280

# K

knowledge  1, 2, 3, 4, 5, 7, 8, 9, 10, 15, 32, 33, 34, 35, 36, 37, 38, 48, 59, 60, 76, 84, 96, 116, 129, 130, 138, 141, 142, 143, 144, 145, 147, 155, 156, 170, 171, 172, 173, 175, 177, 178, 179, 180, 185, 198, 203, 206, 216, 233, 236, 244, 245, 246, 249, 250, 252, 258, 259, 261, 264, 268, 269, 270, 274, 275, 276

# M

management  1, 2, 4, 6, 7, 8, 10, 11, 12, 13, 14, 15, 16, 17, 18, 19, 20, 21, 22, 23, 24, 25, 26, 28, 30, 31, 32, 33, 35, 36, 37, 38, 39, 42, 43, 44, 45, 47, 48, 49, 52, 55, 56, 59, 60, 61, 62, 63, 64, 65, 66, 67, 69, 71, 74, 75, 76, 77, 78, 79, 80, 81, 83, 84, 85, 87, 88, 90, 94, 95, 96, 97, 98, 100, 101, 103, 104, 110, 111, 112, 120, 121, 129, 131, 136, 137, 142, 143, 158, 159, 160, 161, 162, 163, 165, 167, 176, 178, 179, 180, 181, 182, 195, 196, 197, 200, 201, 204, 207, 208, 211, 213, 215, 216, 217, 218, 219, 220, 222, 223, 224, 225, 226, 227, 228, 231, 232, 233, 236, 237, 238, 241, 242, 244, 245, 246, 247, 248, 249, 250, 251, 252, 258, 262, 263, 264, 268, 269, 270, 271, 272, 273, 274, 275, 276, 278, 279, 280, 281

market  1, 2, 3, 5, 10, 11, 12, 16, 20, 25, 28, 29, 30, 31, 37, 38, 44, 45, 47, 50, 51, 52, 53, 54, 55, 58, 59, 60, 61, 62, 63, 64, 67, 70, 71, 72, 74, 75, 76, 77, 78, 79, 80, 81, 83, 84, 85, 86, 87, 89, 90, 92, 99, 101, 102, 103, 104, 106, 107, 108, 112, 115, 116, 117, 118, 119, 120, 121, 122, 123, 124, 125, 126, 127, 128, 129, 130, 131, 132, 133, 134, 137, 139, 142, 148, 152, 159, 165, 166, 171, 185, 190, 191, 192, 195, 197, 198, 199, 200, 201, 203, 204, 205, 206, 207, 209, 211, 213, 216, 221, 225, 228, 232, 237, 243, 244, 248, 251, 253, 254, 264, 265, 266, 267

# O

opportunities  1, 2, 3, 4, 16, 22, 25, 27, 31, 32, 49, 52, 53, 54, 55, 56, 61, 62, 63, 64, 69, 72, 73, 74, 79, 84, 85, 96, 101, 104, 106, 116, 119, 120, 121, 122, 125, 126, 127, 128, 135, 141, 142, 162, 172, 184, 188, 197, 198, 199, 200, 201, 202, 203, 204, 236, 237, 239, 241, 243, 245, 251, 253, 254, 259, 260, 261, 265, 267, 268, 270, 275, 276, 277

# P

profit  1, 2, 4, 6, 12, 15, 16, 17, 18, 24, 28, 29, 30, 37, 41, 47, 53, 54, 56, 85, 91, 92, 93, 101, 120, 124, 129, 130, 131,

132, 136, 141, 142, 143, 145, 154, 162, 171, 182, 184, 191, 192, 201, 212, 213, 215, 222, 223, 228, 243

## S

self-employed 1, 2
skills 2, 5, 6, 8, 9, 40, 76, 95, 96, 112, 118, 135, 142, 145, 165, 171, 176, 178, 180, 181, 182, 213, 218, 220, 221, 222, 233, 244, 245, 246, 249, 250, 252, 255, 259, 264, 267, 269, 279

stability 1, 2, 16, 22, 23, 25, 26, 27, 30, 31, 33, 38, 42, 50, 59, 60, 61, 62, 64, 67, 68, 69, 72, 75, 78, 85, 87, 94, 95, 98, 101, 119, 120, 124, 139, 141, 142, 159, 169, 170, 174, 178, 180, 191, 193, 195, 196, 199, 202, 210, 240, 252, 253, 281

## T

tendency 1, 2